**Capital punishment and
the American agenda**

Capital punishment and the American agenda

FRANKLIN E. ZIMRING
GORDON HAWKINS

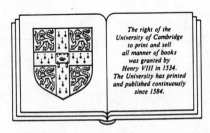

The right of the
University of Cambridge
to print and sell
all manner of books
was granted by
Henry VIII in 1534.
The University has printed
and published continuously
since 1584.

CAMBRIDGE UNIVERSITY PRESS

Cambridge
New York   New Rochelle   Melbourne   Sydney

Published by the Press Syndicate of the University of Cambridge
The Pitt Building, Trumpington Street, Cambridge CB2 1RP
32 East 57th Street, New York, NY 10022, USA
10 Stamford Road, Oakleigh, Melbourne 3166, Australia

First published 1986
Reprinted 1987

Printed in the United States of America

Library of Congress Cataloging-in-Publication Data

Zimring, Franklin E.

Capital punishment and the American agenda.

Includes index.

1. Capital punishment – United States.
2. Executions and executioners – United States.
3. Capital punishment. I. Hawkins, Gordon, 1919–
II. Title.
HV8699.U5Z56 1987   364.6'6'0973   86–21588

British Library Cataloging-in-Publication Data

Zimring, Franklin E.

Capital punishment and the American agenda.

1. Capital punishment – United
States
I. Title. II. Hawkins, Gordon
364.6'6'0973   HV8699.U5

ISBN 0 521 33033 5

To L. J.

      – f. z.

Contents

Foreword

BY TOM WICKER

"Every Western industrial nation has stopped executing criminals, except the United States."

Opening their book with that assertion, Franklin E. Zimring and Gordon Hawkins give us a lucid account of how that shocking situation came to be, and a guardedly hopeful assessment of the possibility that the United States might yet bring itself into line with the civilization of which it professes to be the leader.

In a radical departure from other books on the death penalty in America, they even argue that its abolition would not be so much a profound advance as "society . . . catching up with itself." In their view, Americans "have in fact already outgrown the social and political conditions in which capital punishment can continue to be practiced."

That might seem a quixotic conclusion in view of the fact that within two years after the Supreme Court in 1972 had seemed to outlaw the death penalty in *Furman* v. *Georgia,* twenty-eight states had written new capital statutes; by 1976 that number had grown to thirty-five, with more than 460 persons sentenced to death.

That year, too, in *Gregg* v. *Georgia,* the Supreme Court virtually reversed itself, at least partially on the grounds that the "legislative response to *Furman*" had indicated strong public support for death sentences in murder cases. Actual executions resumed in 1977 and after a slow start their frequency seems to be increasing.

Zimring and Hawkins (they unabashedly call their book an example of "advocacy scholarship") point out, however, that thirty-two of the thirty-five states enacting new death penalty laws after *Furman* had capital statutes at the time of that decision; but only Oregon turned to the death penalty in response (the other two, California and New Jersey, were reacting to state court invalidation, before *Furman,* of their capital punishment laws).

The states that recently have been executing criminals, moreover, are primarily the same Southern states that most often carried out executions before *Furman*. Southern states put 1,887 persons to death from 1935 to 1969, more than in all other regions combined; among the leaders were Georgia, Texas, and Florida. They are also the leaders in post-*Furman* executions.

Regional influences are still the most powerful factor in death sentences and executions, Zimring and Hawkins contend. Pennsylvania, for example, responded to *Furman* with a new death penalty statute similar to that of Georgia. With more than twice Georgia's population but a roughly equal number of homicides, Pennsylvania had thirty-three persons on death row at the end of 1983 and had executed no one since *Furman;* Georgia had 102 on death row and had executed six others.

From such facts, the authors argue that death penalties can be imposed today just about where they could be before *Furman;* that the splurge of new capital statutes after *Furman* was primarily a states'-rights, anti–Supreme Court response; that execution is still primarily a Southern phenomenon; and that nothing demonstrates a "resurgent national perception of capital punishment as the solution to the problem of criminal homicide."

In their view, *Furman* itself was the culmination of a century-old process in this country and other Western nations in which capital punishment gradually had been pushed into disuse, as inconsistent with modern attitudes on human rights and human dignity. The United States was not an exception to this process; in fact, the Michigan Territory abolished capital punishment for all crimes except treason in 1846, more than twenty years before any European country. Rhode Island and Wisconsin also abolished the death penalty long before Portugal, the first European country to do so.

Sixteen American states and six European nations had abolished the death penalty by 1929, though some of those states later had restored it; and after 1935 the number of executions carried out annually in the United States declined steadily from 199 – mostly in the South – to none in 1969. By then eight more states, all European nations, Australia, and New Zealand had either abolished the penalty or stopped executing criminals.

Thus it *was* a culmination of sorts when the Supreme Court in 1971 handed down the *Furman* decision, holding the death penalty, as then administered, to be "cruel and unusual punishment" that violated the Eighth Amendment. The legal scholar Philip Kurland had good reason to suggest, in a review of the case, that "the inevitable came to pass."

But the court, as Chief Justice Burger pointed out in dissent, had not reached "the ultimate issue" – whether capital punishment was unconstitutional *in and of itself* (only Justices Brennan and Marshall so held). The majority had ruled only that the imposition of the death penalty was so infrequent, arbitrary, and capricious that "as then administered" it violated the Eighth Amendment.

Zimring and Hawkins argue plausibly that the strong legislative and public reaction was only to be expected, given the antipathy of the states to being overruled by the Supreme Court, the "ritual" fear of the public that it was being deprived of protection (the authors regard the death penalty as having more symbolic than actual value to those who favor it), and the fact that in no European country had public opinion favored abolition when it took place.

Abolition, in their view – strongly supported by the historical record – is an issue that always has required leadership "from in front" of a reluctant public; but few American political figures tried to provide such leadership after *Furman,* and by the time the issue again reached the Supreme Court in 1976, the majority was *following* public opinion. As Chief Justice Burger, no longer in dissent, stated:

[I]t is now evident that a large proportion of American society continues to regard [capital punishment] as an appropriate and necessary criminal sanction. The most marked indication of society's endorsement of the death penalty for murder is the legislative response to *Furman* . . . [A]ll of the post-*Furman* statutes make clear that capital punishment itself has not been rejected by the elected representatives of the people.

Zimring and Hawkins openly consider *Gregg* to be primarily a judicial surrender to the perceived wishes of the public. Their limited optimism as to the eventual abolition of capital punishment in the United States relies heavily on their view that the court erred in also holding that the post-*Furman* capital statutes had removed the arbitrary and capricious way in which the death penalty was administered. In their opinions, no legal reforms can do that because the task is inherently impossible.

The Pennsylvania–Georgia comparison already cited is evidence that arbitrariness has hardly been eliminated. A study of the Texas and Georgia appellate review procedures lauded by the Supreme Court discloses that these procedures have not helped much either; they invalidated death sentences in only two percent of Georgia cases and one percent in Texas.

"The number of people sentenced to death has increased substantially since *Furman,*" the authors also point out, "to a rate of well over two hundred per year, but the percentage executed has been reduced to less than two percent of the death row population." The resulting situation therefore is all but "indistinguishable from the system that, in the years before *Furman,* permitted 'this unique penalty to be so wantonly and freakishly imposed.' "

For this among other reasons, Zimring and Hawkins believe that the Supreme Court, though they are well aware of its limitations, most likely will yet be the instrument of what they firmly predict: the abolition of the death penalty in the United States, sooner rather than later.

"Historical trends will produce the pressure of abolition and the national court seems the path of lowest resistance to achieving that objective," they write. "We see the court changed not by personnel or a single event but by a sense of the necessity of living up to history's demands."

That would have been a bold outlook even in the last years of the Burger Court, and some will consider it impossible in the forthcoming era of the Rehnquist Court. However, the authors' faith seems as strong as their meticulously researched and argued thesis.

An end to the power of the state to execute its citizens represents to them not just an evolving attitude toward offenders but "a statement about the proper limit on governmental power, a conception of the nature of democratic government with implications far beyond the field of criminal justice . . . [I]t constitutes the kind of statement that only a progressive society can make. It provides countries throughout the world with an index of the degree of recognition accorded to human rights" in this one.

New York, 1986

Preface

Another book about the death penalty? There were so many good arguments against this project that listing them may provide a useful beginning to the book. Capital punishment is a tired subject – overwritten, embedded in cliché and sentiment, unlikely to provoke fresh thought. Sophisticates on both sides of the death penalty debate agree that the presence or absence of executions is irrelevant to the magnitude of crime. Moreover, fewer people will be executed in the United States next year or in any year than will be killed on the highways of Rhode Island. So even bleeding hearts can find more productive avenues for pursuing personal or social salvation.

What more is to be said on this tiresome topic? Quite a bit in our opinion. This book is an attempt to measure what is known about the social, political, and moral realities of the United States of the 1980s against policy options on the death penalty. The basic questions are whether capital punishment can fit into a coherent vision of the American future, and if not, how it can be ended. We explore the experience of other Western nations and compare that record with recent American history. We explain how the question of executions has bounced around the branches of federal and state government and has affected the interplay between national authority and states' rights. We try to set the debate about the death penalty and the Eighth Amendment in the larger framework of the national political process. We place the problem of identifying those who shall die in the reality of the operation of criminal justice. We try to comprehend the political systems that produce seventy condemned prisoners on death row for each execution,[1] and that have generated, in the past ten years, death penalties nationwide but capital punishment as an active policy in only four Southern states.

Most important, we look for the path out of morass, for leading indicators in the next few years, and for the institutions and methods that will finally and decisively bring policy toward capital punishment into harmony with a progressive vision of the American future.

Capital punishment is an issue of largely symbolic importance, but symbols count. In the mid-1980s, the debate about executions is a dispute about the proper limits of governmental power with implications far beyond the administration of criminal justice. The reintroduction of the death penalty nationwide, if it occurs, will reverse a trend away from executions in the United States as old as the Republic and reintroduce the practice, after sustained disuse, for the first time in the history of the Western world.

The book is divided into two parts, each containing four chapters. Part I concerns the way present circumstances came about in the United States and Part II addresses what is likely to happen next.

Although our focus is on the death penalty in its uniquely American setting, our first chapter deals with the status of capital punishment in Western Europe and the former Commonwealth countries. The modern history of the death penalty in these countries explains much about how the death penalty fits into larger social and political contexts. The pattern of abolition in Western democracies is a necessary background to intelligent discussion of capital punishment in the United States. A failure to study the politics of capital punishment in other countries has led to misunderstanding public opinion at home. The rest of Part I reconsiders aspects of the American experience with the perspective of Chapter 1 as an organizing principle.

Chapter 2 provides a panoramic (if capsule) history of the movement toward abolition of capital punishment in the United States with roots in the eighteenth and nineteenth centuries. Our broad reading of American history argues that the Supreme Court decision in *Furman* v. *Georgia*[2] (1972) was a step toward abolition of capital punishment consistent with earlier developments and issued from the appropriate branch of government (the judiciary) and the appropriate level of government (federal) for the late stages of abolition. The reaction to *Furman* v. *Georgia* in public opinion and state legislation was typical of responses to steps away from capital punishment in other countries and to civil rights decisions by the Supreme Court in the United States.

If the *Furman* decision and its aftermath were consistent with a long-term trend toward abolition of capital punishment, what happened to reverse the trend? What happened was the United States Supreme Court's decision in *Gregg* v. *Georgia* in 1976.[3] Chapter 3 discusses the two fateful Supreme Court pronouncements on the death penalty – *Furman* and *Gregg*. We argue that the seeds of the constitutional and historic mistake made in the *Gregg* case were sown in the confused opinions of *Furman*. The failure to put public opinion and legislative reactions to *Furman* in proper historical context influenced the *Gregg* decision. The history of abolition in the rest of the developed world was neither ignored nor rejected; it was unknown.

Chapter 4 completes our historical treatment by outlining the search for standards to determine which offenders should be selected for death. This history shows not only that the search for such standards is futile, but also that it is regarded as unimportant.

The second section of the book turns attention from a history that cannot be unmade to future events. Chapter 5 considers 1986 as a historical moment, providing a snapshot of the circumstances of capital punishment at this juncture and the institutions that have produced these circumstances.

Chapter 6 tells the brief but eventful history of lethal injections as a method of execution in the United States. This subplot of the modern history of the death penalty commands attention because it provides a window into the psychological and political processes operating in the United States in the mid-1980s.

Chapter 7 addresses the career of capital punishment in the United States in the short-range future, when the fate of national policy will probably be determined by state and local governments. This chapter focuses on what is likely to happen over the next five years or so, and how events in the near future might correspond with longer-range trends.

Chapter 8 broadens our perspective to the long term, setting forth our vision of the abolition of capital punishment and its consequences. An appendix then provides a guide to the issue of the death penalty and deterrence, a topic not considered in detail in the text.

Indeed, there are a number of topics of some importance in contemporary disputes about capital punishment that do not receive the emphasis in this book that other analyses have given. The arbitrary pattern of selecting defendants for death, with inherent tendencies toward singling out minorities, the poor, and the socially distant, is central to some arguments against the death penalty in the United States, but not to ours. These serious difficulties compound the problems that would argue for rejection of executions under any regime. The inevitable chance of mistake – either the execution of the innocent or of those wrongly convicted of a capital offense – is well documented and troubling, but it is not an important part of the core case against death as an instrument of the American system of justice. Other concerns, such as a debate about whether executions (with attendant additional legal costs) are more or

less expensive to the state than protracted imprisonment are not given the
serious consideration they do *not* deserve.

The eccentric pattern of our analysis has uncovered issues we feel are
worthy of substantial scholarly attention. The first is the fact that the end
of capital punishment nearly always occurs in democracies in the face of
majority public opposition. Every Western democracy except the United
States has ended executions, but we are aware of no nation where a
democratic consensus supporting abolition was present when executions
stopped. Yet abolition persists, even though public resentment remains
for long periods.

A second puzzle concerns execution behavior in the states in the decade after *Gregg* v. *Georgia.* Although the popular wisdom of the period
was that public opinion had changed about executions in the face of
increasing violent crime, the role of tradition in determining whether and
to what extent executions would take place was dominant. Almost all
executions occur in the South, the traditional stronghold of executions in
America, and over seventy percent of executions have been conducted in
Florida, Texas, Georgia, and Louisiana – four of the top seven executing
states between 1950 and 1960. By contrast, none of the states that had
legislatively abolished the death penalty prior to *Furman* v. *Georgia* has
yet executed a prisoner. This pattern, discussed at length in Chapter 7,
does not yield an easy explanation. It is, however, significant for students
of government and those with serious interest in the future of capital
punishment.

A third pattern, the gradual dissipation of demand for death as retribution long after executions cease, does have a parsimonious explanation.
The victims of terrible crimes, and those who speak for them, demand the
maximum penalty the criminal law provides to underscore the gravity of
their loss. As long as the death penalty is perceived as a legitimate penal
response, it will be demanded, far more often than states are willing to
execute. Once execution is no longer thought of as part of government's
proper arsenal, the retributive demand for the maximum penalty will
persist, but it will be a different maximum penalty. Abolition will be
accommodated in the public demand for retribution only after a period
when it has ceased to be an aspect of the penal system.

These are the kinds of issues that justify, even demand, a fresh scholarly analysis of the death penalty in the United States. Whatever the
shortcomings of this book, we believe we have identified issues that demand substantial effort in the social and policy sciences.

One final preliminary: This book is advocacy scholarship, and the
reader might well wonder whether that phrase is a contradiction in terms.

Our commitment to the abolition of the death penalty is as strong as on any social question we know. Certainly our beliefs have colored the nature of our inquiry and our conclusions. But can there be any truly dispassionate analysis of a question so one-sided? Should there be?

The answers lie more in the text that follows than in anything we can say here. We hope that strong feelings do not disqualify us from insight and understanding. We believe the perspectives that follow are necessary to understanding the issue of capital punishment and of value to its resolution.

Notes

1. *See* NAACP Legal Defense and Educational Fund, Inc., *Death Row, U.S.A.* 3 (Oct. 1, 1985) (1,500 prisoners on death row, but only 21 executions in peak year of 1984).
2. 408 U.S. 238 (1972).
3. 428 U.S. 153 (1976).

Acknowledgments

A substantial number of individuals and institutions contributed to this venture. Our work was supported by the Center for Studies in Criminal Justice at the University of Chicago and the Program in Criminal Justice at the Earl Warren Legal Institute at the University of California at Berkeley. Two law deans, Jesse Choper and Gerhard Casper, provided tolerance, good humor, and hard currency. Early research on the topic was facilitated by a grant from the American Civil Liberties Union to the Earl Warren Legal Institute and by a Visiting Research Fellowship to Gordon Hawkins at Berkeley.

Three of our colleagues read the manuscript in its entirety as it was prepared – John Kaplan at Stanford, Jan Vetter at Berkeley, and Norval Morris at Chicago. Their criticisms and support were essential. Reading and reaction for portions of the book were provided by Gerhard Casper, Albert Alschuler, and Frank Easterbrook at Chicago; Martin Shapiro, Meir Dan-Cohen, Sanford Kadish, and Phil Johnson at Berkeley; Francis Allen and Richard Lempert at the University of Michigan; James Jacobs at New York University, as well as by Mark Miller, Herbert Wechsler, Michael Tonry, and Maurice Zimring.

Richard Rosenthal, Boalt Hall '86, served as a research assistant during 1984–5. Our young colleague Michael Laurence edited, researched, and midwifed the manuscript. Patricia Uebel word-processed more drafts than we can count or she would care to. Janice Gillmore finished the manuscript.

I

The road to 1987

1

The rest of the Western world

The pattern is so simple it is stunning. Every Western industrial nation has stopped executing criminals, except the United States. The unanimity is quite recent. Most Western nations executed prisoners in this century, and many states killed some offenders after World War II. Then the executions ceased, in most cases followed by formal abolition of the punishment some years later.

Yet public opinion in these countries invariably has opposed abolition of capital punishment when the change occurred. How did these countries abandon the death penalty? What can we learn about current and future events in the United States from the experience of the rest of the Western world? These are issues we raise in this chapter and use as a point of reference throughout the book.

Some would argue that, in this case, the lessons from history are minimal. Consider the following statement by a vocal supporter of the death penalty: "I cannot give much weight to the argument suggested by Professor Conrad that, because many countries have abolished the death penalty, we too should abolish it. If many countries follow the Soviet lead and institute cruel concentration camps, should we follow? Should our national decisions follow international fashions . . . ?"[1]

This riposte by Ernest van den Haag to an argument, which incidentally was *not* advanced by Professor John Conrad, provides among other things a good example of the logical fallacy known as *ignoratio elenchi* – that is, the fallacy of obscuring the point by interjecting, through emotional appeal, a proposition other than the one at issue. The statement also furnishes a convenient introduction to the issue missed by van den Haag.

In reality, there is not one, but a multiplicity of lessons to be examined. First, the argument that Conrad actually advanced deserves some attention. Briefly, in presenting "The Retributivist Case Against Capital Punishment," Conrad asked, "Why, then, should retributive justice demand

3

death as the penalty for murder?"[2] He answered that question as follows: "So far as the law is concerned in nearly all the countries of Europe, with the exception of the Soviet Union and the insecure regimes that that nation has imposed on its satellites, that question has been clearly answered. Retributive justice does not require the death penalty to maintain its credibility."[3]

Though Conrad's ultimate argument may be ambiguous, he certainly was not arguing that "because many countries have abolished the death penalty, we too should abolish it" or that "our national decisions [should] follow international fashions." Indeed, it seems unlikely that, despite the immense profusion of literature on the death penalty, one could find any examples of arguments of that kind being advanced.

However, examples of arguments that may seem similar to that which van den Haag caricatures can be found in many contexts. It would be odd indeed if debates about the desirability of any human institution, policy, or practice were conducted without any reference to what happens in other countries. Even the most detached, neutral, academic observation of society would be severely limited if all reference to any other society were excluded. It would also be not merely pointless but scientifically derelict to permit such an irrational restriction on inquiry.

For participants in the death penalty debate to ignore information about imposing and carrying out the penalty in other countries results in shallow and even illogical discourse. Moreover, correlations between execution policy and other features of the policy within countries (for example, shifts in public opinion after abolition or the human rights records of those nations that have retained executions) are legitimate considerations to the death penalty controversy in this country. Failing to address those correlations does not deny their validity or their moral persuasiveness. Death penalty supporters, like the proverbial ostrich with its head in the sand, must eventually recognize the lessons that can be learned from the experiences of others.

A. The abolitionist trend

We begin our examination by observing the death penalty policies of the principal Western European countries. Table 1.1 indicates the current status of the penalty in those countries. All of the states commonly referred to as the Western democracies are found in this table. These are countries that have abolished the death penalty completely; have abolished the death penalty for all offenses committed in peacetime but permit it for certain offenses committed during war; or have retained it for

Table 1.1. *Western Europe: the disappearing death penalty*

Total abolition	Abolition except for specific offenses in wartime	De facto[a]
Austria	Denmark	Belgium
Finland	France	Cyprus
Germany (FRG)	Italy	Greece
Iceland	Netherlands	Ireland
Portugal	Norway	United Kingdom
Sweden	Spain	
	Switzerland	

[a]This heading includes countries that have retained the death penalty in law for certain offenses, but have not had an execution in the past decade.
Source: Amnesty International, *Report: The Death Penalty* (1979).

certain offenses committed in peacetime (such as treasonable acts and terrorist murders) but have not used it in recent years, and in many cases have a longstanding policy against its use expressed by a tradition of commuting death sentences. Belgium, for example, although it retains the death penalty has not had an execution for a civil crime since 1918.

In the past half-century, these countries have shown a clear trend toward abolishing the death penalty either in law or in practice. Within the past fifty years, five of these states have formally abandoned it; five have restricted its application to a narrow list of offenses; and five, although retaining it, have ceased to use it. Two other nations have announced that they propose to abolish the death penalty.[4]

In 1983 the twenty-one member states of the Council of Europe, recognizing "the evolution that has occurred," agreed to add a protocol, "concerning the abolition of the death penalty," to the European Convention for the Protection of Human Rights and Fundamental Freedoms.[5] Article 1 of Protocol Number Six states: "The death penalty shall be abolished. No one shall be condemned to such penalty or executed," although Article 2 reserves for the states the right to retain the death penalty for acts committed "in time of war or imminent threat of war."[6]

Beyond Europe abolition of the death penalty is the standard policy of most developed countries. Canada, after a period of suspension beginning in 1967, eliminated the death penalty for civilian offenses in 1976. It has been retained only for a number of offenses under the National Defense Act.[7] In Australia the death penalty was first abolished in Queensland in 1921, and that example has since been followed both by the federal government and by the remaining states with the exception of Western

Australia where abolition legislation is pending.[8] In New Zealand, where
the last execution was in 1957, the death penalty was abolished in 1941,
restored in 1950, and finally abolished, except for treason, in 1962.[9]

A country deserving special mention because of the provocations en-
dured without resorting to capital punishment is Israel. For more than
two decades, in the face of external force and domestic terror, Israel has
not used the death penalty.[10] The discretionary death penalty is available
for genocide, crimes against humanity, crimes against the Jewish people,
and "acts of inhuman cruelty," but no death sentences have been imposed and no executions carried out since the hanging of Adolf Eichmann
in 1962. Apart from that case, prosecutors have followed a consistent
policy of not asking for a death sentence.

B. The retentionist states

Contrary to van den Haag's characterization, the abolitionist trend in
the West hardly constitutes nations following "international fashions."
There is no international fashion in the sense of a generally accepted,
prevailing style or mode of penal policy and practice. Rather, when one
compares the nonexecuting countries with the principal practitioners of
capital punishment, a clear disjunction between executing and nonexecuting states emerges. Moreover, the contrasting approaches to penal
policy are not accidental. The comparison provides an index to essential
differences in political philosophy and organization. It is no coincidence
that the list of actively executing countries matches that of politically
repressive countries.

The negative correlation between execution policy and governmental
respect for human rights appears throughout the world. For many countries with extensive capital punishment policies, reliable information concerning the rate and frequency of death penalty use is unavailable. What
information is obtained demonstrates a striking positive correlation between capital punishment use and human rights violations.

South Africa, for example, for some years has had one of the highest
rates of judicial execution in the world as well as a very high death rate
for detainees in police custody.[11] The political regime responsible for this
extensive use of capital punishment has also severely curtailed civil and
political rights by discriminatory and repressive legislation. This policy,
involving extensive restrictions on residence, movement, employment,
expression, and association, is enforced by torture, political imprisonment, detention without trial, preventive detention, and the banning of
opposition newspapers and organizations.

South Africa's prominence in executions, however, may be in part a product of reporting practice. Certainly in Africa, many countries officially report no executions, even though mass arrests and executions of political opponents are routine. For example, in Uganda under President Idi Amin, between 1971 and 1979, estimates of the number killed by security forces range from 50,000 to 300,000.[12] Indeed, in many African countries the use of summary, as opposed to judicial, executions is not so much an index of disregard for human rights as the principal method for expressing it.

Latin America is another area where the death penalty cannot be considered only in terms of judicially imposed sentences. In Argentina under the military junta no one was sentenced to death by the military tribunals established to try those suspected of involvement in subversive activities. Yet at that time Argentina was considered a leading practitioner of extrajudicial or extralegal executions, with thousands of people disappearing after arrest or abduction by military or security agents.[13] Here too, murder committed or acquiesced in by government was the principal feature of a consistent pattern of gross human rights violations.

The People's Republic of China is only one of the Asian governments utilizing the death penalty both as a method of maintaining law and order and for enforcing a wide range of political offenses.[14] Capital offenses include provoking dissension, conducting counterrevolutionary propaganda and agitation, and spreading rumors. According to Article 18 of the 1978 Constitution: "The State safeguards the socialist system, suppresses all treasonable and counter-revolutionary activities, punishes all traitors and counter-revolutionaries, and punishes new-born bourgeois elements and other bad elements."[15] The punishment is frequently death, although no official statistics of death sentences or executions are published.

The Soviet Union also publishes no official statistics on the number of death sentences imposed or executions performed, but in the past two decades the Soviet Union steadily has increased the number of offenses subject to the death penalty, and Soviet "dissenters" estimate the yearly number of persons sentenced to die in the hundreds.[16] The list of offenses punishable by death in all fifteen Union Republics includes actions disrupting the work of corrective labor institutions, making or passing counterfeit money or securities, stealing state property, and taking a bribe. The media publicly report only some of the death sentences and executions.

In the Middle East no country has formally abolished the death penalty. The only state without an execution in the last decade is Israel.

Although Israel has committed some civil rights violations, by comparison with such countries as Iran, Iraq, Egypt, Libya, and Syria, Israel's record is remarkably restrained. Moreover, the contrast between executing and nonexecuting countries remains striking. In Iran thousands of executions take place annually; hundreds occur in Iraq.[17]

This brief demonstration of the contrast between executing and non-executing nations is incomplete, for the differences are not confined to policies on the imposition and application of the death penalty. The contrast is also pronounced in the judicial procedures under which people may be sentenced to death, in appeal mechanisms and opportunities for appeal, and in the rights of defendants. In the executing countries these procedures are, respectively, arbitrary, inadequate, and severely restricted. Nor is that all. These countries for the most part publish no official statistics on death sentences or executions, or even details of trial and appeal procedures or commutation mechanisms; the statistical yearbooks omit references to the criminal jurisdiction; and Amnesty International and United Nations questionnaires are ignored. Moreover, governmental reticence in response to requests for death penalty information provides only one example of these countries' extensive use of domestic secrecy and suppression.

C. The decline of the death penalty

Focusing attention on other features of regimes committed to the death penalty is not a rhetorical gambit. The relationship between this aspect of penal policy and the other features is too consistent to be merely coincidental. Nor is it a matter of evaluative judgment but rather one of demonstrable fact that repressive and authoritarian governments employ the death penalty.

The logical conclusion that emerges is that the decline of executions in the West constitutes part of a long-term evolutionary process – the development process of civilization, in fact. It is therefore not surprising that it has been seen as an inexorable progression, "the slow but absolutely certain progress of maturing civilization that will bring an inevitable end to punishment by death."[18]

The development, however, has been neither linear nor uniform. Each country has abandoned executions in its own way, at its own pace, and often with regressions that in retrospect can now be characterized as temporary. What may now be viewed as part of a long-term worldwide evolution often appeared to contemporaries as an eccentric deviation.

Indeed, the history of the decline consists of unconnected events in the several nations. The fact that in Belgium the last execution for a civil crime (apart from the execution of a soldier for murder in 1918) occurred in 1863 is apparently unrelated to the fact that in Queensland, Australia it happened fifty years later in 1913; and in Great Britain the relevant date is just over a century later in 1964. Nor is there any evident relationship between the total abolition of the death penalty for civil and military offenses in Iceland in 1928 and in Portugal half a century later in 1977. How do we explain that although Portugal was the first country in Western Europe to abolish the death penalty for civil crimes (1867), its neighbors Spain (1978) and France (1981) were among the last? Viewed in historical perspective, however (for example, in the context of the centuries since the Middle Ages), the proximity of these events is immediately apparent.

Similarly, what often appeared as decisive policy reversals at the time can be now seen as short-lived. New Zealand abolished capital punishment in 1941, restored it in 1950, and abolished it again in 1962. Italy abolished it in 1890, restored it in 1931, and again abolished it in 1944. Switzerland abolished it in 1874, restored it in ten out of fifteen cantons in 1879, and finally abolished it in 1942. In the years immediately following World War II several formerly enemy-occupied European countries, which had not performed an execution for civil crimes for over half a century (for example, the Netherlands, Norway, and Denmark), executed a number of collaborators and then returned to a nonexecution policy.

Another significant feature of the movement away from the death penalty is frequently long periods between the last execution and official abolition of capital punishment. In most countries formal abolition has been preceded by a period in which no executions took place. Table 1.2 illustrates this phenomenon.

Furthermore, abeyance often had been preceded by a period in which the number of executions gradually decreased. In the Netherlands, for example, there had been no executions in the ten years preceding the last executions in 1860. Denmark had only three executions in the quarter of a century prior to 1892. In Sweden no executions occurred in the six years prior to the last execution in 1910, and the death penalty had been rarely used after the 1865 Penal Code was enacted. In Switzerland twenty-nine years without an execution preceded the last one in 1924, and executions in the cantons that retained capital punishment between 1879 and 1942 were rare.

The long periods between the last execution and abolition make it difficult to determine the point at which the threat of the death penalty

Table 1.2. *Year of last execution versus abolition of capital punishment*[a]

Country	Year of last execution for civil crime	Formal abolition
Netherlands	1860	1870
Belgium[b]	1863	Still in force
Norway	1875	1905
Italy[c]	1876	1890
Denmark	1892	1930
Sweden	1910	1921
Queensland, Australia	1911	1921
Switzerland[d]	1924	1942
New Zealand[e]	1935	1941

[a]This table excludes executions of collaborators after World War II.
[b]Except for the execution of a soldier for a civil offense in 1918.
[c]Restored in 1931 and again abolished in 1944.
[d]Previously abolished in 1874 with limited restoration in 1879.
[e]Restored in 1950 and again abolished in 1962.
Source: Royal Commission on Capital Punishment 1949–1953 Report 340, App. 6 (1953).

ceased to have any meaning. For this discussion, however, these data illustrate an important aspect of the social evolution process: The dates when changes in practice occur rarely coincide with the dates when legislative changes are made. In progressive societies the common pattern of political locomotion is subsequent rather than precedent to social evolution. From de facto to de jure is the usual sequence of abolition in Western democracies.

What at first sight looks like a curious anomaly in Belgium – the retention of the death penalty and the passing of death sentences that, with one exception, have not been carried out for over a century – is in fact merely an extreme example of the normal order in those Western European countries that have retained the death penalty. Only one of those countries retaining the death penalty for specific offenses in wartime has executed anyone for a civil offense in the past ninety years. None of those countries that authorize the punishment for some offenses in peacetime has executed anyone for a decade. Death sentences may be imposed but they are not carried out; clemency applications are invariably granted.

D. Capital punishment as ritual

The experience of other Western countries illuminates an important aspect of death penalty legislation: its symbolic character. It also demonstrates the ritual or ceremonial function of the capital punishment statute, even if not invoked, and of the death sentence. The extensive ethnographic literature on ritual and symbolism focuses mainly on "primitive" societies, tending to overlook the collective ceremonials and focal rituals of large and complex modern societies. Our own twentieth-century institutions and practices, in which what Durkheim called the "collective consciousness"[19] is expressed, have been largely ignored. But it seems likely that the symbolic significance of death penalty legislation, the ritual nature of the murder trial, and the incantatory power of the death sentence constitute a large part of the appeal for supporters of the death penalty.

This may suggest an explanation for the curious ambivalence in contemporary societies that want to preserve death penalty legislation and murder trials yet appear to feel no need for executions. In a simple, homogeneous tribal society a human sacrifice performed with the intention of influencing or manipulating the course of human events is required. In larger, more complex societies the same psychological need is fulfilled, without an actual sacrifice, by the performance of the preliminary rituals. The latent social function is the same.

If this analysis accurately interprets the significance of the death penalty in contemporary cultures, it indicates why, absent a revolution, abolition has always required transition periods in countries committed to it. Long-established institutions or practices that reflect and satisfy fundamental intentions, beliefs, and needs defy instant dissolution by administrative fiat. Indeed, those who place reliance on revolution as a means of achieving abolition will find little encouragement in history. In Russia, for example, after the February 1917 revolution, the provisional government abolished the death penalty within ten days of coming to power, only to revive it a few months later. The Bolshevik government once more abolished it in October 1917 but restored it in 1918. It was again discarded in January 1920 and restored later in the same year. The last time it was abolished was in 1947, but it was reinstated in 1950 and is currently in force throughout the country.

At the same time, the history of those countries that have abolished the death penalty and not restored it indicates that the success of the abolition movement is more than merely fortuitous. As with the other great humanitarian movements of the nineteenth and twentieth centuries, penal reforms often have been achieved in a piecemeal and incremental fashion, but they have also proved immutable. Such movements acquire a momentum that ultimately brings them to a point at which reversal is no longer possible. The British Royal Commission on Capital Punishment confronted this situation in 1949 when it was required to consider "whether the liability under the criminal law in Great Britain to suffer capital punishmer.t for murder should be limited or modified."[20]

The campaign against capital punishment in Britain began in the late eighteenth century when Jeremy Bentham and Sir Samuel Romilly introduced the ideas of Cesare Beccaria to the British political establishment.[21] By the middle of the twentieth century the scope of the death penalty had been so reduced that, as the Royal Commission put it, "a stage has been reached where there is little room for further limitation short of abolition."[22] The Commission reported that it was unable to find a satisfactory solution to the problem of finding "some practicable half-way house between the present scope of the death penalty and its abolition" and concluded that "the real issue is now whether capital punishment should be retained or abolished."[23] In 1964, just over ten years after the Commission published its report, the last execution in Britain took place; and in 1969 the penalty was abolished for all offenses except treason and certain forms of piracy.

The inexorability of this pattern is strikingly illustrated by the fact that even a cataclysm of the magnitude of World War II brought about only a temporary policy reversal in those German-occupied countries that were abolitionist either in law or in practice. In Belgium, 242 collaborators were sentenced to death by councils of war or military tribunals, and were shot. In Denmark, penal legislation was temporarily suspended and forty-six collaborators were sentenced to death and executed under the Military Penal Code. The Netherlands also reinstated the death penalty for war crimes committed during the German occupation. But the revival of the death penalty was temporary; since that time no executions have occurred in any of these countries.

The inevitable progress of the abolition movement is all the more remarkable when the role of public opinion is examined. Successful and sustained abolition has never been a result of great popular demand. In Great Britain, for example, both when the Murder (Abolition of Death Penalty) Act of 1965 suspended the death penalty for murder for an experimental period, and also when abolition was made permanent in 1969, public opinion polls indicated a substantial majority favored retaining the death penalty for murder. A 1964 Gallup poll found only twenty-one percent in favor of abolishing the death penalty, and in 1966, after suspension, seventy-six percent favored reintroduction. In the 1970s, after abolition was made permanent, support for restoring the death penalty continued, rising to eighty-two percent by 1975.[24] Britain's experience appears typical; in most abolitionist countries, if the issue had been decided by direct vote rather than by the legislature, the death penalty probably would not have been repealed.

Table 1.3. *German public opinion: The death penalty, 1948, by percent*

For retention	74
For abolition	21
Undecided	5
Total	100

Source: The Germans: Public Opinion Polls 1947–1966 (E. Noelle-Neumann & E. Neumann eds. 1967).

Table 1.4. *German public opinion: The death penalty, 1980, by percent*

In favor of death penalty	26
Opposed to death penalty	55
Undecided	19
Total	100

Source: The Germans: Public Opinion Polls 1967–1980 (E. Noelle-Neumann ed. 1981).

Capital punishment supporters often cite public opinion as a reason for retaining it, but public opinion or perception almost invariably follows tradition, and the death penalty as symbol is certainly traditional. Indeed, few reforms would have been approved in any area if a nationwide referendum had determined their passage. For most people the death penalty is not a matter of great concern, at least not sufficiently to generate the upsurge of popular dissatisfaction required to repudiate traditional practices.

The public's lack of interest also partially explains why, once abolition is accomplished, the death penalty, though previously the subject of widespread debate, ceases to be a pressing public issue. Furthermore, after-abolition support for the death penalty diminishes. Public opinion polls conducted in the Federal Republic of Germany before and after abolition in 1949 provide a dramatic illustration of this process. In October 1948 pollsters asked respondents: "If a new German penal code were to be introduced, would you be for the retention or abolition of capital punishment?" For another poll, in January 1980, respondents were asked: "Are you in principle opposed to or in favor of the death penalty?" The results of both polls are seen in Tables 1.3 and 1.4.

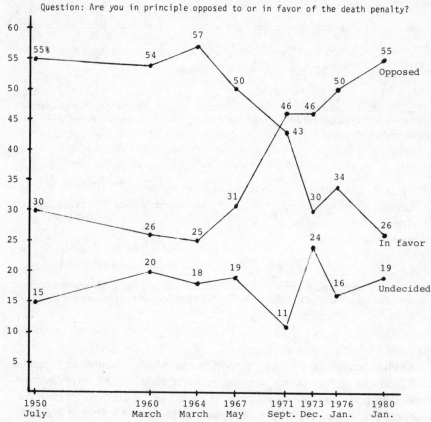

Figure 1.1.   German public opinion: the death penalty (1950–80). *Source: The Germans: Public Opinion Polls 1967–1980,* at 171 (E. Noelle-Neumann ed. 1981).

The change in German public opinion on the death penalty after abolition over the years 1950–80 is illustrated in Figure 1.1.

The symbolic character of death penalty legislation probably explains the strong support for the punishment after abolition, which diminishes until, after several years, opposition dominates public opinion. Because the death penalty symbolizes governmental willingness to employ ultimate power against those who threaten collective moral order, when a government relinquishes that power much of the public believes that society will be incapable of protecting itself. In reality, the death penalty is about as relevant to controlling violent crime as rain-dancing is to controlling the weather. So long as rain dances continue to be performed, as they have been since time immemorial, the belief that they have some

influence on rainfall cannot be tested. When they cease to be performed, and the amount of precipitation remains unchanged in the subsequent years, the ritual's influence dissipates. Similarly, as time passes after abolition and increases in violent crime do not materialize, the felt necessity of the capital sanction diminishes gradually.

The death penalty's symbolic or ritual character is also illustrated by the fact that in countries retaining the death penalty rarely will a noncapital sentence for a capital crime or a commutation of a death sentence rouse any great public interest, much less opposition. Just as in primitive communities sacrificial rituals have evolved from human sacrifice to animal sacrifice and ultimately to token sacrifice, it appears that in modern communities the public is usually satisfied by the performance of a ritual that does not actually terminate in the sacrificial slaughter of a human being. This also explains both the lack of popular demand for the abolition of the death penalty and the relative indifference to whether executions are carried out. Whatever functions the death penalty is seen to fulfill – whether it be the demonstration of the community's abhorrence of murder, a declaration of determination to do something about it, the satisfaction of retributive feelings, or the deterrence of potential murders – the pronouncement of the death sentence may often be accepted as satisfying these ends. Eventually a time comes when, although the penalty remains on the statute book, death sentences are no longer required and ultimately the penalty itself is abolished.

This evolutionary process is illustrated by the experience in New Zealand from the restoration of the death penalty in 1951 to its final abolition in 1962. During 1951–7 the death penalty was imposed eighteen times for murder, but only eight executions occurred. Between 1958 and 1961 not only were executions in abeyance but despite seven convictions for murder, no death sentences were imposed. Finally, the death penalty for murder was abolished in 1962.[25] Thus, a period in which the death penalty was imposed but carried out in less than fifty percent of cases was followed, first by a period in which the death penalty was available but not imposed, and ultimately by abolition.

E. The issue of public opinion

The abolition process indicates that an important distinction should be drawn between public attitudes on capital punishment and public attitudes on executions. A considerable amount of research has been carried out on public attitudes toward capital punishment in the United States. Public opinion surveys have consistently found that since the late 1960s a two-to-one majority of the population has favored the death penalty.

There has been a good deal of disagreement, however, about the significance of these findings.

Considerable research effort has also gone into attempts to identify the determinants of public support for capital punishment. In some cases, determinants identified as strongly correlated to support for capital punishment have been personality characteristics such as punitiveness, authoritarianism, dogmatism, and intolerance. Other studies have been directed to discovering the extent to which either utilitarian or retributive sentiments play a determinative role in ensuring continuing public support for the death penalty. Unfortunately, in neither case have researchers paid any attention to the symbolic importance not merely of the death penalty as part of the criminal justice system but also of the casting of a vote for or against it.

Yet this is clearly a matter of crucial importance. Ellsworth and Ross conducted a close examination of the views of abolitionists and retentionists and found that two-thirds of the respondents would support the death penalty even if it were proved to be no better as a deterrent than life imprisonment, and that one-half professed they would support it even if it caused as many murders as it prevented.[26] In the same vein, the June 1973 Harris survey of public attitudes toward the death penalty found that fifty-four percent of those who favored capital punishment said they would favor it even if it had no deterrent effect.[27] Similarly, Neil Vidmar found that fifty-five percent of Canadian adults who favored capital punishment indicated that they would favor it regardless of its deterrent value.[28]

Some concern other than deterrent efficacy, which has loomed so large in the capital punishment literature, played an important part in producing those responses. One explanation offered by Vidmar and Ellsworth is what they call "the retribution hypothesis": the idea "that retribution may be an important motive in capital punishment attitudes."[29] It seems highly probable, however, that an equally substantial proportion of death penalty supporters would have reaffirmed their commitment if they had been told that it had been demonstrated that the death penalty was not a retributively necessary punishment for murder. Hugo Bedau probably more accurately described American attitudes toward the death penalty: "One question that has proved more difficult to answer than all others is *what* the present high levels of public support for the death penalty really support. Is it only the *legal threat* of the death penalty, coupled with the judicial ritual of trying, convicting, and occasionally sentencing a murderer to death, rather than *actual executions?*"[30]

One reason why this question has not been answered, some might

think, is that it has not been addressed. For it is true that in all those surveys dealing with such matters as general levels of support for the death penalty, levels of support among various subpopulations, social and psychological correlates of death penalty attitudes, and the public's factual knowledge about the death penalty, the question Bedau raised has somehow escaped attention. Yet if it is correct to suggest that the reason for support – which is more important, for instance, than deterrent efficacy or retributive aptness – relates to the significance of the death penalty as a symbol, it would be sanguine to expect this to be elicited through questionnaires.

The problems involved here are not such familiar ones as that of respondents giving answers they regard as socially acceptable, or think are compatible with the opinions of the interviewer, or may make them look good in the interviewer's eyes. Of course, these difficulties cannot be entirely ignored. One wonders, for example, what proportion of the eighty-six percent of respondents who, in a 1977 Harris Survey,[31] opposed televising executions, would view a televised execution.

The basic problem in detecting the significance of the death penalty as a symbol is deeper. Symbolic or ritual institutions and practices are commonly supported quite unreflectively, without any clear conception on the part of those supporting them as to why they do so. This is one reason why responses to questionnaires framed in terms of official rationales and penal theories so often seem paradoxical, inconsistent, and difficult to interpret.

What importance, for instance, should policymakers, legislators, governors, or appellate judges give to popular support for the death penalty "even if it caused as many murders as it prevented"? What are the policy implications of the 1973 Harris survey which found that while fifty-nine percent of respondents favored the death penalty there was no clear majority on the offenses that should carry mandatory capital punishment? What significance should be attached to the finding in the same survey of a substantial discrepancy between respondents' general attitudes toward capital punishment and their self-predicated behavior as jurors?[32]

One answer to the problem of discrepancies, inconsistencies, and apparently "frivolous" or "uninformed" responses is that additional empirical investigation is required. What is needed, say Vidmar and Ellsworth, is "more sophisticated research which can better examine people's understanding and underlying attitudes about the death penalty."[33] This suggests that sufficiently refined questionnaires that, for instance, succeed in distinguishing such common misconceptions in the public mind as the confusion of deterrence with incapacitation, will be able to extract some unambiguous meaning from opinion and attitude surveys and will ultimately clarify precisely what the public wants and why it wants it.

There are, however, a number of objections to this solution. First, although much of the survey research conducted on this topic has been unsophisticated – for example, the questions were unclear or respondents were offered an insufficient range of alternative responses – a lot of it has been, if anything, too sophisticated. In particular, much of it has been based on the assumption that people's nonratiocinative beliefs translate into explicit policy options.

Some of the principal problems encountered by practicing sociologists and anthropologists investigating the beliefs of those engaged in ritual or symbolic activities are relevant. It is by no means easy to be sure to what extent those who profess a belief intend it literally or even understand what they are saying. "The diligent field worker," one anthropologist has said, "may . . . conclude not only that his native informants neither quite believe nor disbelieve what they tell him, but even that they sincerely believe without knowing quite what it is that they are believing."[34]

What is true of people in other cultures with exotic beliefs, practices, and institutions is equally true in Western society. It is unlikely that many of those who claim to believe in the existence of God could explain precisely what it is that they are claiming. However, more sophisticated research probably would do little to illuminate their understanding or their underlying attitudes about deism. Does faith in the death penalty fall into a very different category?

An attempt to clarify public attitudes to capital punishment by Sarat and Vidmar[35] sought to assess support for or opposition to the death penalty in a sample of Massachusetts residents by means of a questionnaire, using a seven-alternative scale. The questionnaire was part of an experiment designed to test whether "information manipulations" would produce "evaluative and cognitive changes regarding the death penalty."[36] What emerged was that there were relatively minor changes among "persons who were moderate in their initial attitudes."[37] The authors reported that "[t]he magnitude of such change was not great; when change occurred it generally involved movement to the very next alternative rather than an alternative several steps away."[38] Nevertheless, they concluded that "an informed public opinion about the death penalty may differ substantially from one that is uninformed."[39]

Whatever one's interest in the nature of support for the death penalty, the most striking finding was that those who either strongly or very strongly favored the death penalty were, with few exceptions, unswayed by the information presented. This raises the fundamental question about the nature of "death penalty attitudes" that the questionnaire was designed to assess. Yet the appearance of precision in this attempt to discriminate more precisely between, and objectively measure, different levels of support for the death penalty is illusory. It is quite impossible, for instance, either to determine the denotation of such statements as "I am somewhat in favor of the death penalty," "I am somewhat opposed to the death penalty," or "I am uncertain about the death penalty," or to tell what evaluative, cognitive, or other mental elements form the states of mind expressed by them.

Nevertheless, the almost complete indifference of the more unequivocal death penalty supporters to "information manipulations" suggests very strongly that support for the death penalty is generally not a matter of cognition (that is, knowing something), or of evaluation (that is, determining the worth, value, or utility of something). The lack of reaction appears to indicate that what is involved is not judgment based on empirical evidence or ethical argument but rather such mental states as are connoted by terms like "faith," "belief," or "conviction," or even such affective conditions as "allegiance" or "loyalty." This is precisely what would be expected if, as we have suggested, the appeal of the death penalty derives not from its function as a particularly effective or appropriate penal method, but rather from its symbolic significance.

F. Unconscious parallelism

It is important to note at some length the absence of international coordination or cooperation because of the similarity in the patterns leading to the end of execution in Western democracies. The common elements in each nation's path toward abolition are not attributable to the central administration of a single strategy or to conscious appropriation of tactics that have proved successful in other countries. Instead, the parallelism is unconscious. The path to abolition has similar elements simply because this is how the abolition of capital punishment happens in modern democracies.

Truly international organizations did not become involved until very late in the movement. The proceedings and transactions of the regular quinquennial congresses convened by the International Prison Commission (after 1930 called the International Penal and Penitentiary Commission) from 1872 to 1935 record only one discussion of the death penalty.[40] This was at the Washington Congress in 1910, but no resolutions were passed on the subject. This is not suprising for, as Negley Teeters explained in his account of those deliberations: "The prevailing point of view appeared to be that of the criminal jurist, marked by cautiousness in phrasing proposals for a change in the present penal system, and hesitation in recommending changes of a too specific or too radical character."[41]

After World War II the United Nations, by a General Assembly Resolution adopted on December 1, 1950, assumed the role and functions of the International Penal and Penitentiary Commission, which had held its last meeting in 1935. Not until the fall of 1959 was abolition of the death penalty placed on the agenda of the General Assembly; and not until 1968 did the United Nations Consultative Group of Experts on the Prevention of Crime and Treatment of Offenders to which the subject had been referred recommend abolition.[42]

In the late 1950s the Council of Europe's European Committee on Crime Problems also began to address capital punishment. According to Marc Ancel, who chaired the committee, "it was understood that the question of abolition or otherwise of the death penalty was not to be examined as such," and the committee's report, *The Death Penalty in European Countries,* published in 1962, is a survey of "the law and current practice in the Council countries" at that time.[43]

It was not until the 1970s that another international organization, Amnesty International, took an unequivocally abolitionist position on capital punishment. In 1965 it circulated a resolution at the United Nations for "the suspension and eventual abolition of the death penalty for *peacetime political offenses.*"[44] In 1973 the Council of Amnesty International decided that the death penalty "must now be seen as a violation of the human right not to be subjected to torture and cruel, inhuman, or degrading treatment."[45] Finally, an international conference convened by Amnesty International in December 1977 "marked the beginning of work on a worldwide scale for the abolition of the death penalty."[46]

Each of the major Western European countries discarded the death penalty in its own way and at its own pace but toward the same end. By the time international organizations became involved the battle was almost over. The situation at that time is described in the final paragraph of the 1962 Council of Europe report:

The whole survey shows . . . that among Members of the Council of Europe abolitionist countries are well in the majority. Elsewhere . . . capital punishment simply survives in theory and its application is declining steadily. An impartial glance at the facts clearly shows that the death penalty is regarded in Europe as something of an anachronism, surviving precariously for the moment but perhaps doomed to disappear.[47]

The authoritative transnational statement came after the fact, in 1983, when the Council of Europe formally abolished the death penalty.

If the common elements in the ending of executions in Europe are not attributable to coordinated effort or shared tactics, the recurring themes have significance as the likely results when democratic governments move toward abolition. These recurrent themes include: (1) the lag between de facto and de jure abolition, (2) public opposition, (3) political leadership from the front, and (4) the linkage between abolition of capital punishment and other civil liberties.

1. De facto versus de jure

The difference between "de facto" and "de jure" abolition of the death penalty involves more than the passage of years. The preservation of death penalty legislation as a potential weapon of last resort, although there is no need to use it under ordinary conditions of civil society even for the most serious individual crimes, may represent an acceptable political compromise. In practice, even when the rare death sentence is imposed, executions are not carried out and applications for clemency are almost always successful. But theoretically the lethal weapon is available for an emergency.

Preservation of the death penalty for specific offenses in wartime when the civil order is totally threatened, on the other hand, may reflect an important distinction. In such circumstances the death penalty is seen not so much as a retributive punishment, but rather as part of the war. This distinction was probably operative to some degree in the use of the death penalty for wartime collaborators in countries where the nonexistence of the death penalty had become a national tradition. It is possibly also reflected in what Jonathan Power referred to as "in many people's minds one powerful argument in favor of capital punishment – its use to punish terrorists."[48] "The morality or immorality of killing terrorists," he wrote, "is difficult to distinguish from the morality or immorality of killing enemy soldiers in a war."[49] In countries such as Italy, Israel, Great Britain, Ireland, and the Federal Republic of Germany, however, where terrorism has been not merely a threat but a reality, that "difficult" distinction has been consistently drawn. The record of those abolitionist countries faced with actual terrorism in peacetime, as opposed to the almost universal acceptance of the necessity of killing enemy soldiers in wartime, indicates the problematic character of Power's analogy.

2. Public opposition and acquiescence

Popular opposition to abolition is inevitable. Majorities of two-thirds opposed to abolition were associated with abolition in Great Britain in the

1960s, Canada in the 1970s, and the Federal Republic of Germany in the late 1940s. Indeed, there are no examples of abolition occurring at a time when public opinion supported the measure.

Even so, public opinion does change slowly over time. In 1962 the Council of Europe reported in relation to Italy, Belgium, the Netherlands, Denmark, Norway, and Sweden that "there seems to be no question of capital punishment nowadays in any of those countries."[50] In Sweden, the most recent public opinion poll revealed that twenty-eight percent of the respondents were for capital punishment, which the press described as an extraordinarily high proportion in favor of an "outmoded punishment."[51] In Norway a poll found seventy percent opposed the death penalty, fifteen percent favored it, and fifteen percent had no opinion.[52] In none of these countries had there been any public clamor for reintroducing the death penalty, or any significant struggle between those in favor and those against it.[53] This is the common pattern in countries that have not executed for decades, and it is difficult to believe that it represents a political compromise. A more plausible conclusion would be that when a country has been abolitionist in practice for a number of years, controversy tends to end.

3. Political leadership

When democratic countries cease to execute and subsequently repeal death penalty legislation, this is accomplished by institutions of representative democracy; but, as an English commentator wrote in 1973: "In the case of capital punishment legislators lead from the front."[54] In this context public opinion is invariably led, not followed. An important reason for this is that the public mainly views the death penalty, as Hugo Bedau has put it, as "an important legal threat, abstractly desirable as part of society's permanent bulwark against crime,"[55] rather than in terms of gassing, poisoning, electrocuting, shooting, or hanging large numbers of human beings.

Those who make and implement government policy, on the other hand, are much closer to the nexus between policy and practice, between "the death penalty" as statute, and killing people as punishment. Thus, the difference between public attitudes and the government's or legislators' view may often be, in part, not so much a difference in opinion as a difference in perspective. One method for dealing with this difference is the "moratorium" device that suspends the death penalty for a trial period. This may, as it did in Great Britain from 1965 to 1969, facilitate the transition from de facto to formal abolition of the death penalty.

4.   *The human rights linkage*

We have noted a correlation between an absence of execution
ernmental respect for human rights. This association is not, c
fortuitous. Both nonexecution and human rights policy are derived irom
the same conception of the proper relationship between citizen and government in the political and social order. That conception involves a
negative constraint on government regarding its use of individuals as a
means to political ends.

Today's limits on the extent to which human beings may be manipu-
lated for social purposes have been defined, in terms of a concept of
rights with Lockean antecedents, in the United Nations' Universal Declaration of Human Rights: "Everyone has the right to life, liberty and the
security of person. . . . No one shall be subjected to torture or to cruel,
inhuman or degrading treatment or punishment."[56] Amnesty International has declared that its "main ground of opposition to the death
penalty is that it is a cruel, inhuman and degrading punishment and a
violation of the right to life."[57] But opposition to the death penalty is not
merely a matter of protecting criminals from a particular kind of penalty;
it is directed at the protection of all citizens from the power of governments to pursue their own needs

We stop short of trying to determine how many issues require the kind
of leadership from the front found in capital punishment, nor do we
attempt to discuss what elements separate these issues from topics better
suited to simpler theories of democratic representation. Our point is that
these elements accompany the end of capital punishment, the normal
pattern of abolition that provides a standard of comparison with developments in the United States in recent years.

Notes

1.   E. van den Haag & J. Conrad, *The Death Penalty: A Debate* 34 (1983).
2.   *Id.* at 24.
3.   *Id.*
4.   However, this trend is not entirely confined to Western Europe. In some of the
     Eastern European countries with the notable exception of the Soviet Union there has
     been a trend towards the introduction of new penal codes reducing the number of
     crimes punishable by death. In Albania the 1977 Penal Code reduced the number of
     crimes for which a discretionary death sentence was provided from forty to thirty-two
     and the amended 1968 Bulgarian Penal Code reduced the crimes punishable by death
     from fifty to twenty-nine. Moreover, in most of these countries (including East Ger-
     many, Poland, Czechoslovakia, Hungary, Rumania, and Bulgaria) there appears to
     have been a diminution in the number of both death sentences and executions over the
     past two decades. Unfortunately, in most Eastern European countries no official statis-
     tics on death sentences or the use of the death penalty are published; where published
     they are known to be incomplete. U.S. News & World Report, "Death Penalty: A
     World Survey," in *The Death Penalty* 13 (I. Isenberg ed. 1977).

5. European Convention on Human Rights Protocol No. 6, 5 *European Human Rights Reports* 167 (1983).
6. *Id.*
7. Amnesty International, *Report: The Death Penalty* 160 (1979) (hereafter Amnesty International Report).
8. *Id.* at 69.
9. *Id.* at 92–3.
10. *Id.* at 175–6.
11. *Id.* at 58.
12. *Id.* at 198.
13. *Id.* at 144–5.
14. *Id.* at 66.
15. Amnesty International, *Report 1978,* at 154 (1978).
16. Amnesty International Report, at 130.
17. *Id.* at 171–5.
18. A. Amsterdam, "Capital Punishment," *The Stanford Magazine,* Fall/Winter 1977, at 42.
19. *See Durkheim and the Law* (S. Lukes & A. Scull eds. 1983).
20. *Royal Commission on Capital Punishment 1949–1953 Report* iii (1953) (hereafter *Royal Commission Report*).
21. *See* C. Phillipson, *Three Criminal Law Reformers – Beccaria, Bentham, Romilly* (1923).
22. *Royal Commission Report,* at 212.
23. *Id.* at 212, 214.
24. 1 *Gallup International Opinion Polls, Great Britain, 1937–1975,* at 774, 1462 (G. Gallup ed. 1976); *see also* H. Erskine, "The Polls: Capital Punishment," 34 *Pub. Opinion Q.* 300 (1970).
25. Amnesty International Report, at 92–3.
26. P. Ellsworth & L. Ross, "Public Opinion and Capital Punishment: A Close Examination of the Views of Abolitionists & Retentionists," *cited in The Death Penalty in America* 68 (H. Bedau 3d ed. 1982) (hereafter *The Death Penalty in America*).
27. *The Harris Survey* (Louis Harris & Associates, Inc.), *cited in The Death Penalty in America,* at 74 (poll conducted June 1973).
28. N. Vidmar, "Retributive and Utilitarian Motives and Other Correlates of Canadian Attitudes Toward the Death Penalty," 15 *Canadian Psychologist* 337–56 (1974).
29. N. Vidmar & P. Ellsworth, "Research on Attitudes Toward Capital Punishment," in *The Death Penalty in America,* at 68, 75.
30. H. Bedau, "American Attitudes Toward the Death Penalty," in *The Death Penalty in America,* at 68 (emphasis in original) (hereafter H. Bedau, "American Attitudes").
31. *The Harris Survey* (L. Harris & Associates, Inc.), *cited in* Bedau, "Recent Survey Research Data on the Death Penalty," *The Death Penalty in America,* at 92 (poll conducted 1976).
32. *Id.* at 89–90 (polls conducted in 1973 and 1977).
33. N. Vidmar & P. Ellsworth, "Public Opinion and the Death Penalty," in *Capital Punishment in the United States* 125, 131 (H. Bedau & C. Pierce eds. 1976).
34. W. G. Runciman, *A Treatise on Social Theory Vol. I,* at 67–8 (1983).
35. A. Sarat & N. Vidmar, "Public Opinion, the Death Penalty, and the Eighth Amendment: Testing the Marshall Hypothesis," in *Capital Punishment in the United States,* at 190.
36. *Id.* at 205.
37. *Id.* at 202.
38. *Id.*
39. *Id.* at 203.
40. N. Teeters, *Deliberations of the International Penal and Penitentiary Congresses: Questions and Answers 1872–1937* (1949).
41. *Id.* at 137–8.
42. B. Alper, *Crime: International Agenda: Concern and Action in the Prevention of Crime and Treatment of Offenders 1846–1972,* at 79 (1972).

43. Council of Europe: European Committee on Crime Problems, *The Death Penalty in European Countries* 3 (1962) (hereafter Council of Europe).
44. J. Power, *Amnesty International: The Human Rights Story* 32 (1981) (emphasis added) (hereafter J. Power, *Amnesty International).*
45. *Id.* (emphasis added).
46. Amnesty International Report, at 1.
47. Council of Europe, at 55.
48. J. Power, *Amnesty International,* at 34.
49. *Id.*
50. Council of Europe, at 53.
51. *Id.*
52. *Id.*
53. *Id.*
54. R. Buxton, "The Politics of Criminal Law Reform: England," 25 *Am. J. Compar. L.* 244 (1973).
55. H. Bedau, "American Attitudes," at 68.
56. United Nations, *Yearbook on Human Rights for 1948,* at 466 (1950).
57. Amnesty International Report, at 3.

2

The long-term trend that failed

In the first chapter of *Executions in America,* published in 1974, William J. Bowers wrote of "the abandonment of capital punishment" and "the demise of executions in America" as something that "has not been adequately explained from a historical viewpoint."[1] The same year Hugo Bedau predicted "we will not see another execution in this nation in this century."[2] Many others probably felt that there would never be another execution in America; that an era or epoch had ended; and that the time for historical analysis and explanation had come.

At the time, these observations seemed accurate. There had not been a legal execution in this country since 1967, and there had been a dramatic decline in the number of executions per year over the preceding three decades: from 199 in 1935 to 1 in 1966.[3] In light of subsequent events, however, these predictions were premature.

Historians usually provide more or less systematic accounts of what has happened in the life or development of a people, a country, or an institution, although they occasionally speculate about what might have happened. The task we attempt in this chapter is of a different character: an explanation of something that did not happen.

Figure 2.1 shows the trend in legal executions in the United States over the past fifty years.

By this writing the history of capital punishment in the United States should have ended with abolition of the practice. All the landmarks are there – the last execution in 1967, the *Furman* decision in 1972, a decade without execution. This chapter briefly sets out the long history of the move toward the end of capital punishment in America. Chapter 3 discusses the two Supreme Court cases that first culminated and then apparently reversed the momentum of many decades toward abolition.

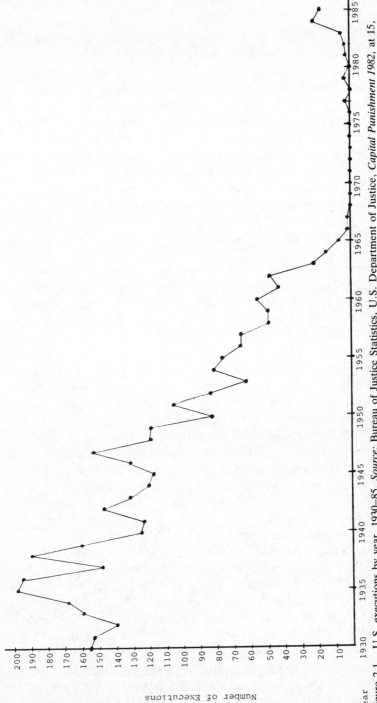

Year

Figure 2.1. U.S. executions by year, 1930–85. *Source:* Bureau of Justice Statistics, U.S. Department of Justice, *Capital Punishment 1982*, at 15, Table 2 (1983); NAACP Legal Defense and Educational Fund, Inc., *Death Row U.S.A.* 2 (Aug. 1, 1986).

Number of Executions

A. America as pioneer

To many observers in the early nineteenth century, America seemed to
be, in Alexis de Tocqueville's words, "a new universe" with distinctive
qualities and characteristics that "seemed to distinguish the citizens of the
United States from all Europeans."[4] "Civilized in externals but a savage
at heart," wrote Herman Melville, "America is, or may yet be, the Paul
Jones of nations."[5] The contrast between the United States and the rest
of the Western world was striking in many sociopolitical areas and not
least in the penal system that de Tocqueville came to America to study.
Nevertheless, as the century passed, even in the notably inelastic area of
penal policy a remarkable parallelism, and a degree of reciprocity, developed – probably influenced to some extent by de Tocqueville's own
writing.[6] This parallelism is particularly clear in relation to the death
penalty.

Chapter 1 discussed the decline of the death penalty in the rest of the
Western world, and America, far from being excluded, has an indisput-
able claim as a pioneer in this development. When the Territory of Michigan in 1846 voted to abolish capital punishment for all crimes except
treason, effective March 1, 1847, it preceded the first European country
to do so by twenty years. Indeed, two American states, Rhode Island in
1852 and Wisconsin in 1853, had eliminated the penalty for all crimes
including treason before Portugal, the first European nation to abolish,
did so in 1867. America retained its position in the forefront of the
abolitionist movement in the twentieth century. When, in 1927, E. Roy
Calvert published his eloquent and influential statement of "the case
against capital punishment," he devoted eleven pages, three tables, and a
graph to the American situation in his chapter on "The Position in Other
Countries." Moreover, he classified America as an "abolitionist country."[7] Table 2.1 indicates that some evidence existed at that time to
support this categorization.

As indicated above, America's entry into World War I led to restoration of the death penalty in a number of states. Moreover, in the four
decades between 1917 and 1957 there was not a single repeal of death
penalty legislation. Nevertheless, in the years following 1930 the movement away from the death penalty continued. This is clear from the
consistent decline in the number of executions despite the absence of
formal abolition. Table 2.2 shows the trend in executions from 1935 to
1969 by year and by the average for five-year intervals. This progressive
decline in executions was accompanied in the latter years by a resumption
of abolitionist legislation. Once again this paralleled developments in
Europe, and in other Western countries, as Table 2.3 demonstrates.

Table 2.1. *Abolition of the death penalty by jurisdiction in the United States and Europe, 1840–1929*

Decade	United States	Europe
1840–9	Michigan (1846)[a]	
1850–9	Rhode Island (1852)[b]	
	Wisconsin (1853)	
1860–9		Portugal (1867)[m]
1870–9	Iowa (1872)[c]	Netherlands (1870)[n]
	Maine (1876)[d]	Switzerland (1874)[o]
1880–9	Maine (1887)[d]	
1890–9	Colorado (1897)[e]	Italy (1890)[p]
1900–9	Kansas (1907)[f]	Norway (1905)[q]
1910–19	Minnesota (1911)	
	Washington (1913)[g]	
	Oregon (1914)[h]	
	North Dakota (1915)	
	South Dakota (1915)[i]	
	Tennessee (1915)[j]	
	Arizona (1916)[k]	
	Missouri (1917)[l]	
1920–9		Sweden (1921)

[a] Death penalty retained for treason until 1963.
[b] Death penalty restored in 1882 for a life term convict who commits murder.
[c] Death penalty restored in 1878 and abolished again in 1965.
[d] Death penalty restored in 1883 and abolished again, as shown above, in 1887.
[e] Death penalty restored in 1901.
[f] Death penalty restored in 1935.
[g] Death penalty restored in 1919.
[h] Death penalty restored in 1920 and abolished again in 1964.
[i] Restored the death penalty in 1939.
[j] Restored the death penalty in 1917.
[k] Restored the death penalty in 1918.
[l] Restored the death penalty in 1919.
[m] Retained for some military crimes until 1977.
[n] Restored the death penalty in 1943 for war crimes committed during World War II.
[o] Limited restoration in 1879 and totally abolished in 1942.
[p] Restored the death penalty in 1931 and abolished it again in 1944.
[q] Military Penal Code retains death penalty for acts of treason during wartime, and after World War II thirty-eight collaborators were executed.
Source: Royal Commission on Capital Punishment 1949–1953 Report App. 6, at 340 (1953); W. Bowers, *Executions in America* 6 (1974); Amnesty International, *Report: The Death Penalty* 121 (1979).

Table 2.2. *Executions by year and average for five-year intervals in the United States, 1935–69*

Years	No. of executions	Five-year averages	Years	No. of executions	Five-year averages
1935	199		1955	76	
1936	195		1956	65	
1937	147		1957	65	
1938	190		1958	49	
1939	160	178	1959	49	61
1940	124		1960	56	
1941	123		1961	42	
1942	147		1962	47	
1943	131		1963	21	
1944	120	129	1964	15	36
1945	117		1965	7	
1946	131		1966	1	
1947	153		1967	2	
1948	119		1968	0	
1949	119	128	1969	0	2
1950	82				
1951	105				
1952	83				
1953	62				
1954	81	83			

Source: Bureau of Justice Statistics, U.S. Department of Justice, *Capital Punishment 1978,* at 16, Table 1 (1979).

B.   Two countries?

The national figures shown in Table 2.2, like many other American aggregates, can be somewhat misleading. They mislead if they suggest that the decline in executions was a national phenomenon – a consistent and uniform development throughout the country. In fact, the national aggregates mask considerable regional variations, and these variations are important to analyzing the progressive abandonment of executions in America.

The crucial regional difference is that between the South and the rest of the United States. Between 1935 and 1969, as Table 2.4 demonstrates, more executions took place in the South than in all the other regions combined.

Of the fourteen states, each of which performed over 100 executions between 1930 and 1969, ten were Southern. Those Southern states together accounted for 1,901 executions: approximately half of the 3,859

Table 2.3. *Abolition of death penalty by jurisdiction in the United States, Europe, and other Western countries, 1930–69*

Decade	United States	Europe and Western countries
1930–9		Denmark (1930)^c
1940–9		Iceland (1940)
		Switzerland (1942)^c
		Italy (1944)
		Australia – Federal (1945)^b
		W. Germany (1949)
		Finland (1949)
1950–9	Alaska (1957)	Greenland (1954)
	Hawaii (1957)	Australia (NSW) (1955)^d
	Delaware (1958)^a	
1960–9	Oregon (1964)	New Zealand (1961)^d
	Iowa (1965)	U.K. (Great Britain) (1965)^{d,e}
	West Virginia (1965)^b	U.K. (Northern Ireland) (1966)^d
	Vermont (1965)^b	Canada (1967)
	New York (1966)^b	Australia (Tasmania) (1968)
	New Mexico (1969)^b	

^{a} Restored in 1961.
^{b} Retained for certain extraordinary civil offenses.
^{c} Retained for certain wartime offenses.
^{d} Retained for treason and piracy.
^{e} Suspension in 1965 was made permanent in 1969.
Source: W. Bowers, *Executions in America* 6, Table 1–1, 178, Table 7–3 (1974).

total for all the United States in that period. The distribution of those executions is shown in Table 2.5.

The South's execution policy can be distinguished in other respects from the rest of the country. The Southern states had more extensive lists of capital statutes than did the others, the four states with ten or more capital statutes being Alabama (17), Arkansas (13), Kentucky (11), and Virginia (10). By 1965 only one of the seventeen Southern states (the border state of West Virginia) did not retain the death penalty. Of the 455 persons executed for rape between 1930 and 1969, 443 or 97.4 percent were executed in the South. Moreover, of those executed 398, or 90 percent, were black. In the South, eleven men were executed for burglary, all of whom were black. In the South, twenty-three men were executed for armed robbery, nineteen of whom were black.[8]

At first sight, so striking is the contrast between the South and the other regions that the South appears to be "another country." Yet over the years from 1930 to 1969 a number of the top ten executing states were not in the South. The heavily populated states of New York (329), Cali-

Table 2.4. *Executions in five-year intervals for four regions of the United States, 1935–69*

Five-year intervals	Northeast	North central	West	South
1935–9	145	113	100	524
1940–4	110	42	73	413
1945–9	74	64	76	419
1950–4	56	42	65	244
1955–9	51	16	51	183
1960–4	17	16	45	102
1965–9	0	5	3	2
Total	453	298	413	1,887

Source: Bureau of Justice Statistics, U.S. Department of Justice, *Capital Punishment 1981,* at 15, Table 2 (1982).

fornia (292), Ohio (172), and Pennsylvania (152) each executed more than did a number of Southern states: Alabama (135), Louisiana (133), Arkansas (118), and Kentucky (103). Furthermore, the decline in executions, as shown in Table 2.5, did not follow a uniform course in the South, so that there is no characteristic pattern for that region. Texas, for example, experienced a sharp drop in executions in the early 1940s but thereafter continued to execute with some regularity until the mid-1960s. In Georgia, North Carolina, and South Carolina the steepest decline came later, in the early 1950s. In Florida, Mississippi, and Louisiana it came even later, in the late 1950s and early 1960s.

Because of the Southern states' dominant role in use of the death penalty, they largely determined the national pattern in executions. Thus, the major decline in executions in that region during the 1950s and 1960s was the numerically dominant factor in the "demise" of executions in America. It is necessary, therefore, to examine the circumstances that led to the sharply decreased use of the death penalty in the South between the late 1950s and the late 1960s.

According to de Tocqueville, "there is hardly a political question in the United States which does not sooner or later turn into a judicial one."[9] It is not surprising, therefore, that the judiciary played an important role in the abolitionist movement. Indeed, in his discussion of "the judicial assault on capital punishment in America," William Bowers argued that "growing receptivity of higher courts to appeals in capital cases may have played a *crucial role* in the demise of executions by encouraging death row prisoners to appeal their cases and by discouraging penal authorities from scheduling and performing executions."[10]

Table 2.5. *Executions in five-year intervals for Southern states performing over 100 executions from 1930 to 1969*

Five-year intervals	GA	TX	NC	FL	SC	MS	AL	LA	AR	KY
1930–4	64	48	51	15	37	26	19	39	20	18
1935–9	73	72	80	29	30	22	41	19	33	34
1940–4	58	38	50	38	32	34	29	24	20	19
1945–9	72	36	62	27	29	26	21	23	18	15
1950–4	51	49	14	22	16	15	14	14	11	8
1955–9	34	25	5	27	10	21	6	13	7	8
1960–4	14	29	1	12	8	10	4	1	9	1
1965–9	0	0	0	0	0	0	1	0	0	0
Total	366	297	263	170	162	154	135	133	118	103

Source: Bureau of Justice Statistics, U.S. Department of Justice, *Capital Punishment 1981*, at 15, Table 2 (1982).

Nor is it suprising that the focus of this "judicial assault" was in the Southern states, beginning with *Powell* v. *Alabama* (1932), when the U.S. Supreme Court ruled that the accused in a capital case "requires the guiding hand of counsel at every step in the proceedings against him."[11] *Powell* guaranteed that defendants could obtain both the legal advice necessary to identify the grounds for appeals and the assistance necessary to carry such appeals forward. This case and the other early landmark Supreme Court cases such as *Patton* v. *Mississippi* (1947), which prohibited racial discrimination in jury selection; *Fikes* v. *Alabama* (1957), which provided protection against coerced confessions; and *Shepherd* v. *Florida* (1951) and *Hamilton* v. *Alabama* (1961), which elucidated and developed the rulings in *Powell* and *Patton*, all "typically involved the rights of black defendants in southern trial courts."[12] Furthermore, it was in the 1950s and 1960s in the South that the American Civil Liberties Union and the NAACP Legal Defense and Education Fund, Inc. (Legal Defense Fund) became active, "appealing the cases of condemned offenders, particularly black rapists, in Southern states and, by implication, challenging the law enforcement and judicial practices that resulted in the death sentence for such offenders."[13]

C. The moratorium strategy

Only in the mid-1960s did the Legal Defense Fund develop a strategy for direct systematic challenge to the institution of capital punishment. Termed the "moratorium strategy," the plan involved presenting the entire range of anti–capital-punishment arguments in all cases in which execution appeared imminent and representing every death row inmate who sought Legal Defense Fund assistance. Michael Meltsner has summarized the rationale underlying the moratorium strategy as follows:

The politics of abolition boiled down to this: for each year the United States went without executions, the more hollow would ring claims that the American people could not do without them; the longer death-row inmates waited, the greater their numbers, the more difficult it would be for the courts to permit the first execution. A successful moratorium strategy would create a death-row logjam.[14]

The strategy was undeniably successful, but it is impossible to determine precisely how successful because what has been called the "pileup on death row"[15] had begun some time before the Legal Defense Fund launched its campaign in the mid-1960s. As Hugo Bedau put it, the campaign was "superimposed upon a trend that was already underway . . . throughout most of the nation during the previous two decades."[16] The result was that the number of prisoners under sentence of death increased by 277 percent in one decade; from 219 at the end of 1960 to 607 at the end of 1970.[17]

It is not necessary here to recount all the details of the moratorium campaign up to *Furman* v. *Georgia* (1972) in which the U.S. Supreme Court ruled that the death penalty was "cruel and unusual" punishment because it had been used in an arbitrary and discriminatory fashion.[18] It is necessary, however, to distinguish some of the principal legal claims and challenges that combined to force the Supreme Court to consider the constitutionality of capital case procedures.

Hugo Bedau described the story of the campaign as one of "losing every major battle except the first and the last."[19] The first successful battle began with class action habeas corpus petitions filed in federal district courts in Florida and California by the Legal Defense Fund on behalf of death row prisoners. The federal courts granted a stay of execution to all death row inmates in both states pending review of constitutional objections to the death sentence.[20] Thus began the steady buildup of persons under sentence of death, which reached a total of 620 at the end of 1972.[21]

Table 2.6 illustrates how litigation in the U.S. Supreme Court and various state courts led to this accumulation of prisoners on death row.

Of importance in some subsequent cases was the application of social science research to demonstrate racial discrimination in death sentencing and execution practices. A variety of studies since 1940 provided evidence of this discrimination, the extent of which is most apparent in cases of death sentences for rape. This evidence was ably summarized by Marvin Wolfgang, who in 1965 cooperated with the Legal Defense Fund in con-

Table 2.6. *Moratorium on executions and death row populations, 1961–72*

Year	No. of prisoners executed during year	No. of prisoners under sentence of death Jan. 1
1961	42	219
1962	47	266
1963	21	268
1964	15	298
1965	7	322
1966	1	351
1967	2	415
1968	0	434
1969	0	479
1970	0	524
1971	0	607
1972	0	620

Source: U.S. Department of Justice, National Prisoner Statistics Bulletin, *Capital Punishment 1971–1972*, at 20, Table 4 (1974).

ducting an examination of the relationship between race and sentencing for rape in a number of Southern and border states where rape was a capital crime. He found that "during the twenty year period from 1945 to 1965 in seven southern states . . . there has been a systematic, differential practice of imposing the death penalty on blacks for rape and, most particularly, when the defendants are black and their victims are white."[22]

Attorneys presented Wolfgang's statistical analyses as evidence in state and federal appellate courts to support the contention of racial discrimination in the imposition of the death penalty. Nevertheless, courts maintained that such evidence, whatever it might demonstrate about the past or other localities, was irrelevant to any particular case under review. For example, in *Maxwell* v. *Bishop* (1968) in which Wolfgang appeared as a witness, the court of appeals held that "whatever it may disclose with respect to other localities, we feel that the statistical argument does nothing to destroy the integrity of Maxwell's trial . . . [The statistics do not] relate specifically to Garland county where this particular offense was committed and where Maxwell was tried and convicted."[23]

Witherspoon v. *Illinois* (1968) was another case in which social science research was used. Here the petitioners argued before the Supreme Court that to exclude persons opposed to the death penalty from juries in capital cases – a practice common to almost every capital punishment state – deprived the defendant of the right to a jury that was representative of the community.[24] The evidence offered consisted of opinion survey results suggesting that jurors who favored capital punishment were more prone to convict than were jurors who opposed the penalty. The Supreme Court rejected the available evidence as too "tentative and fragmentary," avoiding the issue of whether Witherspoon's jury was lawfully chosen from a random cross section of the community. It did rule, however, that the Constitution prohibited challenging jurors opposed to the death penalty in order to obtain a "hanging jury."[25] Although the Court made the ruling fully retroactive, the immediate effect was slight, and only a few subsequent cases have vacated death sentences because they violated *Witherspoon.*[26]

Death penalty opponents also challenged its use for crimes other than murder. The year after *Witherspoon* the death penalty was attacked in *Boykin* v. *Alabama* (1969), the argument being that Edward Boykin's execution for robbery, in light of the infrequent and discriminatory use of the death penalty for that crime, constituted "cruel and unusual punishment" under the Eighth Amendment. The Supreme Court avoided the constitutional issue and returned the case to the state trial court on procedural grounds.[27] However, in 1970 the Fourth Circuit Court of Appeals, in *Ralph* v. *Warden,* ruled that the death penalty for rape was "disproportionate" to the crime and therefore was unconstitutional because it amounted to "cruel and unusual punishment."[28] As Meltsner explained, this was "an important psychological breakthrough," even though the ruling was inapplicable to the majority of death row prisoners, because they had been convicted not of rape but of murder.[29]

Another unsuccessful constitutional challenge to the death penalty was *McGautha* v. *California* (1971).[30] In this case the procedural issue of sentencing standards and practices that had earlier been unsuccessfully argued in *Maxwell* v. *Bishop* was again the issue. The argument in *McGautha* focused on whether it was constitutional, in the absence of standards or guidelines, to give the jury complete discretion to impose the penalty. The Supreme Court by a vote of six to three held that the "due process" guarantee of the Fourteenth Amendment did not require states to establish standards or guidelines that juries must follow in sentencing.[31] Writing for the majority, Justice Harlan stated that to identify death cases "before the fact" and to fashion the criteria in an intelligible formula "appear to be tasks which are beyond present human ability."[32] Commenting on Justice Harlan's defense of the standardless process, Professor Harry Kalven, Jr. wrote that the Court's reasoning disclosed "a fatal flaw, a kind of reductio ad absurdum in the death penalty itself."[33] "What does it mean about the nature of the death penalty," he wrote, "that either it cannot, so we are told, be administered through a set of rules guiding its allocation or that no responsible organ of government is willing to take on the burden of allocating it?"[34]

In the final stages of the moratorium campaign two cases were notable. In the first, *People* v. *Anderson* (1972), the California Supreme Court declared that the state's death penalty was unconstitutional under California's prohibition against cruel or unusual punishments.[35] Thus California, with the largest death row population in the nation, produced "the first holding by any court that the death penalty per se violates constitutional provisions."[36]

The second, *Furman* v. *Georgia* (1972), was already in progress when the California court announced its decision in *Anderson* in February 1972. In the three cases combined under *Furman* v. *Georgia*[37] the Supreme Court had granted review on the question: "Does the imposition and carrying out of the death penalty in this case constitute cruel and unusual punishment in violation of the Eighth and Fourteenth Amendments?" The Supreme Court was under unusual pressure to resolve this issue, not only because of the great number of appeals that had been brought before it, but also because no executions had occurred since 1967 and there were more than 600 persons on death rows in thirty-two states.

On June 29, 1972, the Supreme Court, in a five-to-four decision, held that, to carry out the death penalty in the cases under review would be cruel and unusual punishment, in violation of the Eighth and Fourteenth Amendments, and it reversed the lower courts' imposition of death sentences.[38] The Justices entered similar orders in 120 other death penalty appeals pending before the Court and effectively prevented the execution of all prisoners on death row at the time.

Commentators viewed the decision as a milestone in the abolition movement. "At one stroke" said Hugo Bedau, "this ruling in effect abolished all death penalties throughout the nation."[39] "By implication," wrote Daniel Polsby, "most or all extant statutes in American jurisdictions that prescribe the death penalty are unconstitutional."[40] Jack Greenberg of the Legal Defense Fund issued a statement asserting that "there will no longer be any more capital punishment in the United States."[41] Philip Kurland in his review of the Supreme Court's 1971 term wrote: "[O]ne role of the Constitution is to help the nation to become 'more civilized.' A society with the aspirations that ours so often asserts cannot consistently with its goals, coldly and deliberatley take the life of any human being no matter how reprehensible his past behavior. . . . In the *Furman* v. *Georgia* decision the inevitable came to pass."[42]

In his account of the Legal Defense Fund campaign against the death penalty, Michael Meltsner said that in the early 1960s "no one could have predicted that within a few years gas chambers and electric chairs would be dismantled; and that the Supreme Court would rule the death penalty had been administered in so random, illogical, and discriminatory a fashion that it was unconstitutional."[43]

Kurland was not alone in considering *Furman* as inevitable. Over half a century earlier one of the first sociologists to study the history of capital punishment in America had predicted that "in the course of the present century the use of the death penalty will finally pass away."[44] In 1952 another sociologist wrote that "the death penalty has become an unacceptable and ineffective method of punishment and has been largely replaced by imprisonment."[45] In 1964 Bedau had observed that the death penalty was being used so sparingly in the United States that "the obvious inference is that the death penalty in our country is an anachronism, a vestigial survivor of an earlier era."[46]

Such foresights did not require precognitive powers. Frank Hartung, twenty years before *Furman,* noted that "the over-all, international trend is toward the progressive abolition of capital punishment."[47] America had long been a part of that prevailing tendency or course of events. The essential question is not why the *Furman* v. *Georgia* decision came when it did, but why the general trend toward abolition was subsequently reversed.

D.   The *Furman* backlash

Some of the initial reaction to this seeming judicial abolition of the death penalty bordered on hysteria. Michael Meltsner[48] gave some characteristic examples: Georgia's Lieutenant Governor Lester Maddox described the decision as "a license for anarchy, rape, murder." Alabama's Lieutenant Governor Jere Beasley claimed that "a majority of this nation's highest court has lost contact with the real world." Atlanta Police Chief John Inman spoke of the loss of a "definite deterrent to major crimes." Memphis Police Chief Bill Price asserted that those who had "hesitated to pull the trigger before just might go ahead now."

Many commentators also predicted a swift legislative reaction. The *New York Daily News* urged state legislators to readopt the death penalty with all its "old time" severity to see "what the Supreme Court does about that."[49] Tom Wicker in his *New York Times* column predicted that there would be "a flurry of state laws requiring, for instance, mandatory death sentences" for such crimes as vicious rapes and killing police officers or prison guards.[50] Members of Congress discussed the possibility of a constitutional amendment to permit the death penalty.[51] Wicker's prediction about legislative activity proved accurate. Bedau's words explain the story concisely:

Table 2.7. *American public opinion on death penalty for murder*[a]

Survey date	Percent opposed	Percent in favor
November 1953	28	72
March 1960	41	59
February 1965	48	53
July 1966	53	47
June 1967	40	60
January 1969	44	56
October 1971	46	54
February 1972	45	55
March 1972	43	58
March 1973	37	63
March 1974	34	67

[a] Figures rounded to nearest decimal point; noncommittal responses (e.g., "Don't know") deleted.
Source: Smith, "A Trend Analysis of Attitudes toward Capital Punishment 1936–1974," *in* 2 *Studies of Social Change Since 1948*, at 263, Table IB (J. Davis ed. 1976).

Within a year after *Furman,* commissions had been formed in several states to make recommendations on the issue, and bills to restore capital punishment had been introduced in three dozen state legislatures. By midsummer such bills had already been signed into law in twenty states. On the second anniversary of *Furman,* twenty-eight states had new death penalty legislation and more than 100 persons in seventeen states had been sentenced to death under these new laws.[52]

The legislative backlash corresponded to, though it was not guided by, a parallel movement in public opinion. American public opinion on the death penalty has been measured in a variety of national surveys since 1936, and the results clearly reveal *Furman's* impact on public opinion. Opposition to capital punishment had gained ground steadily from 1953 until, in 1966, a majority opposed capital punishment. Between 1953 and 1966 support for the death penalty declined by twenty-five percent. In 1967 opposition to the death penalty declined, but this was quickly reversed and opposition remained high until 1972 (the year of *Furman*) when a dramatic decline occurred.

National surveys conducted by the American Institute of Public Opinion (Gallup) and the National Opinion Research Center put the question: "Are you in favor of the death penalty for persons convicted of murder?" Table 2.7, derived from survey responses, illustrates the trends in opposition to the death penalty from 1953 to 1974. The dimension of

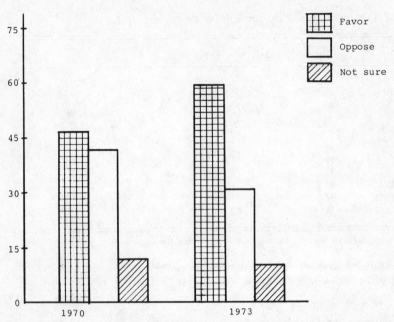

Figure 2.2.   Public attitudes toward capital punishment, United States, 1970 and 1973. *Source:* adapted from U.S. Department of Justice, *Sourcebook of Criminal Justice Statistics 1980*, at 199, Figure 2-7 (1981); constructed by *Sourcebook* staff on the basis of L. Harris, *The Harris Survey* 1 (1977).

the shift in public opinion in reaction to *Furman* is also illustrated in Figure 2.2, derived from the Harris Survey.

The reaction to *Furman* might have been expected. Potent symbols are relinquished only with some misgivings, although the early level of apprehension does not usually persist for long. In Great Britain, for example, the percentage favoring the death penalty increased from seventy percent in February 1965, prior to suspension of the penalty for an experimental period, to seventy-six percent in 1966, the year after suspension. Yet by 1970, the year after abolition was made permanent by resolutions of both Houses of Parliament, support for the death penalty had fallen to sixty-one percent.[53] Of course, a U.S. Supreme Court decision is not the equivalent of resolutions in both the Commons and Lords in Great Britain, or for that matter, an act of our own Congress. Indeed, some observers saw the Supreme Court as having courageously done what the legislative branch was too pusillanimous to do. "For what happened," wrote Burton Wolfe, "should be plain to anyone: the courts abolished the death penalty. . . . The courts ended it because wiser, more honest, and more courageous men than the majority of those in high elected office perceived that abolition of capital punishment was one of the most basic steps toward the creation of a society that solves its problems without resorting to violence."[54]

In fact, the Supreme Court had stopped short of total abolition: "[T]he Court's decision in *Furman* v. *Georgia* was not definitive in character."[55] True, the decision invalidated the capital punishment laws of nearly all the states that retained the death penalty and of the federal government and the District of Columbia. None of the prisoners on death row could be executed nor could anyone be sentenced to death. The death penalty controversy, however, had not been settled in a decisive or final way. As Chief Justice Burger stated in his dissenting opinion:

Since there is no majority of the Court on the ultimate issue presented in these cases, the future of capital punishment in this country has been left in an uncertain limbo. Rather than providing a final and unambiguous answer on the basic constitutional question the collective impact of the majority's ruling is to demand an undetermined measure of change from the various state legislatures and the Congress . . . . I am not altogether displeased that legislative bodies have been given the opportunity, and indeed unavoidable responsibility, to make a thorough reevaluation of the entire subject of capital punishment.[56]

E. The social psychology of backlash

State legislatures, as we have seen, quickly responded to the Court's decision, but instead of conducting a thorough reevaluation of the subject, they enacted whatever statutory revisions they perceived as correcting the constitutional flaws contained in pre-*Furman* capital laws. By 1976 thirty-five states had enacted new death penalty laws, usually based on some variation of the Model Penal Code provisions. Death sentences were swiftly imposed and by the end of 1976 more than 460 persons were subject to the death penalty.[57]

Charles L. Black, Jr., in describing the post-*Furman* legislative frenzy, concluded that it resulted from "the operation of causes which those of us who oppose capital punishment can only guess at."[58] A decade later we think it possible to provide more substantial analysis of this question than random conjecture or surmise.

We have found that the most plausible explanations of the political reaction in those states responding to *Furman* with new death penalty legislation are from the literature of social psychology, either the so-called frustration–aggression hypothesis or the theory of psychological reactance.

According to the frustration–aggression hypothesis, "aggression is always a consequence of frustration."[59] Furthermore, when the frustrating condition appears arbitrary, aggression occurs more readily; "the arbitrariness of the frustration [is] an important determinant of the intensity of the aggression."[60] Might not this image, overdrawn perhaps as a psychological principle,[61] still capture the essence of legislative response to the federal judiciary taking away the power to legislate the death sentence?

Even more descriptive of legislative response is the notion of psychological reactance. The loss of freedom to legislate on the death penalty triggers a strong desire to reassert the legislative power to act.[62] The surge in interest and activity was a response, reasserting authority against federal power as much as acting on criminal justice. Both the shift in public opinion (Table 2.7 and Figure 2.2) and the legislative backlash evidently represent a response to the deprivation of the death penalty option; but it is important to distinguish the political response from the changes in public opinion, because what the legislatures did was not simply a reflection of variations in public opinion from state to state.

Public opinion reacted to *Furman* in the same way – with a hostile response – all over the country: in abolitionist states, in de facto abolitionist states, and in death penalty states. By contrast, the legislative pattern varied among the different states and was highly contingent on each state's previous capital punishment policy. Those states that were abolitionist by legislation prior to *Furman* remained abolitionist with Oregon as the one exception. Nor did any substantial change of policy occur in those states that had special and very restrictive death penalty provisions. For example, New York, where the public is subject to the same passion about the death penalty as in other states, and which has some of the highest crime rates in the country, currently does not employ it. Nor does Massachusetts, despite a referendum vote in favor of the death penalty and the passage of a bill in the legislature that the governor vetoed.

Table 2.8 classifies states by the status of the death penalty in June 1972, when *Furman* was decided. Of the pre-*Furman* abolitionist states, only Oregon – a jurisdiction that vacillated in the years before 1972 – has a death penalty in force. Additionally, both California and New Jersey, whose death penalty statutes were invalidated by state court action prior to *Furman,* reactivated the legislation; perhaps a state level frustration–aggression scenario.

The pre-*Furman* death penalty states are almost unanimous in the opposite direction. Capital punishment laws were enacted in thirty-two of thirty-five jurisdictions that had such legislation prior to the *Furman* decision. In one state, Massachusetts, the legislative attempt was vetoed by the governor and struck down by the state supreme court without subse-

Table 2.8. *Current status of capital punishment by pre-*Furman *legislation, fifty states*

		Post-*Furman* response	
Pre-*Furman*		No death penalty	Death penalty
Non–death penalty states by legislation (9)	Alaska, Hawaii, Iowa, Maine, Michigan, Minnesota. Oregon, West Virginia, Wisconsin	All, except Oregon (8)	Oregon
Non–death penalty states by judicial invalidation (2)	California, New Jersey	None	California, New Jersey
Restrictive death penalty states (5)	New Mexico, New York, North Dakota, Rhode Island, Vermont	New York,[a] North Dakota, Vermont[b]	New Mexico, Rhode Island
Death penalty states (35) (plus District of Columbia)	Alabama, Arizona, Arkansas, Colorado, Connecticut, Delaware, District of Columbia, Florida, Georgia, Idaho, Illinois, Indiana, Kansas, Kentucky, Louisiana, Maryland, Massachusetts, Mississippi, Missouri, Montana, Nebraska, Nevada, New Hampshire, North Carolina, Ohio, Oklahoma, Pennsylvania, South Carolina, South Dakota, Tennessee, Texas, Utah, Virginia, Washington, Wyoming	District of Columbia, Kansas, Massachusetts[c]	All others (32)

[a] Death penalty statute enacted in 1974; declared unconstitutional by state supreme court in 1977 and 1984.
[b] Death penalty statute remains unchanged, but constitutionally infirm.
[c] Death penalty statute enacted in 1979; declared unconstitutional by state supreme court in 1980.

quent moves to reinstitute the penalty. Two jurisdictions, the District of Columbia and Kansas, are the only pre-*Furman* death penalty states without subsequent authorizing statutes; in all others, the penalty is in force.

This near-perfect legislative pattern is as inconsistent with changes in public opinion as one can imagine. In only two of fifty states – Oregon and Kansas – does the electorate seem to have changed the legislature's course. Even in Oregon, the 1978 law continues a stop-and-go pattern that has characterized the issue since midcentury. Everywhere else, past conduct determines present policy.

Almost without exception the states that started executing most promptly after *Gregg* v. *Georgia* were those whose capital punishment laws *Furman* had voided. Far from being representative of national public opinion, they were drawn from the same Southern constituency that provided the bulk of executions over the past half-century. Rather than a resurgent national perception of capital punishment as the solution to the problem of criminal homicide, what this pattern illustrates is a *state* response to a *federal* slight that was seen as arbitrary and unwarranted.

There is, after all, a long history of popular disagreement with, and of political and legislative challenge to, the Supreme Court's antimajoritarian rulings. What has been called "the rejection-of-the-people's-choice function of judicial review"[63] has incurred retaliation by the national and state political branches throughout the existence of the Court. Devotion to states' rights and opposition to the jurisdiction of the federal government and the federal courts is as old as the Union.

There is in fact nothing paradoxical about the zeal of state legislatures in producing new death penalty statutes, or about the fact that "the country did not sigh with relief at the Court's having taken on itself the burden of eliminating this vestigial cruelty, bringing the United States into line with most civilized nations."[64] There may be no consensus about what democracy means, but being brought into line by an unelected, authoritative, elite body would not fit most popular definitions.

Moreover, there are a number of symbolic issues on which state legislatures annually and deliberately test the patience of the constitutional courts, including school prayer, pornography, and abortion. The parallels between the reaction to *Furman* and the reaction to the Supreme Court's decisions in the school prayer cases are striking. In the early 1960s, the Court decided several controversial decisions involving the constitutionality of religious prayer in public schools. In *Engel* v. *Vitale*, the Court held that the use of a prayer composed by the New York Board of Regents violated the First Amendment requirement of separation of church and state.[65] The next year, the Court declared that religious use of the Lord's prayer and Bible reading in classrooms similarly violated the Constitution.

The public outcry against these decisions was "deafening."[66] Within hours of their being handed down, politicians, newspapers, and religious leaders condemned them. Political leaders throughout the country called for constitutional amendments to overturn the Court's rulings; forty-nine such amendments were introduced in Congress.[67] Initial compliance with the rulings was mixed, but eventually many of those who decried the decisions have since applauded them;[68] and, of course, no constitutional amendments were enacted and no impeachment proceedings against the justices were instituted.

The death penalty was precisely the type of politically charged, symbolic policy issue to which judicial invalidation has always provoked anger and resentment. Anyone familiar with the history of the Warren and Burger Courts alone should have been prepared for the reaction to *Furman.* Nor was it surprising that the *Furman* decision was widely construed as being both contrary to the wishes of the majority of citizens and in the interest only of an unpopular and insignificant minority.

F. The end of the trend

What might be surprising is that four years later the Supreme Court, although not overruling *Furman,* rejected abolition by the judiciary. Arguably, the ruling in *Gregg* v. *Georgia* that "the punishment of death does not invariably violate the Constitution"[69] did not represent a complete reversal of opinion. Nevertheless, it surely represented a retreat from the view that the Supreme Court was "charged with the creative function of discerning afresh and of articulating and developing impersonal and durable principles."[70]

Writing for the *Gregg* majority, Justice Stewart, who had declared in *Furman* that the penalty of death was "unique . . . in its absolute renunciation of all that is embodied in our concept of humanity,"[71] now found that it did not offend our standards of decency:

The petitioners in the capital cases before the Court today renew the "standards of decency" argument, but developments during the four years since *Furman* have undercut substantially the assumptions upon which their argument rested . . . it is now evident that a large proportion of American society continues to regard it as an appropriate and necessary criminal sanction. The most marked indication of society's endorsement of the death penalty for murder is the legislative response to *Furman.*[72]

This passage seems to imply that whatever a large proportion of American society *regards* as appropriate *is* appropriate, and that what legislatures do, with what Chief Justice Burger called "their essentially barometric role with respect to community values,"[73] provides a reliable index of what the community regards as appropriate. The role of the Supreme Court, then, would be to do no more than endorse the views of the majority. It has been said that "to what degree the Justices, individually or collectively are guided by perceived public attitudes" is a "complex psycho-empirical problem."[74] In this case it is hardly complex at all.

The *Gregg* decision was not only the end of a trend but also the beginning of a multiphase drama in the U.S. Supreme Court and in the states themselves that is discussed throughout Part II. Whatever the doctrinal significance of *Gregg* (and this we examine in Chapter 3), the decision announced a new era for the states. It transformed capital punishment at the state level from a solely symbolic issue into a practical possibility. Executions, rather than having ceased permanently, might now begin again. The states had power that many key actors in many states, including those producing large numbers of death sentences, had supposed would never again exist. Death rows, ever-present through the 1960s and early 1970s, took on a new meaning because executions could happen.

The Supreme Court's involvement with the death penalty intensified rather than abated as a consequence of *Gregg* and its companion decisions. Major decisions about the death penalty had been announced four times in the decade that culminated in *Gregg*. Now major cases were coming to the Court every term, frequently in clusters, and the prospect of executions strained the Court's power to select questions for review. A wave of decisions voiding death sentences and sections of state death penalty laws was followed in the early 1980s by a series of cases in which wide latitude was granted to state procedures for capital punishment determination in murder cases.

Even those states with large death row populations seemed unprepared for the power returned to them by *Gregg*. Commentators who had predicted an immediate bloodbath in the wake of the *Gregg* decision were wide of the mark. Gary Gilmore's voluntary execution in 1977 was followed by no executions in 1978, two in 1979, none in 1980, and one in 1981.

One major explanation for this very slow startup was the delay imposed by federal courts as a host of subsidiary issues about death penalty standards and procedures wound their way through elaborate legal processes. But the federal courts were not, and are not, the only force restraining executions. There was in truth little evident enthusiasm for executions in the United States and none outside the South. Even a

decade after *Gregg* only a minority of those states with death row populations have experienced any executions.

Many of the events in the first decade after *Gregg* v. *Georgia* are
consistent with the theory that the license to execute, which that decision extended in principle to the states, was both unexpected and not
altogether welcome. Detailed plans for execution were not in place
then, and are still not pursued with full seriousness in many states with
death row inhabitants. The question of how to execute prisoners was
apparently regarded as moot until *Gregg*. Over the following ten years
capital punishment has actually been reintroduced in less than one-
quarter of American states and in less than one-third of the states with
death penalty laws.

In the popular press and political rhetoric of the 1970s, the step toward
abolition taken by the Supreme Court in *Furman* was regarded as radical,
whereas the position taken in *Gregg* v. *Georgia* four years later was seen
as a return to a normal set of institutional arrangements between the U.S.
Supreme Court and the states. Yet viewed in relation to the long-term
history of capital punishment in the United States and the experience of
other Western nations, the opposite view is plausible: *Furman* was the
culmination of a historical movement of long duration, whereas *Gregg*
signaled a sharp departure from trends in the United States and the
development of capital punishment policy in the rest of the West.

There is literally no precedent for what happened after *Gregg*, and for
what will happen next. Did the Supreme Court Justices know they were
mandating so momentous a departure? On what doctrinal basis did it
rest? These are the concerns of Chapter 3.

Notes

1. W. Bowers, *Executions in America* 21, 29 (1974) (hereafter W. Bowers, *Executions*).
2. Bedau, "Challenging the Death Penalty," *Harv. C.R.-C.L.L. Rev.* 9 (May 1974).
3. Bureau of Justice Statistics, U.S. Department of Justice, *Capital Punishment 1982*, at 14, Table 1 (1984) (hereafter *Capital Punishment 1982*).
4. G. Pierson, *Tocqueville and Beaumont in America* 118–19 (1938).
5. H. Melville, *Israel Potter* 120 (Northwestern Univ. Press 1982).
6. G. de Beaumont & A. de Tocqueville, *On the Penitentiary System in the United States and its Application in France* (F. Lieber trans. 1964).
7. E. R. Calvert, *Capital Punishment in the Twentieth Century*, at v, 50, 77–88 (1927).
8. *Capital Punishment 1982*, at 16, Table 3.
9. A. de Tocqueville, *Democracy in America* 270 (G. Lawrence trans. 1969).
10. W. Bowers, *Executions*, at 28 (emphasis added).
11. 287 U.S. 45, 69 (1932).
12. W. Bowers, *Executions*, at 13. The earlier cases cited are *Patton* v. *Mississippi*, 332 U.S. 463 (1947), *Fikes* v. *Alabama*, 352 U.S. 191 (1957), *Shepherd* v. *Florida*, 341 U.S. 50 (1951), and *Hamilton* v. *Alabama*, 368 U.S. 52 (1961).
13. W. Bowers, *Executions*, at 23.
14. M. Meltsner, *Cruel and Unusual: The Supreme Court on Capital Punishment* 107 (1973) (hereafter M. Meltsner, *Cruel and Unusual*).

48   *I. The road to 1987*

15. B. Wolfe, *Pileup on Death Row* (1973) (hereafter B. Wolfe, *Pileup*).
16. Bedau, "Background and Developments," in *The Death Penalty in America* 26 (H. Bedau 3d ed. 1982).
17. National Prisoners Statistics Bulletin, U.S. Department of Justice, *Capital Punishment 1971–1972,* at 20, Table 4 (1974).
18. For more detailed accounts, see M. Meltsner, *Cruel and Unusual,* W. Bowers, *Executions,* and H. Bedau, *The Courts, the Constitution and Capital Punishment* (1977) (hereafter H. Bedau, *Courts*).
19. H. Bedau, *Courts,* at 84.
20. *Adderly* v. *Wainwright,* 272 F. Supp. 530 (M.D. Fla. 1967); *Hill* v. *Nelson,* 272 F. Supp. 790 (N.D. Cal. 1967).
21. National Prisoner Statistics Bulletin, U.S. Department of Justice, *Capital Punishment 1971–1972,* at 20, Table 4 (1974).
22. Wolfgang, "Racial Discrimination in the Death Sentence for Rape," in W. Bowers, *Executions,* at 120.
23. 398 F.2d 138 (8th Cir. 1968).
24. 391 U.S. 510 (1968).
25. *Id.*
26. H. Bedau, *Courts,* at 71.
27. 395 U.S. 238 (1969).
28. 438 F.2d 786 (4th Cir. 1970).
29. M. Meltsner, *Cruel and Unusual,* at 231–2.
30. 402 U.S. 183 (1971).
31. *Id.*
32. *Id.* at 204.
33. Kalven, "Foreword: Even When a Nation Is at War," 85 *Harv. L. Rev.* 25 (1971).
34. *Id.*
35. 6 Cal. 3d 628, 493 P.2d 880, 100 Cal. Rptr. 152, *cert. denied,* 406 U.S. 958 (1972).
36. H. Bedau, *Courts,* at 85.
37. The other two were *Jackson* v. *Georgia,* 225 Ga. 790, 171, S.E.2d 501 (1969), and *Branch* v. *Texas,* 447 S.W.2d 932 (Tex. Crim. App. 1969).
38. *Furman* v. *Georgia,* 408 U.S. 238 (1972).
39. Bedau, "Capital Punishment," in *Encyclopedia of Crime and Justice Vol. I,* at 136 (S. Kadish ed. 1983).
40. Polsby, "The Death of Capital Punishment? *Furman* v. *Georgia,*" 1972 *Sup. Ct. Rev.* 1.
41. M. Meltsner, *Cruel and Unusual,* at 291.
42. Kurland, "1971 Term: The Year of the Stewart–White Court," 1972 *Sup. Ct. Rev.* 296–7.
43. M. Meltsner, *Cruel and Unusual,* at 4.
44. Bye, "Recent History and Present Status of Capital Punishment in the United States," 17 *J. Crim. L., Criminology & Police Science* 239 (1926); *see also Committee of Philanthropic Labor of Philadelphia, Yearly Meeting of Friends, Capital Punishment in the United States* 101 (1919).
45. Caldwell, "Why is Death Penalty Retained?" 284 *Annals Am. Academy Pol. & Soc. Science* 52 (1952).
46. H. Bedau, *The Death Penalty in America* 31 (1964).
47. Hartung, "Trends in the Use of Capital Punishment," 284 *Annals Am. Academy Pol. & Soc. Science* 19 (1952).
48. M. Meltsner, *Cruel and Unusual,* at 290.
49. *Id.* at 291.
50. *Id.*
51. *Id.*
52. H. Bedau, *Courts,* at 93.
53. 1 *Gallup International Opinion Polls, Great Britain, 1937–1975,* at 774, 1462 (G. Gallup ed. 1976); Erskine, "The Polls: Capital Punishment," 34 *Pub. Opinion Q.* 300 (1970).

54. B. Wolfe, *Pileup,* at 416.
55. W. Bowers, *Executions,* at 29.
56. *Furman,* 408 U.S. 238, 403 (1972) (Burger, C.J., dissenting).
57. National Prisoner Statistics, U.S. Department of Justice, *Capital Punishment 1977,* at 5 (1978).
58. C. Black, Jr., *Capital Punishment: The Inevitability of Caprice and Mistake* 12–13 (1974) (hereafter C. Black, *Caprice and Mistake*). One guess that seems clearly mistaken is that "the zeal with which the state and federal lawmakers rushed to patch the capital laws in the wake of *Furman*" should be perceived simply as the outcome of public pressure generated "through the growth of crime, spreading anger and fear, and increase of punitive attitudes." J. Gorecki, *Capital Punishment: Criminal Law and Social Evolution* 112–13 (1983).
59. J. Dollard, N. Miller, L. Doob, O. Mowrer, & R. Sears, *Frustration and Aggression* 1 (1939).
60. *Id.*
61. *See, e.g.,* Berkowitz, "Frustrations, Comparisons, and Other Sources of Emotion Arousal as Contributors to Social Unrest," 28 *J. Soc. Issues* 77 (1972).
62. *See* J. Brehm, *A Theory of Psychological Reactance* (1966).
63. J. Choper, *Judicial Review and the National Political Process* 132 (1980) (hereafter J. Choper, *Judicial Review*).
64. C. Black, *Caprice and Mistake,* at 12.
65. 370 U.S. 421 (1962).
66. F. Friendly & M. Elliott, *The Constitution: That Delicate Balance* 125 (1984).
67. K. Dolbeare & P. Hammond, *The School Prayer Decisions: From Court Policy to Local Practice* 27 (1971); *see also* Kurland, "The Regents' Prayer Case: 'Full of Sound and Fury, Signifying . . . ,' " in *Church and State: The Supreme Court and the First Amendment* 1, 1 (P. Kurland ed. 1975) (hereafter Kurland, "Prayer Case").
68. Kurland, "Prayer Case," at 33.
69. *Gregg* v. *Georgia,* 428 U.S. 153, 169 (1976).
70. Hart, "Foreword: The Time Chart of the Justices," 73 *Harv. L. Rev.* 84, 99 (1959).
71. *Furman* v. *Georgia,* 408 U.S. 238, 306 (1972).
72. *Gregg,* 428 U.S. at 179.
73. *Furman,* 408 U.S. at 385 (Burger, C.J., dissenting).
74. J. Choper, *Judicial Review,* at 125.

3

The death penalty and the Eighth Amendment

Chapter 2 dealt with the involvement of the United States Supreme Court as an historical event in a larger landscape – an event that influenced trends in executions and death sentences. In this chapter a more focused inquiry is necessary. When a constitutional court becomes a significant force in the destiny of an issue, those seeking comprehensive historical explanations of that question must take legal doctrine seriously.

In the case of capital punishment, the central doctrinal conflict of the 1970s was also the most important development in the public career of the issue. The debate concerned the Eighth Amendment ban on cruel and unusual punishment and its relation to the practice of executions. Although the Eighth Amendment issue has focused national attention only since the 1970s, its importance requires a sustained analysis of this debate. That is our task here.

In addressing this conflict, we offer a discussion of the Eighth Amendment that falls short of a systematic jurisprudential analysis or a fully articulated theory of constitutional interpretation. We do not speculate about how the Founders or the Framers might have construed the Eighth Amendment in today's circumstances. Nor do we deal with the "fine-tuning" of cases involving the mandatory death penalty for killing a police officer[1] or the subsidiary questions generated by permitting the death penalty after *Gregg*.[2]

The heart of the matter lies in two sets of opinions, *Furman* v. *Georgia* (1972)[3] and *Gregg* v. *Georgia* (1976),[4] together with the quartet of cases decided the same day as *Gregg* – *Proffitt* v. *Florida*,[5] *Jurek* v. *Texas*,[6] *Woodson* v. *North Carolina*,[7] and *Roberts* v. *Louisiana*[8] – which rejected the argument that imposing the death penalty under any circumstances constitutes cruel and unusual punishment in violation of the Eighth and Fourteenth Amendments. *Furman* and *Gregg* are the two crucial episodes in the history of capital punishment in this country in this century, and we limit our analysis to the essential questions in these two cases. We argue

50

that *Furman*, rightly construed, provided a basis for extending the prohibition of capital punishment, but that the confusions of *Furman* were a substantial barrier to justifying the historically and doctrinally correct result in *Gregg*.

In *Furman* the Supreme Court held that "the imposition and carrying out of the death penalty in these cases constitute cruel and unusual punishment in violation of the Eighth and Fourteenth Amendments."[9] In *Gregg* the plurality opinion specifically addressed a question that was avoided in *Furman:* "[T]he basic contention that the punishment of death for the crime of murder is, under all circumstances, 'cruel and unusual' in violation of the Eighth and Fourteenth Amendments of the Constitution"; the Court held that "the punishment of death does not invariably violate the Constitution."[10]

Any thorough discussion of *Furman* v. *Georgia* must first consider the extraordinary diffusion of the collective reasoning of the Court in that decision. Though many hailed the Supreme Court's decision in *Furman* as the final renunciation of the death penalty, a close examination of the decision reveals a much less certain result. In *Furman* each justice filed a separate opinion, and as Justice Powell explained in his dissent: "[T]he reasons for that judgement are stated in five separate opinions expressing as many separate rationales."[11] Chief Justice Burger, in his dissent, spoke of "the uncertain language of the Eighth Amendment"; of its being "less than self-defining"; and of its "enigmatic character."[12] He also said that "the widely divergent views of the Amendment expressed in today's opinions reveal the haze that surrounds this constitutional command."[13] Certainly, those who hoped that the Court would dispel the haze and provide "new or useful tools which might be used to help the unenlightened to see why the death penalty is cruel and unusual punishment"[14] have found *Furman* disappointing.

A. A singular opinion

Despite the lack of clarity in the Court's decision, one opinion identified, more than any other, the crucial issues in the case – the opinion of Harry A. Blackmun, one of the four dissenting justices. It is a singular opinion in the literal sense because all the other dissenting opinions were joined by all the other dissenters, but no other justice concurred with Justice Blackmun. It is also singular in the coherence with which it reveals a view of the Supreme Court's role in administering the prohibition against cruel and unusual punishment that ultimately dominated and determined the Court's later decision in *Gregg*.

The opinion begins with a passage that deserves quotation in full:

Cases such as these provide for me an excruciating agony of the spirit. I yield to no one in the depth of my distaste, antipathy, and, indeed, abhorrence, for the death penalty, with all its aspects of physical distress and fear and of moral judgment exercised by finite minds. That distaste is buttressed by a belief that capital punishment serves no useful purpose that can be demonstrated. For me, it violates childhood's training and life's experiences, and is not compatible with the philosophical convictions I have been able to develop. It is antagonistic to any sense of "reverence for life." Were I a legislator, I would vote against the death penalty for the policy reasons argued by counsel for the respective petitioners and expressed and adopted in the several opinions filed by the Justices who vote to reverse these judgments.[15]

Justice Blackmun proceeded to cite a number of cases, from 1879 to 1963, in which it was "either the flat or implicit holding of a unanimous Court" that "capital punishment was . . . not unconstitutional per se under the Eighth Amendment."[16] He then said:

Suddenly, however, the course of decision is now the opposite way, with the Court evidently persuaded that somehow the passage of time has taken us to a place of greater maturity and outlook. The argument, plausible and high-sounding as it may be, is not persuasive, for it is only one year since *McGautha,* only eight and one-half years since *Rudolph,* 14 years since *Trop,* and 25 years since *Francis,* and we have been presented with nothing that demonstrates a significant movement of any kind in these brief periods. The Court has just decided that it is time to strike down the death penalty. There would have been as much reason to do this when any of the cited cases were decided. But the Court refrained from that action on each of those occasions.

The Court has recognized, and I certainly subscribe to the proposition, that the Cruel and Unusual Punishments Clause "may acquire meaning as public opinion becomes enlightened by a humane justice." . . . And Mr. Chief Justice Warren, for a plurality of the Court, referred to "the evolving standards of decency that mark the progress of a maturing society." . . .

My problem, however, . . . is the suddenness of the Court's perception of progress in the human attitude since decisions of only a short while ago.[17]

As a technical matter, the Court had never before faced or decided the issue of whether death was cruel and unusual punishment.[18] But the nature of Justice Blackmun's "problem" is in fact crucial here. In effect, Justice Blackmun posed three questions that the majority justices in *Furman* should have addressed: First, why should the death penalty be regarded as cruel and unusual punishment? Second, what evidence is there to support the claim that "the passage of time" has produced the relevant kind of evolutionary development in standards of decency in the United States, from which the Eighth Amendment "must draw its meaning"? Finally, why is *now* (that is, 1972) the time to strike down the death penalty?

Justice Blackmun's questions are answerable but they were not well addressed in the five opinions that uneasily coalesced to form the *Furman* majority. At the time this was regrettable; four years later the answers should have proved decisive.

B. The majority opinions

Justice Brennan's doctrinal analysis came closest to responding to Blackmun's concerns. He began by describing the purpose of the Bill of Rights, in particular the Eighth Amendment's prohibition of cruel and unusual punishments. Without this clause, "the legislature would otherwise have had the unfettered power to prescribe punishments for crimes."[19] He added that the clause does not function in a vacuum; for it to restrain the legislature, the judiciary must be willing to enforce its prohibition.[20] Justice Brennan acknowledged the imprecise nature of the clause, but he quoted Chief Justice Warren, writing the plurality opinion in *Trop* v. *Dulles* (1958), to interpret the Amendment: "The Clause 'must draw its meaning from the evolving standards of decency that mark the program of a maturing society' "; and that " 'The basic concept underlying the [Clause] is nothing less than the dignity of man. While the State has the power to punish, the [Clause] stands to assure that this power be exercised within the limits of civilized standards.' "[21]

Justice Brennan then suggested four principles to guide the Court when resolving whether a punishment is prohibited by the cruel and unusual punishment clause. The first principle is that "a punishment must not be so severe as to be degrading to human dignity"; the second, "that the State must not arbitrarily inflict a severe punishment"; the third, "that a severe punishment must not be unacceptable to contemporary society"; and the fourth, "that a severe punishment must not be excessive."[22] He concluded that:

[T]he punishment of death is inconsistent with all four principles: Death is an unusually severe and degrading punishment; there is a strong probability that it is inflicted arbitrarily; its rejection by contemporary society is virtually total; and there is no reason to believe that it serves any penal purpose more effectively than the less severe punishment of imprisonment.[23]

Justice Brennan's opinion is lucidly and vigorously argued and is soundly based in its conception of the Eighth Amendment "as posing a core question of values."[24] It draws attention to matters that are directly relevant to answering that core question. His attempt to focus the issue on the principles underlying the clause is well conceived and, although inevitably vulnerable to criticism at some points, well executed. But in the end it fails.

It fails because it does not address two of the key questions posed in Justice Blackmun's opinion. Justice Blackmun had asked why the Court ignored previous decisions that assumed that capital punishment was not unconstitutional per se under the Eighth or the Fourteenth Amendment. What had occurred to warrant the change in opinion? Nothing in Justice Brennan's opinion explains the abrupt leap, this sudden mutation, in the evolution of "standards of decency." Blackmun also argued that legislators were the proper government actors to abolish the death penalty, "these elected representatives of the people – far more conscious of the temper of the times, of the maturing of society, and the contemporary demands for man's dignity, than are we who sit cloistered in this Court."[25] Again, Justice Brennan's opinion is silent on why the Court should reject the will of the majority as expressed by their elected representatives on this issue.

Indeed, Brennan apparently accepted Blackmun's view that the voice of the people should prevail. One principle that he saw as "inherent in the Clause is that a severe punishment must not be unacceptable to contemporary society";[26] and he maintained that "this punishment has been almost totally rejected by contemporary society. . . . [R]ejection could hardly be more complete without becoming absolute."[27] Basing this contention on the fact that "death sentences are rarely imposed and death is even more rarely inflicted,"[28] he concluded that because society is responsible for the infrequency of the punishment, the public has implicitly rejected it. Yet this argument not only does nothing to answer Blackmun's point; it is also vulnerable to the objection that a valid inference from the rare imposition of a penalty would be, not that society has repudiated the penalty, but "that it wishes to reserve its use to a small number of cases."[29] As Chief Justice Burger explained: "If selective imposition evidences a rejection of capital punishment in those cases where it is not imposed, it surely evidences a correlative affirmation of the penalty in those cases where it is imposed."[30]

Justice Marshall was the only other member of the Court to conclude that the Eighth Amendment prohibits capital punishment for all crimes and under all circumstances. His opinion is similar to Justice Brennan's in that he thought the crucial question at issue was the normative one: whether the death penalty accorded with "evolving standards of decency that mark the progress of a maturing society." Marshall enunciated four principles, which he derived from previous judgments of the Court, for determining that a punishment might be deemed cruel and unusual. Two of these principles – that punishments that amount to torture are prohibited and that punishments that were previously unknown as penalties for a given offense may be unconstitutional – were irrelevant to the decision in *Furman*.

Rather, Justice Marshall's argument rested on his other two principles: that a penalty may be cruel and unusual because it is excessive and serves no valid legislative purpose, or because "it is abhorrent to currently existing moral values."[31] In his words, "capital punishment serves no purpose that life imprisonment could not serve equally well" and therefore "there is no basis for concluding that capital punishment is not excessive"; and furthermore, "even if capital punishment is not excessive, it nonetheless violates the Eighth Amendment because it is morally unacceptable to the people of the United States at this time in their history."[32]

Justice Marshall's argument is well articulated and well documented. It includes the legislative history of the Eighth Amendment, a brief history of capital punishment in the United States, and an analysis of the available evidence regarding the deterrent efficacy of the death penalty. Yet, his opinion is no more responsive to the second and third questions posed by Justice Blackmun than is Justice Brennan's.

Marshall acknowledged that the Court, or individual justices, had previously expressed opinions that the death penalty is constitutional or that indicate an acceptance *sub silentio* of capital punishment as constitutionally permissible. He maintained that the last case to imply that capital punishment was still permissible was *Trop* v. *Dulles* (1958). Not only was the language in that case dicta, but also the circumstances had changed in the ensuing fifteen years to justify a reexamination of the issue.[33] He went on to say, correctly: "There is no holding directly in point, and the very nature of the Eighth Amendment would dictate that unless a very recent decision existed, *stare decisis* would bow to changing values, and the question of the constitutionality of capital punishment at a given moment in history would remain open."[34] But this does nothing to answer Justice Blackmun's objection that "we have been presented with nothing that demonstrates a significant movement of any kind" in the "14 years since *Trop*."[35] In other words, it does not (and Justice Marshall does not anywhere else in his opinion) indicate why at that particular "given moment in history" the Court should find capital punishment violative of the Eighth Amendment.

Justice Marshall does address the will-of-the-people argument. That argument, he said, was undercut by "the fact that the constitutionality of capital punishment turns on the opinion of an informed citizenry."[36] If properly informed, "the great mass of citizens" would conclude "that the death penalty is immoral and therefore unconstitutional."[37] He did, however, acknowledge some doubt about this, saying that while the information presently available "would almost surely convince the average citizen that the death penalty was unwise, a problem arises as to whether it would convince him that the penalty was morally reprehensible."[38] What cannot be doubted is that Marshall's unfulfilled conditional proposition, unsupported by evidence, about the possible opinion of an informed electorate fails to meet Justice Blackmun's objection to what he saw as judicial usurpation of the authority of the legislative branch.

The arguments of Justices Douglas, Stewart, and White avoided both "the core normative question with which Justice Brennan and Marshall attempted to grapple"[39] and what the Chief Justice called "the ultimate issue presented in these cases . . . the basic constitutional question."[40] All three justices view the Eighth Amendment in terms that Daniel Polsby has aptly described as depriving it of "a dimension which is latent in almost all of the previous cases, particularly in the *Weems* case and in the Warren opinion in *Trop* – as an independently potent moral force which is at the disposal of the least dangerous branch of government and which may be used to make the most dangerous branch a little less so."[41] All three opinions focused on defects in the sentencing system or sentencing practices that they found to violate the Eighth Amendment rather than on the death penalty itself.

Justice Douglas avoided altogether the question of whether the death penalty per se is a cruel or unusual punishment. Indeed, what he said applies to imprisonment just as much as to the death penalty: "[I]t is 'cruel and unusual' to apply the death penalty – *or any other penalty* – selectively to minorities whose numbers are few, who are outcasts of society, and who are unpopular, but whom society is willing to see suffer though it would not countenance general application of the same penalty across the board."[42]

In another key passage Justice Douglas said: "It would seem to be incontestable that the death penalty inflicted on one defendant is 'unusual' if it discriminates against him because of his race, religion, wealth, social position, or class, or if it is imposed under a procedure that gives room for the play of such prejudices."[43] Because the death penalty statutes were "pregnant with discrimination" and the procedures involved in the imposition of the death penalty were discriminatory, Justice Douglas believed they were not "compatible with the idea of equal protection of the laws that is implicit in the ban on 'cruel and unusual' punishments."[44] Thus, he did not reach the questions raised by Justice Blackmun. Nor, with one exception, did Justices Stewart and White, whose "swing votes" were crucial in *Furman*. As the Chief Justice said, both "stop short of reaching the ultimate question."[45] Justice Stewart acknowledged the uniqueness of the death penalty "in its absolute renunciation of all that is embodied in our concept of humanity" and also that the case for concluding that the death penalty is constitutionally impermissible in all circumstances under the Eighth and Fourteenth Amendments "is a strong one."[46]

We shall refer to these statements again in the context of the plurality opinion and judgment of the Court that Justice Stewart announced in *Gregg.* In *Furman,* however, he did not develop these thoughts because he thought it unnecessary to resolve the constitutionality of capital punishment under all circumstances. Rather, he decided that the petitioners' sentences should be set aside because "the Eighth and Fourteenth Amendments cannot tolerate the infliction of a sentence of death under the legal systems that permit this unique penalty to be so wantonly and freakishly imposed."[47]

Similarly, Justice White believed that questions of whether the death penalty was unconstitutional per se, or whether there was any system of capital punishment that would comport with the Eighth Amendment, were not presented in *Furman* and did not need to be decided. He said, however, that "the death penalty is exacted with great infrequency even for the most atrocious crimes and that there is no meaningful basis for distinguishing the few cases in which it is imposed from the many cases in which it is not."[48] He concluded that this arbitrariness in imposing the death penalty violated the Eighth Amendment.

Unlike Justices Douglas and Stewart, he did say something directly relevant to one of Justice Blackmun's key concerns. Justice Blackmun asked in effect why now was the appropriate time to strike down the death penalty. Although Justice White claimed that he did not resolve whether the death penalty was unconstitutional per se, he did come close to answering that question in the following passages:

I begin with what I consider a near truism: that the death penalty could so seldom be imposed that it would cease to be a credible deterrent or measurably to contribute to any other end of punishment in the criminal justice system. . . . At the moment that it ceases realistically to further these purposes, . . . the emerging question is whether its imposition in such circumstances would violate the Eighth Amendment. It is my view that it would, for its imposition would then be the pointless and needless extinction of life with only marginal contributions to any discernible social or public purposes. . . . It is also my judgment that this point has been reached with respect to capital punishment as it is presently administered. . . . I cannot avoid the conclusion that as the statutes before us are now administered, the penalty is so infrequently imposed that the threat of execution is too attenuated to be of substantial service to criminal justice.[49]

C. The missing links

The majority justices did not completely fail to confront the crucial issues
raised by Justice Blackmun. By collating and consolidating selected passages from all their opinions it is possible to synthesize an opinion that
adequately responds to his challenge. One might begin with Justice
Blackmun's own opinion and his declaration of distaste, antipathy, and
abhorrence for the death penalty "with all its aspects of physical distress
and fear" and its antagonism "to any sense of 'reverence for life.' "[50] This
passage certainly sounds very much like an Eighth Amendment analysis
mandated by previous cases, notably *Trop* and *Weems*.[51] The problem, as
he defined it, was "the suddenness of the Court's perception of progress
in the human attitude since decisions of only a short while ago."[52]

To understand this problem we have to ask: In what sense was the
Court's judgment in *Furman* sudden? The materials discussed in Chapters
1 and 2 are useful in this inquiry. In light of the decline of the death
penalty in the rest of the Western world and of America's participation,
indeed primary role, in that development, it is impossible to regard the
Court's decision that it was "time to strike down the death penalty" as
anything more than the culmination of a long-term movement in Western
societies "down the road toward human decency," to use Justice Blackmun's own words.[53] It was a movement that had begun *in America* one
hundred and twenty-five years earlier[54] and had continued consistently
until, by 1972, there had been no executions in America in the previous
five years.

The relevant "passage of time" to which Justice Blackmun's attention
should have been directed was not the "brief periods" since *McGautha,
Rudolph, Trop,* and *Francis,* but rather the whole period over which the
long-term trend away from execution developed. In that context, the
"significant movement" he sought is plainly manifest over the twentieth
century. To say that "the passage of time has taken us to a place of
greater maturity and outlook" was not a matter of "plausible and high-
sounding argument," but simply a matter of historical fact.

In that perspective, *Furman* cannot be viewed as some kind of precipitate rush to judgment. Justice Blackmun contended that the Court had had
as much reason to invalidate the death penalty in each of the previous
cases, but it had not done so. Indeed, there *was* as much reason when the
earlier cases were decided, for the critical processes of historical change
had been operating, on an incremental basis, for many decades. Philip
Kurland, whose verdict was that in the "*Furman* v. *Georgia* decision the
inevitable came to pass," also said: "The essential surprise is that it came

to pass when it did. Earlier cases had afforded the majority justices the same opportunities to justify the conclusion they reached."[55] The Court's "perception of progress in the human attitude" may have been "sudden" in some sense, but it more properly could be regarded as belated.

Two other aspects of Justice Blackmun's opinion deserve attention. After referring to recently enacted federal death penalty legislation – the 1961 aircraft piracy statute, the 1965 presidential assassination statute, and the 1970 Omnibus Crime Control Act – he said:

> It is impossible for me to believe that the many lawyer-members of the House and Senate . . . were callously unaware and insensitive of constitutional overtones in legislation of this type. The answer, of course, is that in 1961, in 1965, and in 1970 these elected representatives of the people – far more conscious of the temper of the times, of the maturing of society, and of the contemporary demands for man's dignity, than are we who sit cloistered on this Court – took it as settled that the death penalty then, as it always has been, was not in itself unconstitutional. Some of those Members of Congress, I suspect, will be surprised at this Court's giant stride today.[56]

In the first place, the context of death penalty legislation is crucial to comprehending its meaning as political and symbolic action. What Justice Blackmun, "cloistered on this Court," seems to have missed – and what "the many lawyer-members of the House and Senate" will undoubtedly have been well aware of, and sensitive to – is the almost purely symbolic significance of death penalty legislation at the federal level where a virtual moratorium on executions prevailed and was the most important indication of the Eighth Amendment status of putting people to death.

Over the years in which the legislation mentioned was enacted, out of a federal prison population averaging 22,430[57] there were never more than two federal prisoners on death row.[58] Moreover, despite the many federal crimes for which the death penalty was available only one prisoner was executed in that period. That execution took place in 1963 prior to the passage of two of the federal death penalty laws. There have been none since then, and at this writing there have been no federal prisoners on death row for the past nine years.

What is also puzzling about this passage is that its conception of the cruel and unusual punishment prohibition is apparently so restrictive that it makes the clause almost meaningless. If public opinion as interpreted by the "elected representatives of the people" conclusively determines the range of punishments available, it is difficult to understand the function of a prohibition on cruel and unusual punishment or what could constitute a violation of the Eighth Amendment in this context. What is the significance of a curb on majority and legislative will that cannot be employed to check or restrain that will?

If, on the other hand, "one role of the Constitution is to help the nation to become 'more civilized,' "[59] then public opinion must be accorded a different and necessarily subsidiary position. As evidenced by the experience of the rest of the Western world, the abolition of capital punishment never takes place with evident public support. Majorities on the order of two-thirds of the population support the continuation of the death penalty at the time of abolition.[60] Then they dissipate.[61] The role of a constitutional court operating within the Eighth Amendment is to facilitate this transition to a more civilized society.

The history of the abandonment of capital punishment demonstrates the need for a "lead from the front." With rare exceptions, this type of leadership in American political life is a function of the Supreme Court. By according current public opinion a subsidiary role, the judiciary may make difficult decisions regarding punishment policy and eventual public acceptance. In making those decisions the Court cannot be guided solely by the present will of the people. As Justice Blackmun rightly said: "I do not sit on these cases, however, as a legislator, responsive, at least in part, to the will of constituents."[62]

To what extent the justices should be guided by perceived public attitudes, however, is a different matter. According to Justice Jackson, writing the Court's opinion in the Flag Salute Cases: "The very purpose of a Bill of Rights was to withdraw certain subjects from the vicissitudes of political controversy, to place them beyond the reach of majorities and officials . . . ."[63] The Court should not attempt to reflect and endorse every shift in majority wishes or legislative patterns. On the contrary, it should (and in the past often has), by "its appeal to conscience as well as political ideals and its invocation of fundamental tenets" lead the people "to reconsider the merit and virtue of previously formulated popular decisions."[64]

What the justices are called on to do in many instances is to act in accordance with Edmund Burke's view of the popular role of a legislator in the British Parliament:

> I am to look, indeed, to your opinions; but to such opinions as you and I must have five years hence. I was not to look to the flash of the day. I know that you chose me, in my place, along with others, to be a pillar of the state, and not a weathercock on top of the edifice . . . of no use but to indicate the shiftings of every fashionable gale . . . When [and only when] we know that the opinions of even the greatest multitudes are the standard of rectitude, I shall be obliged to make these opinions the masters of my conscience.[65]

According to Burke, a Member of Parliament had no "obligation . . . to be popular" or to advocate positions that would "reflect that of his constituents."[66] Rather his duty is "to act upon a very enlarged view of things," to respect "the broad claims of general humanity," and sometimes therefore to act contrary to "the opinion of the people, which some think . . . is to be implicitly obeyed."[67]

It is unlikely that legislators in either England or America do more than "partially perform the role of 'Burkean Trustee' rather than 'Instructed Delegate.' "[68] In both countries, "the safer the district, the stronger the legislator's display of independence of popular will on specific issues."[69] But unlike England, in the United States the existence of the Supreme Court, with its power of judicial review, must make it easier for legislators who fear that an unpopular stand may cost them votes among their constituents to leave the task of acting upon an "enlarged view of things" to the Court. The school prayer issue provides a case in point. "Only the Court," as Jesse Choper noted, "could speak for religious nonconformists against devotional exercises in the public schools . . . because legislators could not oppose God and retain their seats."[70]

Certainly, on many such issues legislators feel freer to indulge in simplistic instinctive reactions or to pander to populist feelings. "It is impossible convincingly to refute," wrote Choper, "the propositions that lawmaking would be more sensitive to individual liberties if it were conducted with the knowledge that its resolutions were final, and that the ever present potential of judicial disapproval actually encourages popular irresponsibility and stultifies the people's sense of moral and constitutional obligation."[71]

The difference between the English parliamentary system and the American national political process is most marked in relation to symbolic issues of this kind. In what are called questions of conscience, Members of Parliament, although not immune to political reprisals, view themselves much more as ultimate arbiters having the kind of fundamental responsibilities that in this country are vested in the Supreme Court; and in this role they do not feel themselves as having to be automatically responsive to arguments based on the popular will supported by opinion poll findings. The most notable (although by no means only) example of this is the abolition of the death penalty in Britain. R. J. Buxton said: "The capital punishment issue raised in acute form the relationship between the actions of an individual M.P. [Member of Parliament] and the opinions of his constituents."[72] Nevertheless, although "throughout this period opinion polls consistently showed sixty or seventy percent of the electorate as being in favor of retention" the legislation abolishing the death penalty for murder for five years was passed by a substantial majority in 1965.[73] What are the implications of this analysis? According to

Chief Justice Burger in *Furman:* "[I]n a democratic society legislatures, not courts, are constituted to respond to the will and consequently the moral values of the people. . . . [I]n a democracy the legislative judgment is presumed to embody the basic standards of decency prevailing in the society."[74] But if legislatures play only the "essentially barometric role" assigned to them by the chief justice (an image that calls forcibly to mind Edmund Burke's "weathercock") and the Supreme Court adheres to what he referred to as "our traditional deference to the legislative judgment," who in America will take that "enlarged view of things" or respond to "the broad claims of general humanity" that Burke saw as the duty of the Member of Parliament?

It is interesting in this context to recall Justice Marshall's hypothesis in *Furman* that, given the kind of information necessary to make informed judgments about capital punishment, "the great mass of citizens would conclude . . . that the death penalty is immoral and therefore unconstitutional."[75] Marshall has been criticized for taking "such an apparently 'nondemocratic' position":

His argument suggests a disbelief in genuine ethical pluralism. Reasonable men do not differ, at least not in their attitudes toward the death penalty: informed judgment produces moral consensus. To adopt such a view is to go beyond the requisites for judging the value of public opinion; it is to express a profoundly elitist belief in the superiority of knowledge.[76]

In fact, Marshall never claimed that the creation of an informed public opinion would necessarily lead to universal rejection of the death penalty; and in any case, the true function of the Court is to be on occasion both nondemocratic and elitist.

The Supreme Court is, of course, undemocratic in both structure and function. It remains largely aloof from the political system, "insulated from political responsibility and unbeholden to self-absorbed and excited majoritarianism."[77] Functioning as "the censurer of the consensus of the popular will, which is the task of the Court in judicial review,"[78] may not be autocratic (for the Court does not have absolute power), but it is plainly undemocratic. Moreover, it constitutes an elite in the straightforward sense that, although attempts at political manipulation through the use of appointment occur, the Court's members are essentially a group selected as among the finest, most distinguished members of their profession.

In *Furman* the Court's attention was drawn to the decline of the death penalty in the rest of the civilized world. Chief Justice Burger, dissenting, referred to this worldwide trend, but denied its relevance to the issues because it "hardly points the way to a judicial solution in this country under a written Constitution."[79] "Our constitutional inquiry," he said, must be "confined to the meaning and applicability of the uncertain language of the Eighth Amendment."[80]

The chief justice's rubric might suggest that the Court should confine itself to a purely semantic analysis designed to determine the denotation of the phrase "cruel and unusual punishments." But even semanticists are concerned with the development of, and changes in, the meaning of speech forms. Furthermore, they do not confine their attention to parochial or regional usage or to a fixed point in time.

With regard to the Framers' "true" meaning of the Amendment, it is informative to read Raoul Berger's account of the history of the clause relating to cruel and unusual punishments. Berger contested what he calls "the spurious doctrine that the clause, borrowed from the Bill of Rights of 1689, prohibits excessiveness in punishment":[81]

One thing is clear beyond peradventure: the "cruel and unusual punishments" clause left death penalties untouched. Writing seventy years after the appearance of the clause in the 1689 Bill of Rights, Blackstone said of "deliberate and wilful murder, a crime at which human nature starts," that it is "punished almost universally throughout the world with death," striking testimony by the great commentator that the death penalty was not affected by the clause.[82]

Blackstone's statement, however, is also striking evidence that the great commentator regarded contemporary policy and practice in countries other than his own relevant to considering the death penalty. Is it conceivable that the Supreme Court would have considered it irrelevant if the position in 1972 had been, as it was in Blackstone's day, that deliberate and wilful murder was punished almost universally throughout the world with death?

The experience of Western democracies with the issue of capital punishment is indeed relevant to Justice Blackmun's concerns. Detailed knowledge of the processes leading to abolition in other countries would certainly have provided a better context for the Court's deliberations in *Furman* and might have dispelled Justice Blackmun's unease.

The performance of the majority in *Furman* was typical of the significant moves toward abolition in Western nations. The Court's leadership of public opinion was no more dramatic than that of the executive branch and parliament in many other nations. Even the nonultimate issue decided in *Furman,* the death penalty "as administered," resembles the incremental approaches, including suspension of executions and de facto abolition, in other countries. Furthermore, the Court that ventured the decision in *Furman* was in that branch of the federal government historically relied upon to initiate such changes.

One consequence of regarding *Furman* v. *Georgia* as a typical step toward abolition of capital punishment is to center attention to *Gregg* v. *Georgia* as a historical discontinuity. From a long-term perspective, the United States Supreme Court did not produce two surprises in the 1970s, but only one, and serious study of the origins, reasoning, and context of *Gregg* v. *Georgia* becomes even more pertinent.

D.   From *Furman* to *Gregg*

To many observers, *Furman* had, for all practical purposes, ended the practice of executions in America.[83] Yet the Supreme Court was less certain of *Furman's* effect.

On July 2, 1976, when the Supreme Court announced its decision in *Gregg* v. *Georgia,* it became clear that executions would indeed resume. With Gary Gilmore's death before a firing squad in Utah on January 17, 1977, "nearly ten years without any executions came to a violent end."[84] Justice Blackmun asked in *Furman* what had happened in the brief periods since *McGautha, Rudolph, Trop,* and *Francis* to justify the Court's striking down the death penalty in *Furman;* it is pertinent here to ask what had happened in the four years between *Furman* and *Gregg* to bring about an apparently outright reversal of opinion.

One commentator's version of the transformation from *Furman* to *Gregg* is phrased in nakedly political terms: The dissenters in *Furman,* "all Nixon-administration appointees and led by Chief Justice Warren E. Burger, were a solid bloc in defense of the death penalty."[85] The retirement of Justice Douglas and his replacement by Justice Stevens, who was appointed by President Ford, ensured that there was no longer a majority on the bench with the kind of judicial philosophy that produced the *Furman* decision. But the idea that patterns of constitutional decision making are determined by the unvarying policy positions of members of the Court and that changes in those patterns are thus simply a function of changes in personnel is contradicted, rather than supported, by the available evidence.[86] Moreover, in *Gregg* it was the "swing votes" of justices Stewart and White, who were with the majority in *Furman,* which created a solid majority. Indeed, the central opinion was written by Justice Stewart and supported by Justice White. A bloc of three justices – Stewart, Powell, and Stevens – apparently with Justice Stewart as the leader, were the only ones to vote with the majority in all five death penalty opinions issued that day.

Another interpretation of the change is that in *Gregg* the Court simply reversed the spirit if not the substance of *Furman.* At least one of the justices – Blackmun – appears to have seen it in that way. He did not write an opinion in the case nor did he join in the opinion of others in the majority, though he did concur in the result. In *Gregg* he wrote: "I concur in the judgment. See *Furman* v. *Georgia,* 408 U.S. 238, 405–414 (1972) (Blackmun, J., dissenting), and *id.,* at 375 (Burger, C.J., dissenting); *id.,* at 414 (Powell, J., dissenting); *id.,* at 465 (Rehnquist, J., dissenting)."[87] What is striking here is that Justice Blackmun's references with approval are confined to the four *Furman* dissents, implicitly disapproving the majority reasoning in *Gregg.* And he said the same thing in a slightly abbreviated form when concurring in *Proffitt* and *Jurek,* and also when dissenting in *Woodson.*[88]

E. The central issue

To understand the transition from *Furman* to *Gregg* it is necessary to examine the plurality opinion and judgment of the Court announced by Justice Stewart and joined by Justices Powell and Stevens. For it is there, particularly in the passages dealing with the petitioners' argument that a death sentence for murder was a per se violation of the Eighth and Fourteenth Amendments, that the determining factors are found.

The petitioners in *Gregg* argued, as those in *Furman* had, that standards of decency had evolved to the point where capital punishment could no longer be tolerated. They argued that the evolutionary process had been completed and that standards of decency required that the Eighth Amendment be construed as prohibiting capital punishment. The *Gregg* Court acknowledged that "an assessment of contemporary values concerning the infliction of a challenged sanction is relevant to the application of the Eighth Amendment."[89] The plurality opinion added that "this assessment does not call for a subjective judgment. It requires, rather, that we look to objective indicia that reflect the public attitude toward a given sanction."[90]

The Court addressed this question in the following passages:

The petitioners in the capital cases before the Court today renew the "standards of decency" argument, but developments during the four years since *Furman* have undercut substantially the assumptions upon which their argument rested. . . . [I]t is now evident that a large proportion of American society continues to regard it as an appropriate and necessary criminal sanction.

The most marked indication of society's endorsement of the death penalty for murder is the legislative response to *Furman.* The legislatures of at least 35 States have enacted new statutes that provide for the death penalty for at least some crimes that result in the death of another person. And the Congress of the United States, in 1974, enacted a statute providing the death penalty for aircraft piracy that results in death. . . . [A]ll of the post-*Furman* statutes make clear that capital punishment itself has not been rejected by the elected representatives of the people.

In the only statewide referendum occurring since *Furman* and brought to our attention, the people of California adopted a constitutional amendment that authorized capital punishment, in effect negating a prior ruling by the Supreme Court of California in *People* v. *Anderson* . . . that the death penalty violated the California Constitution.[91]

The opinion continues:

The jury also is a significant and reliable objective index of contemporary values because it is so directly involved. . . . The Court has said that "one of the most important functions any jury can perform in making . . . a selection [between life imprisonment and death for a defendant convicted in a capital case] is to maintain a link between contemporary community values and the penal system." . . . [T]he actions of juries in many States since *Furman* are fully compatible with the legislative judgments, reflected in the new statutes, as to the continued utility and necessity of capital punishment in appropriate cases. At the close of 1974 at least 254 persons had been sentenced to death since *Furman,* and by the end of March 1976, more than 460 persons were subject to death sentences.[92]

Justice White also wrote an opinion in *Gregg,* which the chief justice and Justice Rehnquist, concerning in the judgment, joined. Justice White concluded his opinion by saying: "For the reasons stated in dissent in *Roberts* v. *Louisiana,* . . . neither can I agree that the petitioner's other basic argument that the death penalty, however imposed and for whatever crime, is cruel and unusual punishment."[93] In *Roberts* v. *Louisiana* Justice White argued, in dissent, that events since 1974 disputed the conclusion in *Furman* that the death penalty offended society's prevailing attitudes. Congress and thirty-five state legislatures had decided that the death penalty was a legitimate and appropriate punishment by reenacting the penalty for one crime or another.[94]

The significance of these passages from the opinions written by Justices Stewart and White is that they reveal what had happened in the interim between *Furman* and *Gregg* to change the minds of the two justices who cast the crucial "swing votes" in *Furman.* Justice Stewart had said in *Furman* that the case advanced by Justices Brennan and Marshall for concluding that the infliction of the death penalty was constitutionally impermissible in all circumstances under the Eighth and Fourteenth Amendments was "a strong one."[95] Justice White had said that the death penalty was exacted with such a "degree of infrequency" that it had ceased "realistically" to further "any discernible social or public purposes," and that it was therefore "patently excessive and cruel and unusual punishment violative of the Eighth Amendment."[96]

What had happened to undermine the strong case advanced by Justices Brennan and Marshall? What had restored viability to a penalty that had, in Justice White's words, "for all practical purposes run its course"?[97] Two phenomena appear to have strongly influenced Justices Stewart and

White: the impact of *Furman* on public opinion and the legislative response to *Furman*.

Consider first the matter of public opinion. Both justices referred to the fact that California, after the invalidation by the California Supreme Court of the state's death penalty in *People* v. *Anderson,* had adopted a constitutional amendment authorizing capital punishment. Both referred to a 1968 referendum on the Massachusetts death penalty in which a majority voted to retain the death penalty. Both also cited public opinion polls on capital punishment including (in the case of Justice Stewart) a December 1972 Gallup poll indicating that fifty-seven percent of the people favored the death penalty and a June 1973 Harris survey that showed support of fifty-nine percent.[98]

It is notable that Justice White mentions, in regard to public opinion polls on capital punishment, that "their validity and reliability have been strongly criticized."[99] Yet, as we have pointed out, however, the universal experience is that public opinion invariably favors the death penalty and it is invariably led, not followed, in relation to abolition.[100] If America waits until the death penalty has "become unacceptable to the great majority of the people," or "has been rejected by or is offensive to the prevailing attitudes" in the community, before abandoning it, then it may never do so. Yet experience shows that a shift in public opinion to support abolition would occur at some time after the penalty had been abolished. Moreover, the Court did not discuss the possibility that the post-*Furman* poll results represented no more than a predictable political reaction to *Furman.*

The jury may in some circumstances be "a significant and reliable objective index of contemporary values," but the jury behavior considered crucial by Justice Stewart is equivocal in this case. First, we have no reliable data on jury decisions before and after *Furman* because we do not know how frequently prosecutors asked jurors to make death penalty decisions under pre- and post-*Furman* statutes. Estimating the propensity of juries toward death penalties without those key figures is like trying to construct a fraction without a denominator.

Second, using outcomes in death penalty cases as an index of contemporary values is misleading because prospective jurors with strong scruples against the death penalty are systematically eliminated from capital trials.[101]

Third, the number of death verdicts handed down by juries is small in comparison to the number of death-eligible cases. The death sentence total is less than ten percent of robbery-homicide convictions, and that figure is exclusive of all other death-eligible convictions. Again, we do not know how much of this to attribute to jury behavior because the denominator of death sentence requests is unavailable. However, if we are concerned about a penalty that, according to Justice Stewart, strikes like lightning, the relative infrequency of death sentences after *Furman* remains salient.

Fourth, it is a dubious premise to regard the post-*Furman* jury death sentences as an index of jurors' attitudes. Jurors primarily view their legal and civic duty as a matter of following instructions. *Furman* and the statutes it spawned changed those instructions in ways that increased death verdicts quite independently of juror attitudes. The new "discretionary" statutes contained much more directive language than pre-*Furman* laws. Thus, in imposing death sentences juries may have simply been trying to follow what were perceived as orders; orders, moreover, that legislatures devised as a response to *Furman*.

Finally, the number of death sentences reported in the Stewart opinion in *Gregg* included those imposed under post-*Furman* mandatory legislation. After *Furman,* eighteen states adopted mandatory death penalty statutes that completely removed jury discretion.[102] In fact, that was why these statutes were struck down on the same day that *Gregg* was decided![103]

The legislative deluge of new death penalty statutes that followed *Furman* is reminiscent of the "pouring panic of capital statutes" that was a feature of the history of the criminal law in eighteenth-century England.[104] Whatever the social psychology of that development may have been, the post-*Furman* reaction in America, as we argued in Chapter 2, might best be characterized as a typical case of psychological reactance. Like parallel incidents in school prayer and pornography, legislative backlash came as no surprise to anyone familiar with the history of judicial invalidation in this country.

In short, these "objective indicia" cannot be viewed as providing an accurate reflection of public attitudes on execution. Yet in *Gregg,* the Court apparently accepted them as such, regarding them as decisive on the issue of evolving standards of decency. This is disturbing because, in considering the constitutional validity of a penalty described by Justice Stewart as unique "in its absolute renunciation of all that is embodied in our concept of humanity," such matters should not go unquestioned but rather be subjected to rigorous scrutiny.

One way to examine the complex and crucial issue of capital punishment and public opinion is by asking: What would have happened if the Court had ruled the other way in 1976? We think the reaction would have changed the course of later events. Undoubtedly, a 1976 reaffirmation of the end of the death penalty might have evoked direct-mail campaigns, proposals in Congress for constitutional amendment, and fervent calls for the impeachment of standing judges. That is the American way.

But the dust would probably have settled. Earlier on, we drew a parallel between the capital punishment and school prayer decisions. School prayer amendments do not pass. Neither, we suspect, would the proposed capital punishment amendment of 1976 or 1986 have passed. A ten-year hiatus in executions in the United States, stretched to twenty years, would in retrospect have seemed inevitable. In those circumstances, *Furman* in 1972 and not *Gregg* in 1976 would have been viewed as the landmark case.

The structure of political democracy in America is such that the Supreme Court plays "a vital role in the preservation of the American democratic system."[105] It is vital in the sense that if the Court does not act, then in many cases no action will be taken. It may be true that widescale implementation of the Court's ban on legally imposed school segregation in *Brown* v. *Board of Education* in 1954[106] "was accomplished only after the political branches afforded coercive support in the Civil Rights Act of 1964."[107] But if the Court had not decided as it did, there would have been nothing for Congress to support.

"Today, just ten years later," wrote Dallin Oaks in 1974, "the controversy seems as if it had come from another century. With the passage of the Civil Rights Act we not only changed our law, but we also changed our minds. Today the proposition adopted in that legislation is well accepted from coast to coast and from north to south."[108] It should be remembered, however, that the initiative came twenty years earlier from the justices who in Alexander Hamilton's words "had courage and magnanimity enough to serve [the people] at the peril of their displeasure."[109] If the Supreme Court had adopted as unwavering an approach to the death penalty as it did in *Brown,* that controversy too might now seem to have come from another century and there would not be 1,700 prisoners on death row.

F. The future of the Eighth Amendment

Some basic questions regarding the doctrinal future of *Furman* and *Gregg* deserve attention. The first is whether *Furman*, in spirit and in substance, is still good law. Apparently Justice Blackmun regards *Gregg* as having reversed *Furman*. But again he appears to stand alone; the other eight justices think that the two cases can comfortably coexist. The second and related question is whether, after *Gregg*, any doctrine remains for an assault on execution, either per se or as currently administered, as cruel and unusual punishment in violation of the Eighth Amendment.

There are two obvious but unlikely ways in which the Court could invalidate death penalty laws: *Gregg* v. *Georgia* could be reversed by a Court majority confessing the error of its ways; or, since the Eighth Amendment is not regarded as static but as deriving its meaning from evolving standards of decency over time, a future Court majority could conclude that such standards as they had evolved since 1976 required abandoning the death penalty. The second way is the more probable, but not to be expected in this decade; possibly not the twentieth century.

Thus, having mentioned these unlikely steps, what we shall explore here is whether the statutory systems and capital-sentencing procedures approved in principle in *Gregg* (and in *Proffitt* and *Jurek*) could be struck down in practice under the authority of *Furman,* and in light of the practices that have evolved since 1976 in the administration of capital punishment. To do this it is necessary to narrow the issue from Justice Stewart's statement, which involves the death penalty as a punishment for murder "under any circumstances,"[110] to whether the death penalty for the civil crime of murder in its frequently recurrent forms is constitutionally permitted. In fact, that is the only question that can be decided in terms of the *Furman* opinions. No presidential assassins or persons found guilty of treason are among the 1,700 on death row. Moreover, hypothetical cases cannot be addressed with the same experience and moral authority as can those involving recurrent and prevalent homicides eligible for the death penalty, such as felony killings. Since 1977 a precipitating cause of all but a very small number of executions have been homicides committed in the course of other felonies.

On the average, there have been, in the past decade, more than 20,000 criminal homicides per year in America.[111] An estimated current annual rate of twenty to thirty executions per year represents less than 0.2 percent of the homicide rate. In 1979, when John Spenkelink was executed at Railsford Prison in Florida for robbery-homicide, there were about 2,200 robbery-homicides known to the police and more than 3,400 felony killings.[112] We estimate that over half of these events resulted in one or more arrests, and most occurred in states that make such crimes eligible for capital punishment.[113] Spenkelink's execution was thus less than a one-in-a-thousand proposition. To escalate the odds to one in one hundred for robbery-killings would require some national increase in the frequency of execution, even if only those types of killings were so punished. Increasing the chances to ten in one hundred nationwide would result in more executions in the United States every year for robbery-killing alone than have occurred in any one year during this century. We leave it to the reader to perform the calculations of executions required for more evenhanded justice.

What is the significance of ratios of this order in view of Justices Stewart's and White's opinions in *Furman?* We quote the relevant passage in Justice Stewart's opinion:

> These death sentences are cruel and unusual in the same way that being struck by lightning is cruel and unusual. For, of all the people convicted of rapes and murders in 1967 and 1968, many just as reprehensible as these, the petitioners are among a capriciously selected random handful upon whom the sentence of death has in fact been imposed. . . . [T]he Eighth and Fourteenth Amendments cannot tolerate the infliction of a sentence of death under legal systems that permit this unique penalty to be so wantonly and so freakishly imposed.[114]

Justice White, as we have seen, also emphasized the "degree of infrequency" with which the death penalty was imposed. Indeed, he said, its imposition was so infrequent that it constituted "the pointless and needless extinction of life with only marginal contributions to any discernible social or public purposes."[115]

In light of these statements an inescapable question presents itself: To what extent do the new statutory schemes and procedures for imposing the death penalty, adopted since *Furman,* satisfy the constitutional deficiencies identified by Justices Stewart and White? Justice Stewart referred to the congressional testimony of U.S. Attorney General Ramsay Clark that only a "small and capricious selection of offenders have been put to death. Most persons convicted of the same crimes have been imprisoned."[116] Does the record since *Gregg* reveal a significant change in the process for selecting those offenders to be sentenced to death?

One key issue is whether the state review processes lauded by Justice Stewart in *Gregg* and *Proffitt*[117] effectively police the distribution of death sentences and executions in the post-*Gregg* decade. The Court's opinions in the leading cases in this area indicate a belief that appellate review ensures uniformity, fairness, and consistency in capital sentencing.

A study by Professor George E. Dix of the University of Texas directly addresses this matter, evaluating the empirical data and analyzing many of the appellate opinions in capital homicide cases in a number of states. For each state, Dix asked to what extent the state appellate court has invalidated death penalties, has provided a basis for encouraging proper and consistent sentencing, and has resolved procedural problems.

He found that the Georgia and Texas courts have invalidated death sentences in only two and one percent, respectively, of the cases reviewed; and that although the Florida court had reduced death sentences in twenty-three percent of the cases reviewed, in all but one of those cases the trial judge had ignored a jury recommendation of leniency.[118] None of the states had a review process that resulted in appellate opinions providing "an effective basis for the encouragement of proper and consistent sentencing."[119] Further, "the state appellate tribunals have been inconsistent in their approach to procedural problems that relate to the consistency and appropriateness of the application of the death sentence."[120] He concluded his study by saying:

I suspect, however, that the failure of appellate review reflects the impossibility of the underlying task. The expectation of effective appellate review assumes that objective and rational decisions can be made concerning which killers should live and which should die. The appellants, however, have all committed atrocious crimes. Given the enormity of their crimes, the task of identifying specific characteristics that society may use to determine whether a particular appellant should be executed may be impossible. . . .

If objective standards are impossible to achieve, uniformity within a system of individualized discretion may be an illusory goal. The life-death decision in homicide cases seems to be the area in which such uniformity would be most difficult to achieve. If so, the July 1976 Supreme Court decisions mandate pursuit of an impossible goal. The failure of appellate review of death penalties, therefore, may reflect less upon the appellate process than upon the nature of the objective.[121]

There is nothing in Professor Dix's study to suggest that the arbitrariness associated with the death penalty identified by Justices Stewart and White has been resolved. The number of people sentenced to death has increased substantially since *Furman* to a rate of well over two hundred per year, but the percentage executed has been reduced to less than two percent of the death row population.[122] New death penalty schemes have resulted in a situation indistinguishable from the system that, in the years before *Furman,* permitted "this unique penalty to be so wantonly and so freakishly imposed."[123]

The only alternative to a capital punishment system that searches fruitlessly for a formula to choose the one in one thousand killings, or the one in one hundred robbery-murders that merits death is an obscene affirmative action program in which the states execute many more prisoners than would otherwise be the case in order to generate an impression of evenhandedness to satisfy the Supreme Court. This scenario is not fantastic, nor even unlikely. Already, Florida has responded to critics who noted the great majority of its death row inmates were convicted of killing whites with a campaign to increase death sentences for killings of non-whites.[124] We have observed the sharp increase in death sentences associated with the reaction to *Furman* v. *Georgia* in the South that persisted when *Greg* v. *Georgia* returned power to execute to the states.[125] Understandably, the agencies of state government might conclude that the only way to make executions less freakish in distribution would be to broaden the practice of execution substantially, inflicting more cruelty to demonstrate to the Court that such cruelty was not unusual.

What might an appropriate Eighth Amendment analysis of this course of events conclude? The question has never been faced in previous cases, but we think this form of affirmative action displays a pattern of gratuitousness beyond the imagination of the *Furman* majority justices. Executing people to shore up the legitimacy of executing other people is a most offensive violation of Kant's injunction against the use of citizens "merely as a means." That the Court itself may have set these forces in motion should intensify the scrutiny these developments undergo.

This last point has broader application. There is, in 1986, no method of neutralizing the role of the Supreme Court in the execution policy of years to come. A failure to intervene aggressively in the near future will allow the states to maintain levels of execution that have been significantly altered by the previous conduct by the Court. We develop this point at length in Part II. For now, it is sufficient to note that stopping executions would be only one form of judicial activism in an area where the Court, inevitably, has no truly passive stance to choose. The legacy of *Furman* as well as *Gregg* is that the United States Supreme Court will, in future death penalty cases, be reviewing its own creation.

Notes

1. *Roberts* v. *Louisiana*, 431 U.S. 633 (1977) (mandatory death sentence unconstitutional).
2. *See, e.g., Eddings* v. *Oklahoma*, 455 U.S. 104 (1982) (mitigation evidence); *Godfrey* v. *Georgia*, 446 U.S. 420 (1980) (limits on statutory aggravating circumstances); *Coker* v. *Georgia*, 433 U.S. 584 (1977) (death penalty for rape unconstitutional).
3. 408 U.S. 238 (1972).
4. 428 U.S. 153 (1976).
5. 428 U.S. 242 (1976).
6. 428 U.S. 262 (1976).
7. 428 U.S. 280 (1976).
8. 428 U.S. 325 (1976).
9. 408 U.S. at 239–40.
10. 428 U.S. at 168–9.
11. 408 U.S. at 414 (Powell, J., dissenting).
12. *Id.* at 375–6 (Burger, C.J., dissenting).
13. *Id.* at 376.
14. Polsby, "The Death of Capital Punishment? *Furman* v. *Georgia*," 1972 *Sup. Ct. Rev.* 1, 3 (hereafter Polsby, "Death of Capital Punishment").
15. 408 U.S. at 405–6 (Blackmun, J., dissenting).
16. *Id.* at 407.
17. *Id.* at 408–10.
18. In each of the cases cited by Justice Blackmun, the Court was either not confronted with a general cruel and unusual punishment challenge to the death penalty, or it refused to decide the issue. In *Francis* v. *Resweber*, 329 U.S. 459 (1947), the Supreme Court held that the preparation for and mental anguish involved with an execution

after an unsuccessful first attempt did not violate the Eighth Amendment's prohibition. The Court, in dicta, in *Trop* v. *Dulles,* 365 U.S. 86, 99 (1958), did state that the death penalty was constitutional. However, the issue before the Court was whether depriving one of citizenship for desertion from military service was cruel and unusual punishment. The third case that Justice Blackmun cited, *Rudolph* v. *Alabama,* 375 U.S. 889 (1963), was simply the denial of certiorari to a convicted rapist sentenced to death. Finally, in *McGautha* v. *California,* 402 U.S. 183 (1971), although the Court decided a number of death penalty issues, it did not decide specifically whether the punishment was cruel and unusual.

19. 408 U.S. at 263 (Brennan, J., concurring).
20. *Id.* at 268.
21. 408 U.S. at 269–70 [quoting *Trop,* 356 U.S. 86, 100–1 (1958)] (brackets in original).
22. *Id.* at 271–9.
23. *Id.* at 305.
24. Polsby, "Death of Capital Punishment," at 10.
25. 408 U.S. at 413 (Blackmun, J., dissenting).
26. *Id.* at 277 (Brennan, J., concurring).
27. *Id.* at 295, 300.
28. *Id.* at 299.
29. Polsby, "Death of Capital Punishment," at 20.
30. 408 U.S. at 390 (Burger, C.J., dissenting).
31. *Id.* at 330–2 (Marshall, J., concurring).
32. *Id.* at 359–60.
33. *Id.* at 329 n.37.
34. *Id.* at 330.
35. *Id.* at 408.
36. *Id.*
37. *Id.* at 363.
38. *Id.*
39. Polsby, "Death of Capital Punishment," at 26.
40. 408 U.S. at 403 (Burger, C.J., dissenting).
41. Polsby, "Death of Capital Punishment," at 25.
42. 408 U.S. at 245 (Douglas, J., concurring) (emphasis added).
43. *Id.* at 242.
44. *Id.* at 257.
45. *Id.* at 396–7 (Burger, C.J., dissenting).
46. *Id.* at 306 (Stewart, J., concurring).
47. *Id.* at 310.
48. *Id.* at 313 (White, J., concurring).
49. *Id.* at 311–13 (emphasis added).
50. *Id.* at 405–6 (Blackmun, J., dissenting).
51. *Trop* v. *Dulles,* 356 U.S. 86 (1958); *Weems* v. *United States,* 217 U.S. 349 (1910).
52. 408 U.S. at 410.
53. *Id.*
54. In 1846 the Territory of Michigan voted to abolish capital punishment for all crimes except treason, effective March 1, 1847, thus becoming the first jurisdiction in the English-speaking world to do so. W. Bowers, *Executions in America* 6 (1974).
55. Kurland, "1971 Term: The Year of the Stewart–White Court," 1972 *Sup. Ct. Rev.* 181, 297 (hereafter Kurland, "1971 Term").
56. 408 U.S. at 413.
57. U.S. Department of Justice, *Sourcebook of Criminal Justice Statistics 1973,* at 349, Table 6.17 (1973).
58. Bureau of Justice Statistics, U.S. Department of Justice, *Capital Punishment* (yearly bulletins from 1961 to 1970).
59. Kurland, "1971 Term," at 296.
60. *See* Chapter 2.

61. The most complete documentation of this tendency is found in Germany where two-to-one opposition to abolition of capital punishment at the time it was accomplished became two-to-one support for abolition in just over two decades. *See The Germans: Public Opinion Polls, 1947–1966,* at 150 (E. Noelle & E. Neuman eds., G. Finan trans. 1967) (hereafter *German Polls, 1947–1966*); *The Germans: Public Opinion Polls, 1967–1980,* at 171 (E. Noelle-Neuman ed. 1981) (hereafter *German Polls, 1967–1980*).
62. *Furman,* 408 U.S. at 410 (Blackmun, J., dissenting).
63. *West Virginia State Bd. of Educ. v. Barnette,* 319 U.S. 624, 638 (1943).
64. J. Choper, *Judicial Review and the National Political Process* 138 (1980) (hereafter J. Choper, *Judicial Review*).
65. Burke, "Speech to the British Electors: A Defence of his Conduct in Parliament," in *Orations and Arguments by English and American Statesman* 93, 97, 101 (B. Bradley ed. 1894).
66. *Id.* at 103.
67. *Id.* at 121, 138.
68. J. Choper, *Judicial Review,* at 13.
69. *Id.* at 37.
70. *Id.* at 101.
71. *Id.* at 66.
72. Buxton, "Criminal Law Reform: England," 21 *Am. J. Comp. L.* 240 (1973).
73. *Id.*
74. *Furman,* 408 U.S. at 383–4 (Burger, C. J., dissenting).
75. *Id.* at 363 (Marshall, J., concurring).
76. A. Sarat & N. Vidmar, "Public Opinion, the Death Penalty, and the Eighth Amendment: Testing the Marshall Hypothesis," in *Capital Punishment in the United States* 190, 215 n.49 (H. Bedau & C. Pierce eds. 1976).
77. J. Choper, *Judicial Review,* at 68.
78. *Id.* at 132.
79. *Furman,* 408 U.S. at 404 (Burger, C.J., dissenting).
80. *Id.* at 375.
81. R. Berger, *Death Penalties: The Supreme Court's Obstacle Course* 29–30 (1982).
82. *Id.* at 43 (quoting W. Blackstone, *Commentaries* *194).
83. *See, e.g.,* H. Bedau, *The Courts, the Constitution and Capital Punishment* xiii (1977).
84. *Id.* at xiii–xiv.
85. Bedau, "Is the Death Penalty 'Cruel and Unusual' Punishment?," in *The Death Penalty in America* 247, 249 (H. Bedau 3d ed. 1982).
86. R. Scigliano, *The Supreme Court and the Presidency* 125–60 (1971).
87. 428 U.S. at 227 (Blackmun, J., concurring).
88. *See Proffitt,* 428 U.S. 242, 261 (1976) (Blackmun, J., concurring); *Jurek,* 428 U.S. 262, 279 (1976) (Blackmun, J., concurring); *Woodson,* 428 U.S. 280, 307–8 (1976) (Blackmun, J., dissenting).
89. 428 U.S. at 173.
90. *Id.*
91. *Id.* at 179–81.
92. *Id.* at 181–2 (brackets in original).
93. *Id.* at 226.
94. 428 U.S. 325, 351–3 (1976).
95. 408 U.S. at 306 (Stewart, J., concurring).
96. *Id.* at 311–12 (White, J., concurring).
97. *Id.* at 313.
98. *Roberts,* 428 U.S. at 352 n.5 (White, J., dissenting); *Gregg,* 428 U.S. at 181 n.25.
99. *Roberts,* 428 U.S. at 352 n.5 (White J., dissenting).
100. *See* Chapter 2.
101. *Witherspoon v. Illinois,* 391 U.S. 510 (1968); *see also* Fitzgerald & Ellsworth, "Due Process vs. Crime Control: Death Qualification and Jury Attitudes," 8 *Law & Hum. Behav.* 31 (1984).

102. Model Penal Code § 210.6 n.145 (1980).
103. *Roberts,* 428 U.S. 325 (1976); *Woodson,* 428 U.S. 280 (1976).
104. L. Fox, *The English Prison and Borstal Systems* 22 (1952); *see also* L. Radzinowicz, *A History of English Criminal Law from 1750,* at 3 (1948).
105. J. Choper, *Judicial Review,* at 10.
106. 347 U.S. 483 (1954).
107. J. Choper, *Judicial Review,* at 92.
108. Oaks, "The Popular Myth of the Victimless Crime," in *The Pursuit of Criminal Justice: Essays from the Chicago Center* 223 (G. Hawkins & F. Zimring eds. 1984).
109. *The Federalist* No. 71, at 207 (A. Hamilton) (R. Fairfield ed. 1981).
110. *Proffitt* v. *Florida,* 428 U.S. 242, 247 (1976).
111. U.S. Department of Justice, FBI, *Uniform Crime Reports; Crime in the United States* (1974–1983).
112. U.S. Department of Justice, FBI, *Uniform Crime Reports; Crime in the United States 1979,* at 12 (from Table).
113. *See* Zimring & Zuehl, "Determinants of Injury and Death in Urban Robbery," 15 *J. Legal Stud. 1 (1986).*
114. *Furman,* 408 U.S. at 309–10 (Stewart, J., concurring).
115. *Id.* at 312 (White, J., concurring).
116. *Id.* at 310 n.12 (Stewart, J., concurring).
117. *Gregg,* 428 U.S. at 204–6; *Proffitt,* 428 U.S. at 250–3, 258–9.
118. Dix, "Appellate Review of the Decision to Impose Death," 68 *Geo. L.J.* 97, 159 (1979).
119. *Id.*
120. *Id.* at 160.
121. *Id.* at 160–1.
122. Greenberg, "Capital Punishment as a System," 91 *Yale L.J.* 908, 917, 919 (1982).
123. *Furman,* 408 U.S. at 310 (Stewart, J., concurring).
124. Zeisel, "Race Bias in the Administration of the Death Penalty: The Florida Experience," 95 *Harv. L. Rev.* 456 (1981).
125. *See* W. Bowers, *Legal Homicide: Death as Punishment in America 1864–1982,* at 172 (1984) (during 1974–8, average of 187 prisoners added to death row annually).

4

A punishment in search of a crime

To devote a whole chapter to the criminal law in a book of this nature might be regarded as eccentric, or worse, pedantic. Our justification, however, is that the criminal law of homicide, important in its own right, also provides some insight into the problems of selection, moral coherence, and practical administration that bedevil attempts to harness the punishment of death for public purposes. If the criminal law cannot make persuasive distinctions between life and death cases of murder, a modern death penalty has no use. We argue that the current jurisprudence of death demonstrates the futility of the search for a rational death penalty.

In this chapter, we discuss the development of standards for the death penalty in the Model Penal Code, analyze the influence of the code provisions on modern death penalty legislation in the states, and question whether legal standards are closely linked to the propensity to condemn murderers and conduct executions. We conclude by arguing that efforts to provide a legal rationale for executions occurred far too late in the progress toward abolition in Western society to have any hope of success.

A. A penal paradigm

The most ambitious attempt to define the principles of substantive criminal law, at least in this century, is the American Law Institute's Model Penal Code.

A product of reform efforts in the 1950s and 1960s, the Code's drafters undertook to formulate standards for capital punishment even though its advisory committee strongly opposed the death penalty. Yet these death penalty standards have had more substantial impact on state legislation than any others set forth in the Code.

The Code defines murder as follows:

Section 210.2   Murder
(1) Except as provided in Section 210.3(1)(b), criminal homicide constitutes murder when:

(a) it is committed purposely or knowingly; or

(b) it is committed recklessly under circumstances manifesting extreme indifference to the value of human life. Such recklessness and indifference are presumed if the actor is engaged or is an accomplice in the commission of, or an attempt to commit, or flight after committing or attempting to commit robbery, rape or deviate sexual intercourse by force or threat of force, arson, burglary, kidnapping or felonious escape.[1]

This definition of murder differs from those found in the majority of American jurisdictions because it fails to provide for degrees of murder. The most common definitions of first- and second-degree murder originated from the Pennsylvania Act of 1794. First-degree murder included: (1) premeditated and deliberate homicide ("All murder which shall be perpetrated by means of poison, or by lying in wait, or by any other kind of willful, deliberate and premeditated killing"); and (2) homicides occurring in the course of or in the attempt to commit certain felonies ("or which shall be committed in the perpetration or attempt to perpetrate any arson, rape, robbery or burglary"). Second-degree murder was in substance all other homicides that would have been murder at common law ("and all other kinds of murder shall be deemed murder in the second degree").[2]

Wechsler and Michael explained that the primary objective of the division was to limit the use of the death penalty; this was accomplished by dividing murder into two degrees with the death penalty reserved for the first degree.[3] The preamble to the Pennsylvania statute reads: "[I]t is the duty of every government to endeavor to reform, rather than exterminate offenders, and the punishment of death ought never to be inflicted, where it is not absolutely necessary to the public safety . . . ."[4] The function of the deliberation and premeditation formula and the felony-murder rule was simply to identify those homicides that might be subject to capital punishment.

The distinctions between different murders drawn by most statutes have been much criticized. A particular problem has been interpreting "deliberation" and "premeditation." As Judge Cardozo argued:

The presence of a sudden impulse is said to mark the dividing line, but how can an impulse be anything but sudden when the time for its formation is measured by the lapse of seconds? Yet the decisions are to the effect that seconds may be enough. What is meant as I understand it, is that the impulse must be the product of an emotion or passion so swift and overmastering as to sweep the mind from its moorings. A metaphor, however, is, to say the least, a shifting test whereby to measure degrees of guilt that mean the difference between life and death.[5]

In many cases, as the Commentary to the Model Penal Code explains, "it was a task of surpassing subtlety to say what the 'deliberate and premeditated' formula did require."[6]

The felony-murder rule has proved to be no less ambiguous and problematic. As Wechsler and Michael remarked: "Conceding the ever-present legislative necessity for reconciling extremes by drawing arbitrary lines the justice of which must be viewed from afar, the limits of intelligent casuistry have clearly been reached."[7] The Commentary to the Model Penal Code devotes more than twelve pages to discussion of the "essential illogic" of the felony-murder rule.[8]

By contrast with its concise definition of murder, the American Law Institute, while adopting no position on whether death should be an authorized sentence for murder, included a lengthy provision on capital punishment in the Model Penal Code:

Section 210.6   Sentence of Death for Murder; Further Proceedings to Determine Sentence

(1) *Death Sentence Excluded.* When a defendant is found guilty of murder, the Court shall impose sentence for a felony of the first degree if it is satisfied that:
(a) none of the aggravating circumstances enumerated in Subsection (3) of this Section was established by the evidence at the trial or will be established if further proceedings are initiated under Subsection (2) of this Section; or
(b) substantial mitigating circumstances, established by the evidence at the trial, call for leniency; or
(c) the defendant, with the consent of the prosecuting attorney and the approval of the Court, pleaded guilty to murder as a felony of the first degree; or
(d) the defendant was under 18 years of age at the time of the commission of the crime; or
(e) the defendant's physical or mental condition calls for leniency; or
(f) although the evidence suffices to sustain the verdict, it does not foreclose all doubt respecting the defendant's guilt.

(2) *Determination by Court or by Court and Jury.* . . .

(3) *Aggravating Circumstances.*
(a) The murder was committed by a convict under sentence of imprisonment.
(b) The defendant was previously convicted of another murder or of a felony involving the use or threat of violence to the person.
(c) At the time the murder was committed the defendant also committed another murder.
(d) The defendant knowingly created a great risk of death to many persons.
(e) The murder was committed while the defendant was engaged or was an accomplice in the commission of, or an attempt to commit, or flight after committing or attempting to commit robbery, rape or deviate sexual intercourse by force or threat of force, arson, burglary or kidnapping.
(f) The murder was committed for the purpose of avoiding or preventing a lawful arrest or effecting an escape from lawful custody.
(g) The murder was committed for pecuniary gain.
(h) The murder was especially heinous, atrocious or cruel, manifesting exceptional depravity.

(4) *Mitigating Circumstances.*
(a) The defendant has no significant history of prior criminal activity.

(b) The murder was committed while the defendant was under the influence of extreme mental or emotional disturbance.

(c) The victim was a participant in the defendant's homicidal conduct or consented to the homicidal act.

(d) The murder was committed under circumstances which the defendant believed to provide a moral justification or extenuation for his conduct.

(e) The defendant was an accomplice in a murder committed by another person and his participation in the homicidal act was relatively minor.

(f) The defendant acted under duress or under the domination of another person.

(g) At the time of the murder, the capacity of the defendant to appreciate the criminality [wrongfulness] of his conduct or to conform his conduct to the requirements of law was impaired as a result of mental disease or defect or intoxication.

(h) The youth of the defendant at the time of the crime.[9]

We reproduce these sections because they are of intellectual and historical importance and also because they had substantial practical consequences. Having defined murder with elegant economy in Section 210.2, the Model Penal Code in Section 210.6 proceeds to reopen Pandora's Box – with a multitute of fine distinctions and a complex attempt to subdivide murder into penological categories relevant to the choice between life and death. The reform of the law of murder apparently had collided with the requirements felt necessary by the drafters for capital punishment decisions.

Later commentary alleged that the drafters intended the Code to be "a model for constitutional adjudication as well as for state legislation."[10] Moreover, they felt that the Supreme Court's 1976 and 1978 cases were "a broad endorsement of the general policy reflected in the Model Code provision."[11] The most recent Commentary on Section 210.6 concludes that "the Court has left the Model Code provision as the constitutional model for capital sentencing statutes and in the future may transform Section 210.6 into a paradigm of constitutional permissibility."[12] The question that remains is whether this "paradigm" is sufficient for its momentous task.

B. The weight of circumstances

The moral legitimacy of the definition of the various aggravating and mitigating circumstances enumerated in subsections (3) and (4) is questionable. Even an aggravating circumstance as unambiguous as (3)(b) – "the defendant was previously convicted of another murder or of a felony involving the use or threat of violence to the person" – while relevant to sentencing, hardly provides a morally acceptable instrument for making decisions between life and death. More importantly, the inclusion in subsection (3)(e) of all robbery-killings is hard to justify in that ultimate context. Why does that crime warrant a death sentence? The Commentary makes no attempt to provide a rationale for this specification, merely observing that this paragraph "concerns murder committed in connection with designated felonies, each of which involves the prospect of violence to the person."[13]

Subsection (3)(h), which defines a category of murder as "especially heinous, atrocious or cruel, manifesting exceptional depravity" is not only problematically vague[14] but difficult for a jury, confronted by its first experience of murder of any kind, to apply. At the same time, some provision for particularly horrible murders is required if the code is to be morally defensible. Otherwise, some unanticipated but ineffably dreadful murder might not be subject to the death penalty while a relatively mundane murder would be.

The definition of mitigating circumstances is much more elaborately supported in the Commentary and better integrated with the rest of the Code, but even it is flawed. For example, subsection (4)(a), the counterpart to (3)(b), presents the jury with the task of weighing "against each other"[15] the incommensurable. To what extent should the fact that the defendant has no significant history of prior criminal activity mitigate crimes like the Charles Whitman killings in Austin, Texas in 1966, or the McDonald's massacre in San Ysidro, California in 1984? The Commentary provides no rationale specific to the death penalty for this mitigating circumstance. It is certainly the sort of information that a sentencing body should have, but as a factor in making the choice between life or death it seems almost immaterial.

Subsection (4)(d), which specifies as a mitigating factor the defendant's belief in a "moral justification or extenuation for his conduct," as the Commentary explains, concerns the "question of an idiosyncratic belief in a moral basis for homicide" and relates also to "the assassin who kills in furtherance of a political ideology" and claims moral justification for his conduct.[16] The Commentary states that "consideration of this claim should not be excluded, but it is also expected that the defendant's aberrational belief will be discounted by the extravagance of its departure from societal norms."[17] It seems extremely optimistic to expect juries to possess the casuistical expertise required for this type of moral accountancy. How should this paragraph apply, for example, to the cases of Sirhan Sirhan or Charles Manson?

C. Who should die?

The questions at issue in these sections of the Model Penal Code are quite simple: Who should die, and why? But the way they are answered reveals an extraordinary ambivalence. The supporting Commentary is the least persuasive in the whole Code. It is as though those who drafted these sections and the accompanying comments felt that they were engaged in a mission doomed to failure.

The reason for this ambivalence is clear: "By a vote of 18–2, the Advisory Committee . . . recommended that the Institute favor abolition" of the death penalty.[18] The Council of the Institute was divided on the issue and decided that the Institute should not take any position. Nevertheless, the fact that ninety percent of the Advisory Committee were opposed to the death penalty is reflected throughout the Commentary, beginning with the opening question: "[F]irst in what cases should capital punishment be *possible?*"[19]

Ambivalence is also apparent in the remarkable imbalance or asymmetry in the treatment of aggravating and mitigating circumstances in the Commentary. Aggravating circumstances comprise less than one page of the sixty-five devoted to capital punishment; the discussion of mitigating circumstances is more carefully developed and is five times as long.[20] In all, less than two percent of the Commentary text is devoted to the central question of who should die.

Nor does the Code ever indicate under what circumstances an offender *should* be sentenced to death; that decision is always discretionary. The Code indicates only when an offender *cannot* be sentenced to the death. The aggravating factors never mandate but only permit a death sentence. Furthermore, the court may override a jury decision in favor of death, but it may not impose the capital sanction without jury concurrence.[21]

Although the Model Code recognizes no class of cases for which mandatory capital punishment is authorized, it identifies "at least one class of murder" for which the death sentence "should never be imposed" – murder by juveniles.[22] In effect, the Code provides a set of limiting conditions that obviate or preclude the death penalty but nowhere prescribes it. It answers the question "Who should live?" but avoids the question "Who should die?"

Another striking feature of this purportedly comprehensive analysis is the unreasoned character of much of the exposition. Not only is the entire discussion of eligibility for the death sentence relegated to one brief page in more than sixty, but that one page consists mostly of unsupported propositions. In *McGautha* v. *California,* Justice Harlan, delivering the opinion of the Court, said in a celebrated passage:

To identify before the fact those characteristics of criminal homicides and their perpetrators which call for the death penalty, and to express these characteristics in language which can be fairly understood and applied by the sentencing authority, appear to be tasks which are beyond present human ability.[23]

It seems clear that Justice Harlan did not regard the Model Penal Code as counterevidence to this assertion. He appended the relevant subsections of the Code to the *McGautha* opinion. It is also notable that Justice Brennan, in a forceful and lucid dissent, objected to standardless sentencing, but did not defend the Model Penal Code standards.[24] Justice Brennan was correct in insisting that the decision to take a human life should be subject to the rule of law. Ironically, however, that does not mean that Justice Harlan was wrong in insisting that the task of determining the criteria under which capital felons should be chosen to live or die is "beyond present human ability."

Finally, the Code and the accompanying Commentary identifying which persons should be eligible for capital punishment stand strangely isolated from the rest of the Code. The concepts and categories, the principles, and the vocabulary that explain the model statute are abandoned in the discussion of aggravating circumstances. The clarity, precision, and dialectical acumen that characterize the treatment of mitigating circumstances are replaced by bald assertions with scarcely any supporting reasoning.

Two examples previously noted illustrate this point. First, there is no justification for aggravating circumstance as described in (3)(e) of the Code, that is, in felony murders, which alone account for the majority of all death sentences and executions since *Gregg*. The second is the citation of aggravating circumstance in (3)(b) where "[T]he defendant was previously convicted of another murder or of a felony involving the use or threat of violence to the person." The use of this circumstance to generate death eligibility is justified in this way:

Prior conviction of a felony involving violence to the person suggests two inferences supporting escalation of sentence: first, that the murder reflects the character of the defendant rather than any extraordinary aspect of the situation, and second, that the defendant is likely to prove dangerous to life on some future occasion.[25]

In an otherwise well-documented text, no evidence is offered to support these two inferences.

D. The new statutes in practice

It is informative to look at the post-*Furman* murder statutes in the light of Justice Blackmun's remarks in that case about legislators' sensitivity to "constitutional overtones" in relation to death penalty legislation.[26] As we saw in Chapter 3, eighteen states responded to *Furman* by enacting mandatory death penalty provisions.[27] But a number of the other states enacting new capital punishment legislation patterned their revisions on Section 210.6 of the Model Penal Code with its provisions for aggravating and mitigating circumstances.

The new death penalty legislation was specifically designed to avoid the Supreme Court's objections to the previously administered statutes and, in particular, to answer the concerns of Justices Stewart and White regarding the absence of standards to determine who shall receive a death sentence. The availability of the Model Penal Code provisions drafted to address these concerns must have seemed providential, but in adopting those provisions the states introduced many variations, particularly in the clauses containing aggravating and mitigating circumstances.

For instance, the Georgia statute,[28] upheld by the Supreme Court in *Gregg,* contains provisions that grossly distort those in the Model Code. The statute lists ten aggravating circumstances rather than the eight enumerated in the Code, while completely ignoring the extensive list of mitigating circumstances. Failure to specify any mitigating circumstances renders extremely remote the likelihood of proper consideration of all the "main circumstances of aggravation and mitigation that should be weighed and weighed against each other."[29] In short, Georgia adopted and extended that aspect of the Model Code that is weakest in jurisprudential terms and completely disregarded the provisions relating to mitigating circumstances, which are supported by a carefully articulated, if imperfect, rationale. This dubious departure from the Model Code scheme, however, does not appear objectionable to the Court.

The Texas statute,[30] upheld by the Supreme Court in *Jurek,* departs even further from the Model Code and, according to the Commentary, "could be said to mark a rejection of the Code formulation."[31] The Texas Code defines capital murder as intentional or knowing homicide in five situations: murder of a fire fighter or peace officer; murder committed in the course of certain specified felonies; murder committed for remuneration; murder committed in an escape or attempted escape from prison; and murder of a prison employee by an inmate. Upon conviction of capital murder, a separate sentencing proceeding is held. The jury is instructed that it may impose a death sentence only upon a unanimous and affirmative finding on each of the following issues: whether the homicidal conduct was done deliberately and with reasonable expectation of killing another; whether "there is a probability that the defendant would commit criminal acts of violence that would constitute a continuing threat to society"; and, if warranted by the evidence, whether the defendant's conduct was unreasonable in response to provocation by the deceased.

Although Texas adopted neither the Code's formulation of aggravating circumstances nor of its mitigating circumstances, the Supreme Court held that the state's "action in narrowing the categories of murders for which a death sentence may ever be imposed serves much the same purpose."[32] The Court also held that the judicial interpretation of one of the statutory questions (relating to the probability of future violent crimes) on which the jury had to answer in the affirmative before the death sentence was imposed "was broad enough to allow consideration of any mitigating circumstances that might exist."[33]

The Florida statute, upheld by the Supreme Court in *Proffitt* v. *Florida,* altered the Model Code specifications for both aggravating and mitigating circumstances by omitting one of each[34] and adding as a new aggravating circumstance that the murder "was committed to disrupt or hinder the lawful exercise of any government function or the enforcement of laws."[35] The plurality endorsed the Florida scheme as achieving "an informed, focused, guided and objective inquiry" regarding the question of whether the convicted person should be sentenced to death.[36]

None of these statutes attempts to repair the deficiencies in the Model Penal Code. What they and the other legislative reactions to *Furman* illustrate is a "search for a formula that would restore the death penalty, never mind for what. These statutes . . . do not represent a legislative judgment that particular offenses are 'atrocious' in any singular sense."[37] At one extreme is the Texas statute, which has been criticized as "fundamentally defective as originally written, has not been improved by judicial interpretation, and as administered violates the minimal requirements of evenhanded application set forth in the July 1976 decisions."[38] At the other extreme is the Florida statute, described in the Commentary to the Model Penal Code as "closely derived from the Model Code provision on sentence of death."[39]

Because the Florida statute approximates the Code provisions, it carries with it some of the problems involved in implementing that approach. Of crucial importance is whether the statute solves the problem of devising intelligible criteria to select those who shall die, a task that, again to quote Justice Harlan in *McGautha,* is "beyond present human ability." Florida attempted to do so by adopting a statutory specification of aggravating and mitigating circumstances that, with relatively inconsequential changes, "largely tracks Subsections (3) and (4) of the Model Code provision."[40] Like the Model Code, however, the statute fails to provide any guidance for a rational determination of whether sufficient aggravating circumstances outweigh the mitigating circumstances to justify imposing a death sentence.

Under the Florida statute, at the conclusion of the sentencing hearing the jury is instructed to consider "[w]hether sufficient mitigating circumstances exist . . . which outweigh the aggravating circumstances found to exist; and . . . based on these considerations whether the defendant should be sentenced to life [imprisonment] or death."[41] The jury's verdict, determined by a majority vote, is advisory; the sentence is determined by the trial judge, who is also directed to weigh the statutory aggravating and mitigating circumstances when making that decision.[42]

In *Proffitt* the petitioner challenged the failure of the Florida law to assign any specific weight to the various circumstances and argued that the lack of guidance prevented any rational decision. Justices Stewart, Powell, and Stevens attempted to answer this argument:

> While these questions and decisions may be hard, they require no more line drawing than is commonly required of a factfinder in a lawsuit. For example, juries have traditionally evaluated the validity of defenses such as insanity or reduced capacity, both of which involve the same considerations as some of the above-mentioned mitigating circumstances. While the various factors to be considered by the sentencing authorities do not have numerical weights assigned to them, the requirements of *Furman* are satisfied when the sentencing authority's discretion is guided and channeled by requiring examination of specific factors that argue in favor of or against imposition of the death penalty, thus eliminating total arbitrariness and capriciousness in its imposition.
>
> The directions given to judge and jury by the Florida statute are sufficiently clear and precise to enable the various aggravating circumstances to be weighed against the mitigating ones. As a result, the trial court's sentencing discretion is guided and channeled by a system that focuses on the circumstances of each individual homicide and individual defendant in deciding whether the death penalty is to be imposed.[43]

The Court's response entirely fails to answer the petitioner's challenge.

First, to assume that the questions and decisions involved in the comparative weighing of aggravating and mitigating circumstances "require no more line drawing than is commonly required of a factfinder in a lawsuit" is erroneous. There are few parallels between the judgments commonly required in ordinary lawsuits and whatever a jury is required to do when, for example, it "weighs" an aggravating circumstance such as that a capital felony "was especially heinous, atrocious, or cruel" against a mitigating circumstance that "the defendant has no significant history of prior criminal activity."[44]

Second, the analogy with the insanity defense is instructively inept. The Model Penal Code and the Florida statute do not involve a finding of fact, such as whether a defendant's mental condition satisfies a particular legal definition of insanity. Rather, they require determining the degree of the offender's culpability by balancing the mitigating force of his or her insanity against the aggravating circumstance that his or her insanely motivated act was committed during an armed robbery, without any guidance as to the relative weight to be given to either the insanity or the armed robbery.

This impossible task, however, is not entirely without precedent. Analogous requirements arise in other areas of the law, and they are notorious. A notable example is the standard direction to a judge to award custody of a child in a divorce case to the contesting parent whose care would be in the child's "best interest." This decision involves the same combination of comparative balancing of incommensurables, as well as the problems of uncontrollable discretion, involved in the new jurisprudence of death. Not surprisingly, after assessing the "best interest" standard, scholars have suggested that society may be better off by requiring judges to flip a coin.[45]

Third, the assertion that "the requirements of *Furman* are satisfied when the sentencing authority's discretion is guided and channeled by requiring examination of specific factors that argue in favor of or against imposition of the death penalty" suggests that merely examining or inspecting the various factors presented will, in some occult fashion, induce a rational decision. What seems to be required is an immediate apprehension or intuition, not mediated by any conscious reasoning process. In the absence of any specific weights assigned to the circumstances to be considered, and lacking any kind of comparative weighing formula, how else can the sentencing authority be expected to derive any conclusion from all the aggravating and mitigating information presented to it?

Finally, the assertion that "the sentencing authority's discretion is guided and channeled by requiring examination of specific factors that argue in favor of or against imposition of the death penalty" is based on a misconception. The sentencing authority's *attention* may be guided and channeled, but its *discretion* remains unguided and uncontrolled if aggravating and mitigating circumstances are present. The "clear and precise" directions given to the judge and jury by the Florida statute provide no standards or principles by which to make a judgment; no formula regulates the decision to kill. Indeed, the absence of any established weighing process requires that each sentencing authority devise its own scheme for deciding whether to impose death. As a result, the Florida statute actually increases uncontrolled discretion; a different standard for deciding who shall die is utilized in each capital case.

E. Does the law matter?

A decade after the Supreme Court upheld the revised death penalty statutes, a fundamental question remains: Do the various provisions of the Model Penal Code that "satisfy the concerns of *Furman*," as the new Georgia sentencing procedures were said to do,[46] actually control the imposition of the death penalty in a significant manner?

A recent empirical study conducted in Georgia was aimed at illuminating how judges, juries, and prosecutors in that state decide which convicted killers should be sentenced to death.[47] The study focused on the general question: Given the circumstances of a particular murder case, what was the probability the perpetrator would be sentenced to death? It sought an empirical answer based on the details and outcomes of over 600 murder cases, all of which were tried under Georgia's present death penalty statute between 1973 and 1978.

The study found that the cases in which the death penalty was imposed differed from the others on three primary dimensions: (1) the "certainty" the defendant was a deliberate killer; (2) the "status" of the victim; and (3) the "heinousness of the killing."[48] In this classification system the word "certainty" corresponds to the degree of assurance that the defendant was, in fact, the killer, and "deliberateness" relates to whether the defendant acted knowingly to cause the victim's death. The "status" of the victim represents the relationship between the victim and the accused, and reflects the widely observed pattern that stranger-to-stranger killings are more likely to result in death sentences than those in which the victim knew the defendant. "Heinousness" refers to such killings as those with multiple victims, those preceded by psychological torture or sexual abuse, and those involving bizarre weapons or mutilated bodies.

This classification procedure proved to have strong discriminatory and predictive capability. The rules were derived quite independently of, and do not coincide with, the aggravating factors set forth in the Georgia homicide statute. Indeed, the dimension of "status" has no explicit basis in the law. Yet the author of the study concluded: "It is hard to avoid speculating that, in killings in which jurors can imagine themselves or their loved ones as victims, death penalties are more likely to be imposed."[49] The study also found that the statutory reference to creating "a great risk of death to more than one person" appeared "to have little practical importance."[50]

This study suggests that when jurors make death penalty decisions they consider factors that may be unrelated to any statutory provisions or to the weighing of mitigating and aggravating circumstances. As we have seen in the Georgia statute, the list of aggravating factors is not accompanied by a list of mitigating factors, and a Georgia jury is under no obligation to treat any aspect of the case as mitigating. But as jurors' behavior is predictable without referring to the aggravating factors, there is no reason

Table 4.1. *Homicides, death row populations, and executions in Georgia, Florida, and Pennsylvania*

State	State population[a]	No. of homicides[b]	Year end death row population[c]	No. of executions since 1977[d]
Georgia	5,463,105	713	102	7
Florida	9,746,324	1,409	193	16
Pennsylvania	11,863,895	678	33	0

[a]From U.S. Department of Commerce, Bureau of the Census, *County and City Data Book,* at 2, Table A (1983).
[b]In 1982; from U.S. Department of Justice, FBI, *Uniform Crime Reports; Crime in the U.S. 1982,* at 44, Table 3.
[c]Through 1983; from Bureau of Justice Statistics, U.S. Department of Justice, *Capital Punishment 1983,* at 3, Figure 4 (1984).
[d]From NAACP Legal Defense and Education Fund, Inc., *Death Row, U.S.A.* 3 (Aug. 1, 1986).

to believe that any statutory provisions influence them greatly when they make death penalty decisions.

Moreover, the irrelevance of the various sentencing schemes is highlighted by examining the records of different states that have adopted some variation of the Model Penal Code. If sentencing procedures affect the decision to impose the death penalty – an assumption necessary to the *Gregg* Court's conclusion that the new statutes eliminated the pre-*Furman* arbitrariness – we would expect similar patterns in those states with similar death sentencing laws. The three states selected for this comparison are Georgia, Florida, and Pennsylvania. Although Pennsylvania has what some have termed a mandatory death penalty statute,[51] it does not automatically impose a death sentence upon conviction of a certain offense. The Pennsylvania statute, unlike Georgia's, not only provides the defense the opportunity to prove the existence of mitigating circumstances, but also specifies mitigating circumstances broadly defined to include "[a]ny . . . evidence of mitigation concerning the character and record of the defendant and the circumstances of his offense."[52] One commentator correctly labeled his comparison of the Pennsylvania and Georgia statutes a "distinction without a difference."[53]

Table 4.1 presents the relevant comparative data. The striking contrast between Pennsylvania and the other two states reveals that the most powerful predictor of differential imposition of the death penalty is certainly not substantive law, but rather geographical region. Such regional differences as described in Chapter 2 have a long history and display remarkable consistency. This type of consistency, however, is surely not what the Supreme Court referred to when it required "the evenhanded, rational, and consistent imposition of death sentences under law."[54]

Finally, a third aspect of the death penalty's revival demonstrates the irrelevance of the actual provisions in various post-*Furman* statutes. When the states responded to *Furman* by enacting selected provisions of the off-the-shelf Model Penal Code, they were not seeking to develop a coherent, well-reasoned punishment policy or to articulate a rational method for determining who shall live and who shall die. What they were seeking was death penalty "legislation that passes constitutional muster,"[55] to borrow the Supreme Court's description of the Florida statute. That task proved easier than they had probably anticipated. As Robert Weisberg observed, "the Court has asked virtually nothing of the states that they were not doing before *Furman*. . . . It is as if the constitutional strictures on the death penalty are merely a matter of legal aesthetics. The state will satisfy the Court if it can describe its penalty scheme according to some rational-looking form – indeed some metaphor of rational form."[56]

Still, to conclude that the Model Penal Code provisions and their legislative progeny are largely meaningless in the actual administration of the death penalty is not to say that the efforts of the Code's drafters can be ignored. On the contrary, their attempt to resolve the conflict between the state's power to kill and the rule of law[57] deserves close attention.

The standard-setting exercise of the Model Penal Code and the legislative efforts to provide standards for a late-twentieth-century death penalty were doomed for many reasons. Particularly important, these efforts were arguments against history, coming far too late in the progress toward abolition to have any coherence.

Many of the intellectual problems of the Code have historical roots. The efforts to make fine distinctions among murders came after the system based on premeditation had collapsed under scholarly criticism. The standards were constructed at a time when no more than one out of a hundred killings could lead to execution. To define in advance the elements that make some killings more worthy of punishment than others is difficult in any context; but to define criteria for choosing one case in 100 or 200 is impossible. The moral equivalence between murder and execution did not survive into the modern era. The Code drafters did not wish to restore this equivalence. Instead, relatively trivial distinctions were given controlling influence in the decision between life and death.

The Code did not fail because of lack of effort. What the drafters did represents an earnest and sustained attempt to accomplish their objective. It did not fail because of their particular ambivalence, because ambivalence is inherent in the task of condemning people to death. Nor did it fail because of insufficient juristic competence or ingenuity on the part of the drafters; indeed, they were among "the finest artists of criminal law doctrine."[58] It failed because some decisions can never be subjected to legal discipline, and of those the deliberate decision to take human life is, and will remain, preeminent.

Notes

1. American Law Institute, *Model Penal Code and Commentaries* Pt. II, at 13 (1980) (hereafter American Law Institute). Section 210.3(1) (b) refers to circumstances in which "a homicide which would otherwise be murder is committed under the influence of extreme mental or emotional disturbance for which there is reasonable explanation or excuse. The reasonableness of such explanation or excuse shall be determined from the viewpoint of a person in the actor's situation under the circumstances as he believes them to be." *Id.* at 43.
2. Wechsler & Michael, "A Rationale of the Law of Homicide," 37 *Colum. L. Rev.* 704, 705 (1937) (hereafter Wechsler & Michael, "Rationale").
3. *Id.* at 703.
4. *Id.*
5. B. Cardozo, *Law and Literature* 99–100 (1931).
6. American Law Institute, at 126.
7. Wechsler & Michael, "Rationale," at 716.
8. American Law Institute, at 29–42.
9. *Id.* at 107–10.
10. *Id.* at 167.
11. *Id.*
12. *Id.* at 171.
13. *Id.* at 137.
14. *See Godfrey* v. *Georgia*, 446 U.S. 420 (1980) (Georgia's application of aggravating circumstances unconstitutional).
15. American Law Institute, at 135.
16. *Id.* at 111.
17. *Id.*
18. *Id.* at 136–7.
19. *Id.* at 137–42 (emphasis added).
20. *Id.*
21. *Id.* at 143.
22. *Id.* at 133.
23. *McGautha* v. *California*, 402 U.S. 183 (1971).
24. *Id.* at 248.
25. American Law Institute, at 136.
26. *Furman* v. *Georgia*, 408 U.S. 238, 413 (1972).
27. American Law Institute, at 156.
28. *Ga. Code Ann.* § 27-2534.1 (Supp. 1975) (superseded).
29. American Law Institute, at 135.
30. *Tex. Crim. Proc. Code Ann.* § 37.071 (Vernon Supp. 1986).
31. American Law Institute, at 169.
32. *Jurek* v. *Texas*, 428 U.S. 262, 270 (1976).
33. *Id.* at 272.
34. Sections 210.6(3)(c) and 210.6(4)(d).

35. *Fla. Stat. Ann.* § 921.141(5)(g) (West 1985).
36. *Proffitt* v. *Florida,* 428 U.S. 242, 259 (1976).
37. Zimring, Eigen & O'Malley, "Punishing Homicide in Philadelphia: Perspectives on the Death Penalty," 43 *U. Chi. L. Rev.* 227, 250–1 (1976).
38. Dix, "Administration of the Texas Death Penalty Statutes: Constitutional Infirmities Related to the Prediction of Dangerousness," 55 *Tex. L. Rev.* 1343, 1414 n.340 (1977).
39. American Law Institute, at 158.
40. *Id.*
41. *Fla. Stat. Ann.* §§ 921.141(2)(b)–(c) (West 1985).
42. *Id.* § 921.141(3).
43. *Proffitt,* 428 U.S. at 257–8.
44. *Fla. Stat. Ann.* §§ 921.141(5), 921.141(6)(b) (West 1985).
45. J. Goldstein, A. Freud & A. Solnit, *Beyond the Best Interests of the Child* (1979); *see also* Mnookin, "Child Custody Adjudication: Judicial Functions in the Face of Indeterminacy," 39 *Law & Contemp. Problems* 226, 235–7 (1975).
46. *Gregg,* 428 U.S. at 155, 196–207.
47. Barnett, "Some Distribution Patterns for the Georgia Death Sentence," 18 *U.C. Davis L. Rev.* 1327 (1985).
48. *Id.* at 1339.
49. *Id.* at 1341.
50. *Id.* at 1335.
51. The present Pennsylvania statute was amended in 1978. *See* Act of Sept. 13, 1978, No. 141, § 1, 1978 *Pa. Laws* 756 [current version at 42 *Pa. Cons. Stat. Ann.* § 9711 (Purdon Supp. 1982)]. *See* Act of Oct. 5, 1980, No. 142, § 401(a), 1980 *Pa. Laws* 693 (transferred the codification to title 42).
52. *Id.*
53. Ledewitz, "The Requirement of Death: Mandatory Language in the Pennsylvania Death Penalty Statute," 21 *Duquesne L. Rev.* 103, 107 (1982).
54. *Jurek* v. *Texas,* 428 U.S. 262, 276 (1976).
55. *Proffitt* v. *Florida,* 428 U.S. 242, 259 (1976).
56. Weisberg, "Deregulating Death," 1983 *Sup. Ct. Rev.* 305, 354 (hereafter Weisberg, "Deregulating Death").
57. *McGautha* v. *California,* 402 U.S. 183, 249–50 (1971) (Brennan, J., dissenting).
58. Weisberg, "Deregulating Death," at 313.

II

Futures and consequences

5

A game of chicken

On August 12, 1984, these paragraphs appeared in the *New York Times:*

> With 221 condemned prisoners, Florida has the most crowded death row in the country, and the crowd is growing by 25 a year. The Department of Corrections estimates the number of condemned prisoners could grow to 300 by July 1986.
> The agency plans to ask the Legislature for authority to build a separate facility to house the estimated 800 condemned prisoners expected – assuming the pace of executions does not accelerate sharply – by the year 2000.[1]

These projections are remarkable. Even more remarkable is the matter-of-fact manner in which such extraordinary numbers were reported: eight hundred prisoners on death row in one of fifty states, and this in a state where the current governor is "widely known for the speed with which he signs death warrants."[2] How many will be executed? How will they be selected? What will happen next?

The circumstances of capital punishment in the United States of the 1980s are unprecedented. At the midpoint of the decade some 1,700 prisoners were held by state authorities under "active sentences of death," cases where no outstanding court order or executive decision has reversed a death sentence following a murder conviction. The American megaprison now has, increasingly, a mega–death row as its seventh circle. Either we are on the verge of a momentous change in American execution policy, or we are engaged in a gruesome charade.

The enormity of the death row backlog in contemporary America can be demonstrated in a variety of statistical comparisons. This is by far the largest collection of the condemned in American history. It exceeds by a factor of five the total number of executions in the United States and Western Europe in the previous twenty-five years.[3] In many American states, if present trends in both death sentences and executions continue for a very few years, the number of those awaiting execution will equal the number executed in the past half-century.[4]

A. One execution a day?

For the country as a whole, the supply of condemned prisoners vastly exceeds any objective measure of demand for executions. Eleven persons were executed in the United States between 1977 and the end of 1983.[5] During 1984, partially in response to a Supreme Court mandate to curtail and expedite federal court review,[6] the annual rate of execution in the United States reached twenty-one.[7]

Although the increase demonstrates the role that constitutional courts can have on the pace of executions, even twenty-one executions a year leaves an American prison population stocked with seventy times as many condemned as can be executed. And this is not merely a seventy-year supply; it is an endlessly growing stockpile. To keep pace with the number of death sentences issued annually under state penal schemes approved by the U.S. Supreme Court is to live in a nation that executes about 300 per year, and perhaps one for each day of the year.

That number represents almost twice as many as the peak year of executions in the United States in this century[8] and more than three times as many as the annual total reported by South Africa,[9] now the leading executioner among those nations with accurate reporting. Furthermore, this rate would only be a break-even point. More than one a day would be necessary to reduce the large death row population, many more to achieve a swift and certain execution policy. Anything less (and we will not see one execution a day) creates an endlessly rising backlog and a subsidiary selection process to accompany the procedures that have already produced the fraternity of the condemned.

Executive clemency and intentional delay will restrict the number of executions. State appellate courts and state executive branch maneuvers will serve as the major control on death row populations (with death from suicide and natural causes also of significance). Such methods will prove troublesome but necessary for keeping the number of executions within tolerable limits, to the extent that federal courts withdraw as the primary execution management instrument in the American governmental organization. But none of these measures can reduce the ever-growing death row population.

Moreover, these control mechanisms move the question of who shall live and who shall die away from legal guidelines and the judicial process into an area with neither laws nor principles for guidance.[10] This fundamental inequity led the U.S. Supreme Court to strike down the previously administered death penalty laws in *Furman* v. *Georgia*.[11] Yet it is the inevitable result of implementing the penalty in ways that the courts have since approved.

The situation is not temporary. Unless there are tremendous increases in executions or remarkable decreases in death sentences, then backlog, delay, and occasional executions striking "like lightning"[12] must be seen as integral to the American system.

The whole of Part II is about the implications of and possible solutions to the capital punishment impasse, but in this chapter our ambitions are more modest: to convey a sense of the special problems that current conditions generate for American political and judicial institutions, and the general society. Seventeen hundred death row prisoners and a few dozen executions a year – apparently the choice is between a permanent Reign of Terror or an execution policy that makes mockery of the legal standards governing the use of the death penalty. These are circumstances that almost no one would wish as American public policy. How did this situation come to be?

One simple explanation deserves preliminary attention before we examine the complex causes of present conditions. In this view, capital punishment would be no problem but for the meddlesome intervention of the federal courts. The "pileup" or "logjam" on death row was created by judicial interference with the will of elected state legislators, juries, and judges. Thus, the vast disparity between the condemned and the executed resulted from the judicially imposed moratorium that existed from 1967 through 1977, and the country could live at equilibrium with a modest number of executions (whatever that might mean).

Several indications in recent history dispute the accuracy of this view. The backlog of death sentences produced by the first five years of the moratorium was in fact drastically reduced by the Supreme Court's decision in *Furman* v. *Georgia*.[13] Furthermore, the most dramatic growth in death row populations occurred after 1976, when the U.S. Supreme Court gave its constitutional approval to state capital sentencing statutes in *Gregg* v. *Georgia*.[14] The seven years following that landmark decision produced eleven executions and about 100 times that number of death row inhabitants. In this whole period only twelve states, less than a third of those with capital punishment statutes, performed any executions.[15]

Blaming the courts may be a popular indoor sport, but it misinterprets the extent and breadth of ambivalence over capital punishment in the United States and the crisis of political accountability represented by the current contrast between the many who are condemned and the few who are executed. The game of "blame it on the courts" also ignores a fundamental aspect of American public opinion: Those who support the concept of capital punishment do not necessarily want any executions, and most would be horrified by the kind of perpetual bloodbath that would ensue were the criminal law to keep its promises literally. From the standpoint of public opinion, perhaps the best of all possible worlds is one with the death penalty on the statute books, but no executions.

B.   Passing the buck

Current conditions represent a "crisis of statesmanship" in American political life. Insofar as it produces a situation that nobody wants, it may be compared to the game of "chicken" that provides the title of this chapter.

That game was lucidly described by Bertrand Russell:

> This sport is called "Chicken!" It is played by choosing a long straight road with a white line down the middle and starting two very fast cars towards each other from opposite ends. Each car is expected to keep the wheels of one side on the white line. As they approach each other mutual destruction becomes more and more imminent. If one of them swerves from the white line before the other, the other, as he passes, shouts "Chicken!," and the one who has swerved becomes an object of contempt.[16]

In the game of chicken, the one who swerves to avoid a crash loses. The problem is that if neither participant is willing to become that loser, a catastrophe that nobody wants will occur; but if the potentially fatal crash is truly not desired, why does it so frequently happen? Because each participant is also unwilling to pay the price of "chickening out" and will take great risk to pass that cost to his or her opponent.

The comparison between the absurd mathematics of capital punishment policy and the classic game of chicken is both powerful and incomplete. With respect to the disparity between death sentences and executions, and the continuation of executions themselves, many, if not most, key actors in the American government – in our constitutional courts, in the higher reaches of state government, and in state supreme courts – would rather function in circumstances greatly different from those described in preceding pages. The simplest, and for many the best, solution for these key actors would be the end of executions. Further, many of these agents of state and federal government have the power individually or collectively to stop executions, just as both drivers in a chicken game can avert disaster by swerving or stopping.

At all levels of government, however, to halt executions is perceived as an unpopular act, inviting accusations of autocratic and elitist policy, and negative consequences either in electoral politics or with respect to the legitimacy of judicial institutions. Each authoritative actor would prefer that someone else stop executions – the archetypical situation in chicken. The difference is this: The price of action in the capital punishment game is not one of facing the accusation of cowardice, but rather of accepting the consequences of bravery.

This situation is exacerbated by the multiplicity of elements in the distribution of power over criminal justice policy generally and capital punishment in particular. Many government actors are available to halt executions in a particular jurisdiction. In the 1980s no death sentences can be enforced without decisions by local prosecutors; the local judiciary, with or without a jury; state appellate courts; federal courts; the U.S. Supreme Court; and executive clemency review processes, frequently including the governor of the executing jurisdiction.

The result can be two kinds of buck passing. First, all these avenues of decision make it possible for the individual hoping to shift responsibility onto another to envisage a number of potential candidates for that honor. Second, in the later stages of review, those who hold the power to reverse executions face the apparent seal of approval on the decision to execute that has been conferred by all of the preceding review processes. Proponents of execution can remind the governor that six other decision makers have already affirmed the legitimacy of the procedure. This momentum generates an unwillingness to upset a decision so resolutely endorsed by a series of other presumably responsible actors – a form of passing the buck backward.

In Chapter 7 we tell the story of Velma Barfield, a North Carolina grandmother executed in 1984. One aspect of that event will serve here, however, as a classic case of buck passing. Then-Governor Hunt, in rejecting Mrs. Barfield's clemency petition, said: "I cannot in good conscience justify making an exception to the law as enacted by our State Legislature, or overruling those 12 jurors who, after hearing the evidence, concluded that Mrs. Barfield should pay the maximum penalty for her brutal actions."[17]

Students of rhetoric can benefit by studying this pronouncement, a vintage example of passing the buck backward. It is also a notable instance of endorsing "the maximum penalty" without actually naming it.

Ironically, the same theory that leads to passing the buck backward also encourages passing it forward. Prosecutors can tell themselves to leave it to the jury, juries to the judge, the judge to the appellate court, and so on. This avoidance of responsibility recently led the U.S. Supreme Court to invalidate a death sentence after the prosecutor had encouraged the jury to impose the penalty, claiming that any error would be corrected by future review.[18] The prosecutor, in his closing arguments, had said to the jury: "Now [the defense attorneys insinuate] that your decision is the final decision and that they're gonna take Bobby Caldwell out in front of the Courthouse in moments and string him up and that is terribly, terribly unfair. For they know, as I know, and as [the] Judge . . . has told you, that the decision you render is automatically reviewed by the Supreme Court."[19] The Court did hold that Caldwell's sentence was unconstitutional, but the prosecutor in the case was only verbalizing what every decision maker involved in a death penalty case realizes.

Even though successive participants in the process may be looking to future reviews to take the responsibility away from them – and thus pay the cost of being brave – the result may be the opposite, because of the apparent constraint imposed by the unanimity of prior reviews. Those who look to others in the system to be brave unwittingly raise the perceived price of bravery for those who must act after them.

Buck passing has been a crucial problem in the context of capital punishment in the United States since the 1960s. The federal courts were for so long the single agency preventing executions that many other responsible actors began to depend on the courts' assumption of that role and evaded the practice of individualized decision making. Even the state legislatures that enthusiastically enacted capital punishment statutes after *Furman* v. *Georgia* could do so in comfortable anticipation of subsequent federal judicial disapproval.

As Chapter 2 demonstrated, state legislatures could act knowing courts were hostile, thereby daring the courts to rescue the system from the consequences of the new laws. They were free to pass both symbolic legislation – and the buck. By the time U.S. Supreme Court became impatient with this role for the federal courts, and with the institutional criticism it had absorbed, traditional mechanisms of restraint had been literally abandoned. Other processes and practices that might have been developed around a declining trend in executions were probably aborted.

One illustration of the displacement of other control processes, probably caused by federal court intervention, is the pattern of executive commutation of sentences. Official statistics report the number of such commutations in 1960 at twenty-two, a figure equal to more than ten percent of the 210 persons on death row at the end of that year. By the end of 1967, when the death row population had more than doubled to 435, the number of commutations reported dropped to thirteen, and the more significant percentage of commutations to the death row population had dropped from ten percent to three percent.[20] Executive clemency, seldom popular with executives, was believed less necessary in an era when federal court intervention had brought executions to a virtual halt.

Although federalizing of capital punishment disabled local pressures to decrease the use of the penalty, there is nothing wrong with centralizing the control of executions in a branch of the federal government. Federal control is both more efficient and, given the national scope of the issue, more appropriate than a patchwork of state and local controls. After all, during the base year of 1960, when twenty-two sentences were commuted

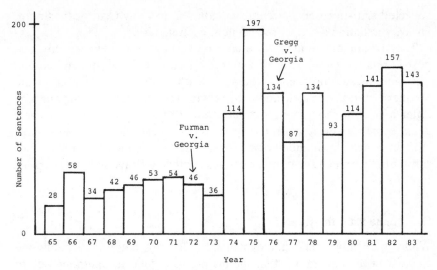

Figure 5.1.   New death sentences by year in the South.

and federal oversight was not prominent, two-and-one-half times as many prisoners were executed as were spared.[21] The point is that the "stop-and-go" character of Supreme Court judgments about the validity of state death penalty provisions probably increased the number of persons sentenced to death over the past ten years and contributed to the high ratio of death sentences to executions.

One illustration of this phenomenon concerns recent trends in executive clemency. Once the governors became accustomed to forgoing responsibility for commutation, they were disinclined to accept political responsibility for death row population control even when the Supreme Court changed course. With the exception of 1976, the year the signals were shifted, government statistics report no post-*Gregg* year in which commutation of sentence reached even four percent of the nation's death row population.[22] Some of the numbers are gallows humor. In 1979, with 588 prisoners on death row, a national total of four sentence commutations was reported, less than one percent of the condemned population. In 1980, when the number on death row at the end of the year jumped 100 to 688, the number of commutations decreased from four to two.[23]

Executive clemency measures behavior at only one point in the complex series of decisions that determines the death row population. A broader gauge of stop-and-go effects on the complex political process that has led to death row inflation is the number of death sentences produced by the constellation of prosecutorial, judicial, jury, and state appellate court decision making referred to earlier. Figure 5.1, taken from federally collected statistics, shows trends in death sentences by year for the South, always the nation's capital punishment capital.

The striking element in these data is the difference between pre- and post-*Furman* v. *Georgia* death sentences. Before 1972, when that decision was announced, the number of new death sentences each year in the Southern states averaged about fifty, with the trend, if any, downward. After a year of rapid legislative adjustment in 1973, the number of new death sentences each year more than doubled, and there is no year after 1973 in which the number of new death sentences in the South did not substantially exceed the number of such sentences issued in any year prior to *Furman*.

C. Blame it on the Court?

While there might be other explanations for this pattern, certainly one element in the equation is that the institutional controls operating before the Supreme Court's apparent preemption of the issue ceased to operate after *Furman*. As with executive clemency, these controls were not reasserted when the court staged its strategic withdrawal from prohibiting capital punishment in 1976. From 1977 through 1983, the annual average of new death sentences in the South was well above double the average in the decade preceding *Furman*.

The matter extends beyond the behavior of prosecutors and judges to that of state legislatures. Relieving the legislative process of ultimate responsibility and then restoring legislative power is an almost certain prescription for a high volume of death sentences. More troublesome is the possibility that a hands-off attitude concerning executions in the future might produce a greater number than would have occurred with a more consistent judicial role.

Although one may only speculate as to what might have happened with a different course of events, one thing seems clear: There is no way for federal courts to play a truly neutral role in execution policy in the United States. The prior role of the courts, and the legislative and popular reactions to it, have set forces in motion that have had significant effect on death sentencing and may have some effect on executions. Whether the Supreme Court contends with this legacy actively or passively in the future, much of what will happen will be attributable to that institution's work. Either way, there is a case for a more sophisticated version of "blame it on the Court."

All of this is complicated by the allocation of responsibility for criminal justice policy in the United States when constitutional values are not implicated. Unlike much of the Western world, the locus of penal policy in the United States is state government, not the national government. State government is both more parochial and traditionally less associated with statesmanship, in the sense of resisting the perceived popular will, than is national government in general and the federal Supreme Court in particular. An illustration of a divergence between federal and state practices with respect to capital punishment emerges from official statistics on executions and death row populations. In the twelve years preceding the Supreme Court's pronouncement in *Furman* v. *Georgia,* despite a multitude of federal crimes for which the death penalty was available, only one prisoner was executed under federal jurisdiction.[24] Less than one-half of one percent of executions during the period occurred under federal jurisdiction.

More important, the federal government has successfully avoided the pileup of death sentences that has produced the disparity between death row populations and any imaginable level of executions in so many American states. During 1960–83, while the death row population in the nation as a whole grew sixfold, the number of prisoners under federal jurisdiction facing death sentences has varied between zero and two and has remained at zero since 1977.[25] The United States is experiencing a de facto moratorium on capital punishment at the federal level, but the allocation of responsibility in criminal justice matters to the states has rendered this fact almost invisible and possibly irrelevant.

D. An inapt analogy?

Is it inaccurate to characterize executions in the mid-1980s as a game of chicken? The car crash in chicken is a circumstance that neither player wishes, but are there not political actors in the United States who really favor current circumstances? Is this not what opinion polls and the pronouncements of candidates for public office are telling us? Not quite.

The behavior of public officials in the period before and after executions is in marked contrast to their discussions of capital punishment during political campaigns. While there is talk about the need for the law to keep its promises, political figures are not usually enthusiastic about specific executions. Indeed, the odd lot of late adolescents who gather around prison boundaries to cheer on the eve of scheduled executions is usually regarded as deviant by the same public that supports capital punishment. James Reston described the hideous performance of the crowd that gathered to witness the execution of Velma Barfield:

[A] clutch of death-penalty boosters egged on the state. "Hip, hip, hurrah . . . K-I-L-L." "Burn, bitch, burn." Their delirious, high-pitched cackles floated over the scene like a bad odor. . . . At 2 a.m. the cheerleaders, inspired by the collective sadism induced by the spectacle, began to chant "Kill her! Kill her! Kill her!" and at 2:15 it was as if the home team had just scored the winning touchdown.[26]

No holder of statewide office has been known to join the cheers anywhere in the United States.

The most that can be said for the opinion of policy makers toward executions is that they are willing to permit executions; there are indeed many responsible government officials willing to allow execution as the cost of maintaining capital punishment statutes. But does this defeat the analogy between teenaged games of chicken and executions? Remember that there are drivers willing to risk catastrophic crashes to avoid the label of cowardice. If there were not, there would be no participants in chicken and no crashes to explain.

Current execution policy and games of chicken are similar in two further respects – the avoidance of personal responsibility for fateful outcomes and the sharp differences between public and private attitudes of key actors. When the cars collide in a chicken game, those involved in the crash tend to avoid ascriptions of personal responsibility for the outcome. The crash is viewed more as the product of fate or an act of God than as anyone's fault. Similarly, executions are regarded as the demand of "the law" as an abstraction or an expression of "the will of the people." The multiplicity of individual decisions necessary for an execution merge into a single depersonalized act of the state. The phenomenon of passing the buck facilitates this imagery, which may be one reason why passing the buck is so common in capital punishment cases. The people who make decisions in these matters frequently talk and think as if no individual is in charge. That this image gives comfort, that this state of diffuse responsibility is felt necessary, seems powerful evidence of ambivalence about legal execution in the United States.

A final parallel between highway bravado and execution policy concerns the distinction between private views and public behavior that may be of critical importance in predicting outcome. The price of chickening out on the highway is public knowledge that the accident avoider lacks the bravado to carry through. If risk-taking behavior of this sort could be decided by truly secret ballot, we doubt that any collisions would occur.

We cannot say that those who hold power on such matters would abolish the death penalty. We *can* say that the public reaction to decisions about capital punishment is regarded as vitally important by decision makers at all levels of government, and that the perceived public reaction has decisive impact on how decisions are made and explained.

The factors we have discussed here provide a context in which the future of capital punishment will be worked out. We shall return to many of the concepts and examples in this chapter as we discuss, successively, each of these aspects of present policy – lethal injection (Chapter 6); the short-term future of executions (Chapter 7); and prospects for the longer term (Chapter 8).

Notes

1. Rangel, "Florida's Death Row Population Booms," *N.Y. Times,* Aug. 12, 1984, at D4, col. 3.
2. *Id.*
3. The number executed under civil authority in the United States from January 1960 to June 20, 1984, was 211. *See* Bureau of Justice Statistics, U.S. Department of Justice, *Capital Punishment 1982,* at 14, Table 1 (1984); Bureau of Justice Statistics, U.S. Department of Justice, *Bulletin: Capital Punishment 1983,* at 1 (1984). The Western world figure was obtained from Amnesty International, *Report: The Death Penalty* (1979).
4. Florida is the first major state to have a death row population (212 in 1984) well in excess of prisoners executed during 1935–85 (178). The total number of legal executions under civil authority in America from January 1900 to August 1, 1985, is 7,312. *See* W. Bowers, *Legal Homicide: Death as Punishment in America 1864–1982,* at 54, Table 2–3 (1984) (hereafter W. Bowers, *Legal Homicide*); Bureau of Justice Statistics, U.S. Department of Justice, *Bulletin: Capital Punishment 1983,* at 1 (1984); NAACP Legal Defense and Educational Fund, Inc., *Death Row, U.S.A.* 3 (Aug. 1, 1985) (hereafter *Death Row, U.S.A.*).
5. *Death Row, U.S.A.,* at 3.
6. *Barefoot* v. *Estelle,* 103 S. Ct. 3383 (1983); *see also* Weisberg, "Deregulating Death," *1983 Sup. Ct. Rev.* 305.
7. *Death Row, U.S.A.,* at 3.
8. *See* W. Bowers, *Legal Homicide,* at 25, Table 1–4; *see also* note 4. The peak year was 1935 with 199 executions.
9. According to South African government figures, 100 executions were carried out in 1982 for criminal offenses. Amnesty International, *Amnesty International Report 1983,* at 81 (1983).
10. *See, e.g.,* Dix, "Appellate Review of the Decision to Impose Death," 68 *Geo. L.J.* 97 (1980).
11. In *Furman* v. *Georgia,* 408 U.S. 239, 310 (1972), Justice Stewart concluded "that the Eighth and Fourteenth Ammendments cannot tolerate the infliction of a sentence of death under legal systems that permit this unique penalty to be so wantonly and so freakishly imposed."
12. *Id.* at 39 ("These death sentences are cruel and unusual in the same way that being struck by lightning is cruel and unusual").
13. The implication of the judgment in *Furman* striking down sentences of capital punishment in the cases before the Court was that most extant statutes in American jurisdictions were unconstitutional and as a result 633 prisoners were removed from death row. *See* M. Meltsner, *Cruel and Unusual: The Supreme Court and Capital Punishment* 292–3 (1974).
14. 428 U.S. 153 (1976).
15. *Death Row, U.S.A.,* at 3.
16. B. Russell, *Common Sense and Nuclear Warfare* (1959).

17. "Carolina Slayer Fails in Her Bid for a Reprieve," *N.Y. Times,* Sept. 28, 1984, at A1, col. 2.
18. *Caldwell* v. *Mississippi,* 105 S. Ct. 2633 (1985).
19. *Id.* at 2640.
20. Statistics for 1960 were derived from U.S. Department of Justice, *National Prisoner Statistics* 2, Figure A (March 1961). Statistics for 1967 were derived from U.S. Department of Justice, *National Prisoner Statistics* 12, Table 4 (June 1968).
21. U.S. Department of Justice, *National Prisoner Statistics* 1 (March 1961).
22. Bureau of Justice Statistics, U.S. Department of Justice, *Capital Punishment* (yearly issues 1976–83).
23. Bureau of Justice Statistics, U.S. Department of Justice, *Capital Punishment 1979,* at Table 17 (1980); Bureau of Justice Statistics, U.S. Department of Justice, *Capital Punishment 1980,* Table 17 (1981).
24. The last federally authorized execution occurred in Iowa in 1963. Bureau of Justice Statistics, U.S. Department of Justice, *Capital Punishment 1982,* at Table 5 (1984).
25. Bureau of Justice Statistics, U.S. Department of Justice, *Capital Punishment* (yearly issues 1960–83).
26. Reston, "Invitation to a Poisoning," *Vanity Fair,* Feb. 1985, at 82, 101.

6

Only in America: some notes on lethal injection

In just nine years, lethal injection has evolved into a parable of multiple parts. It has produced legislation authorizing its use in seventeen states, conflict in the medical profession, one of the most bizarre lawsuits in the nation's history, executions, and the death of a fantasy that the intentional taking of human life could be made acceptable to modern standards of decency by changing the means of execution. The saga of lethal injections is presented here both as a capsule history of capital punishment in America and as a preview of coming attractions. The phenomenon of lethal injection is best understood as an attempt to find a version of execution consistent with a modern society. The quest was an instant failure.

Although the recent history of lethal injection is dramatic, the controversy over its use is hardly unprecedented. The first discussion of this form of inflicting death appears to have occurred in New York in 1888 when that state rejected its use in favor of the more "humanitarian" method of electrocution.[1] Also, nearly three decades before the "discovery" of this issue in America, the whole question of execution methods, including lethal injection, had been given detailed attention by a British Royal Commission. The Commission, which initially viewed lethal injection as a promising, less barbarous method of execution, ultimately rejected it,[2] and there the matter rested until its revival in America in the late 1970s. The Commission's consideration of the concept is an instructive prologue to the more recent developments that are the main concern of this chapter.

A. The Home Secretary's predicament

The British Royal Commission on Capital Punishment was established in 1949 to consider and report on "whether liability under the criminal law in Great Britain to suffer capital punishment for murder should be limited

107

or modified, and if so, to what extent, and by what means."[3] Shortly after
the Commission was appointed, however, it was asked also to consider
execution methods.

The Commission heard evidence from those responsible for executions
in Great Britain, including "the most experienced executioner in this
country"; they inspected a number of execution chambers; and they witnessed demonstrations of execution procedures. In addition, they received evidence about American executions by electrocution and lethal
gas, and on a visit to this country inspected electric chairs in two prisons.

The United Kingdom's practice was, as it had been for many centuries,
to hang ordinary criminals sentenced to death. The Commission's task
was to examine whether any "seemly and practicable" method of execution existed that was both speedy and painless and "free from the degrading associations of that method."[4] They took as a "postulate, that the
requisites are humanity, certainty and decency."[5]

In carrying out this task the Commission did not confine itself to considering the four main methods of execution, other than hanging, used in
the West at that time: electrocution, the guillotine, lethal gas, and shooting. Instead, it pursued its inquiry into whether there was any other
method, still untried, that would inflict death as painlessly and certainly
as hanging, but "with greater decency, and without the degrading and
barbarous associations with which hanging is tainted."[6]

One suggestion made to the Commission was execution by means of a
hypodermic injection of a lethal drug, a method that, according to the
report, "has not, so far as we know, been adopted anywhere as a method
of judicial execution."[7] Nevertheless, the Commissioners felt that to
those who accepted their postulate – that the only requisites were humanity, certainty, and decency – "this is likely to be the alternative to hanging that first suggests itself."[8]

The members were clearly sensitive and civilized people. For example,
the fact that the Home Office received an average of five applications a
week for the post of hangman in their view revealed "psychological qualities of a sort that no state would wish to foster in its citizens."[9] So there is
an air of incongruity about their debating how the deliberate killing of a
human being might best be carried out. Indeed, there is an unconscious,
gruesome humor – the expression "gallows humor" seems apt – in some
of their discussion.

The Commissioners decided, for various reasons, that if lethal injection
were to be instituted as the method of judicial execution, in some cases
intramuscular rather than intravenous injection would have to be used.[10]
But as the intramuscular method is both slower and more painful than

venepuncture, the Commission considered whether a condemned person might be rendered unconscious by the administration of a sedative before being executed. This, however, presented the problem that if the sedative dose were given on the morning of the execution, it would in effect become part of the process of execution, "in which no doctor would think it right to participate."[11] On the other hand, if it were given the night before, because "individual reaction to drugs varies greatly . . . to ensure unconsciousness in the morning it would be necessary to give a dose so strong that it might even prove fatal to anyone specially susceptible to the drug."[12] Here, the Commissioners' report goes on to say, an "objection of principle" arose: "It was represented to us that, if death were thus caused unintentionally, by a method other than that prescribed by law, the Home Secretary might find himself in a most awkward predicament" – that of a murderer.[13]

The scruples of the medical profession, the failure of the human organism to respond conveniently to attempts to destroy it with "decency," and the risk of placing the Home Secretary in an awkward predicament apparently combined to produce a negative collective verdict on lethal injection as a method of execution. The Commissioners did, however, unanimously recommend that "the question should be periodically examined, especially in the light of progress made in the science of anaesthetics."[14]

B.   What happened next

What happened next is that nothing happened. Contrary to the Commission's recommendation, there were no periodic examinations. In the years after publication of the Royal Commission's report, executions in Great Britain declined dramatically from an average of fourteen per year in the decade prior to publication (1943–52) to three per year in the decade prior to the abandonment of the death penalty in Britain (1956–65).[15]

Once the death penalty had been abandoned, whatever progress may have been made in the science of anaesthetics, there was no occasion to reconsider whether lethal injection might be preferable to other means of execution. Nor does any other country in the world, including the United States, appear to have taken up the discussion, even though many jurisdictions employing capital punishment were struggling with the issue. Indeed, just such a struggle had provoked the discussion in Great Britain. Rather than the question of lethal injection having become temporarily dormant, it was as though it had never arisen. This brings up one of the central questions of this chapter: Why, more than two decades later, did it become a salient issue in the United States?

In answering this question, *when* is the key to *why*. For twenty-five years the issue had no constituency; then, quite suddenly, a wave of interest and enthusiasm swept through America. Once the latency period was over, the popularity of the idea of lethal injections was infectious. Oklahoma first legally adopted it in 1977, the year after *Gregg*;[16] Texas, Idaho, and New Mexico soon followed.[17] Withing a few years thirteen states had adopted lethal injection as a method of execution, and many others were considering it.[18] In 1982, Texas performed the first execution by lethal injection.[19] By 1983, it was the second most frequently authorized means of execution in the United States, less popular than electrocution but ahead of such traditional procedures as gassing, hanging, and shooting.[20] Obviously, something significant had occurred in America in the late 1970s to bring about this remarkable upsurge.

It had not happened in 1972 after the decision in *Furman,* although that decision had certainly inspired an explosion of death penalty interest and activity. Interest in lethal injection developed after *Gregg* in 1976. When *Gregg* was decided the United States had not had an execution for nearly a decade. After *Gregg,* America once again faced the prospect of executions: not the death penalty as an abstract issue, but actually putting people to death.

The origins of the American revival of lethal injection are obscure. As early as 1973, then-Governor Reagan of California endorsed the concept with characteristic optimism:

Being a former farmer and horse raiser, I know what it's like to try to eliminate an injured horse by shooting him. Now you call the veterinarian and the vet gives it a shot and the horse goes to sleep – that's it. I myself have wondered if maybe this isn't part of our problem [with capital punishment], if maybe we should review and see if there aren't even more humane methods now – the simple shot or tranquilizer.[21]

Two aspects of Governor Reagan's account deserve comment. First, the analogy he draws neglects a distinction between animal euthanasia and human execution that we regard as decisive: The horse doesn't know the injection is scheduled; the prisoner does. This surely is what Dr. Johnson was referring to when he said that the prospect of hanging "concentrates [the] mind wonderfully." Yet the Reagan excerpt, without any supplement, constitutes the essence of the case for lethal injections in the legislative chambers of several states. It is not so much a summary as the totality of the argument for lethal injections.

Oklahoma became the first state to authorize lethal injections in 1977 as an alternative to the $62,000 expenditure required to repair the state's electric chair and the more than $200,000 capital investment necessary for a functional gas chamber.[22] As far as we can discern, the subsequent enthusiasm for the new scheme was not attributable to a charismatic figure or to an intensely motivated special interest constituency. There was no Johnny Appleseed of lethal injection, no small band of fervent citizen proponents, and certainly no professional group that gave the new proposal a high priority. The concept appealed to legislators with strong interests in reviving executions rather than with particular preferences as to method. And the appeal of this strategy seemed as simple as Reagan's parable of farm management. It is impossible to assess the authenticity of hopes that the method would neutralize opposition to execution, but the legislative language is consistent with such hopes.

It is somewhat ironic that in favoring lethal injection over electrocution, state legislatures were rejecting a form of execution that had itself been adopted as "the most humane and practical method known to modern science of carrying into effect the sentence of death in capital cases."[23] In 1888, when the New York legislature first authorized electrocution, it was less than a decade since Thomas A. Edison had devised a plan for providing electric energy to customers from a common generating system, and only six years after electric power was first made available to the public in New York City. For most people, electricity was profoundly mysterious and newspapers still referred to it as a "fluid."[24] In fact, a New York Commission of Inquiry favored electrocution over lethal injection.

The prompt adaptation for lethal purposes of Edison's methods for generating and distributing electricity followed a lengthy investigation by that New York Commission appointed to identify the most humane method of extinguishing human life. It is also worth noting that the aura of euphemism that surrounded the introduction of lethal injection as a method of execution resembles a contemporary *New York Times* description of the so-called Electrical Execution Law as a means to ensure "euthanasia by electricity."[25]

In the case of *In re Kemmler* the U.S. Supreme Court rejected a constitutional attack on New York's statute by William Kemmler, scheduled to be the first person to be electrocuted, and authorized the state to proceed with the electrocution. The Court held that, because the Eighth Amendment was inapplicable to the states, "the decision of the state courts sustaining the validity of the act under the state constitution is not reexaminable here."[26] But it approved of the state court's conclusion that: "[I]t is within easy reach of electrical science at this day to so generate and apply to the person of the convict a current of electricity of such known and sufficient force as certainly to produce instantaneous and therefore painless death."[27]

In fact, the first electrocution required two attempts before death resulted,[28] and there is considerable evidence that death by electrocution is neither instantaneous nor painless.[29] Nearly a century later there is evidence that lethal injection similarly involves pain and suffering,[30] but neither then nor now have the proponents of these innovations shown any apparent interest in whether these methods proved to be as humane and painless as had been claimed.

C. An ultra-fast-acting barbiturate

Of those states that adopted lethal injection as a method of execution, the great majority had not executed anyone for over twenty years. In one, Montana, there had been no executions for over thirty years.[31] These states were not so much involved in the reintroduction of executions as in their reinvention, so it is not too surprising that some felt that a modern technique embodying the latest methods was needed.

Lethal injections, however, represented more than a technical innovation and a tribute to American know-how; they also were seen as providing a more "acceptable face" for capital punishment. While they could hardly be regarded as harmless, they could be considered "as an alternative, pleasanter, method of execution,"[32] and thus more acceptable to those who might otherwise feel that the readoption of capital punishment was a reversion to barbarism. Indeed, the repetition in the authorizing statutes of such expressions as "an ultra-fast-acting barbiturate" or "an ultra-short-acting barbiturate," which appear in at least eight of the states' provisions for executions, evokes a much more benign image than that evoked by a firing squad, an electric chair, or a gas chamber. The connotation seems to be that of television commercials for fast-acting pain relievers, as though the lethal injection were the ultimate analgesic.

This impression is to some extent reinforced by the fact that some states offer the condemned a choice between a lethal injection and a standard method of execution. Thus, in Montana the prisoner can choose either hanging or the "ultra-fast-acting barbiturate."[33] In Washington the choice is between hanging or a lethal dose of sodium thiopental.[34] In North Carolina the standard method is lethal gas "except that if any person sentenced to death so chooses, he may at least five days prior to his execution date, elect in writing to be executed by the administration of a lethal quantity of an ultra-short-acting barbiturate."[35]

The notion that the condemned might be offered such a choice was considered by the British Royal Commission as affording "a gradual and experimental way of introducing an untried system."[36] The Commission also believed that an incidental advantage of lethal injection could be that it "might facilitate the provision of executioners" because "what was needed of them could be represented rather as an act of mercy than as an execution."[37]

The Royal Commission finally decided against offering the prisoner such a choice on a variety of grounds, including "the vacillation that might be evoked in a prisoner by having to make so crucial a decision, a vacillation tormenting to himself and embarrassing to the authorities, and the need to have the hangman waiting in the background in case his services should be required after all, gradually perhaps losing his skills from disuse."[38] In Montana and Washington, where the hangman had been losing his skills from disuse for the previous forty and twenty years, respectively, the latter consideration presumably weighed very little against the advantage of having execution defined as a type of mercy killing.

Representatives of the American medical profession do not appear to have been consulted formally in advance as they had been in Britain. In New Jersey the statute, while not indicating precisely who is to administer the ultra-short-acting barbiturate, provides that *"Prior to the injection of the lethal substance, the person shall be sedated by a licensed physician, registered nurse, or other qualified personnel,* by either an oral tablet or capsule or an intramuscular injection of a narcotic or barbiturate such as morphine, cocaine or demerol."[39] The medical profession in Britain as we have seen, viewed this role as requiring "unprofessional conduct" from any doctor asked to do it.

Doctors, however, are expressly excluded in the New Jersey statute from administering the lethal dose. The statute provides that the Commissioner of the Department of Corrections:

shall designate persons who are qualified to administer injections and who are familiar with medical procedures, *other than licensed physicians,* . . . to assist in the carrying out of executions, but the procedures and equipment . . . shall be designed to insure that the identity of the person actually inflicting the lethal substance is unknown even to the person himself.[40]

In Montana doctors are not prohibited from carrying out executions. According to the statute:

An execution carried out by lethal injection must be performed by a person selected by the warden and trained to administer the injection. The person administering the injection *need not be a physician,* registered nurse, or licensed practical nurse licensed or registered under the laws of this or any other state.[41]

In Idaho the state prescribes that "any infliction of the punishment of death by administration of the required lethal substance or substances in the manner required by this section shall not be construed to be the practice of medicine."[42] Most of the statutes provide no more than that a licensed physician pronounce the defendant dead after the execution or be present at the execution.[43] Illinois requires that the execution shall be conducted in the presence of two physicians.[44]

D. Organized medicine responds

An insight into this matter is provided by the medical profession's response to execution by lethal injection. The Judicial Council of the American Medical Association (AMA) recommended, and its House of Delegates adopted, the position that a physician should not be a participant in an execution. Rather it affirmed a policy stating that although an individual's opinion of capital punishment is a personal, moral decision, "a physician, as a member of a profession dedicated to preserving life when there is hope of doing so," should not terminate life.[45] In addition to the AMA, the American Public Health Association, the American Psychiatric Association, and the American Nursing Association also resolved that members of their professions should not actively participate in executions.[46]

This reaction parallels a similar response three decades earlier in Britain. Both the British Medical Association and the Association of Anaesthetists told the Royal Commission on Capital Punishment that lethal injection was impracticable for three reasons. They claimed that it was impossible to give an intravenous injection to anyone with certain physical abnormalities and that it is difficult to administer one without the subject's cooperation. The principal objection, however, was that the procedure demanded "professional skill, which the medical profession would be unwilling to use for such a purpose."[47]

The British Medical Association agreed that "if it were *practicable,* the intravenous injection of a lethal dose of a narcotic drug would be a speedy and merciful procedure,"[48] but, in its words:

No medical practitioner should be asked to take part in bringing about the death of a convicted murderer. The Association would be most strongly opposed to any proposal to introduce, in place of judicial hanging, a method of execution which would require the services of a medical practitioner, either in carrying out the actual process of killing or in instructing others in the technique of the process.[49]

The Royal Commission regarded this objection somewhat skeptically:

We of course respect the attitude of the British Medical Association but we think they may have magnified its probable consequences. . . . [I]t is not only within the profession that the necessary skill is to be found. There are many outside it who are fully competent either to give injections themselves or to train others to do it. Laboratory technicians engaged in research work that requires them to give intravenous injections to small animals become extremely skilful. No one can say beforehand to what extent it would be possible either to get volunteer executioners among persons already skilled, or to arrange for training unskilled persons to act as executioners and for giving them the constant practice in venepuncture necessary to maintain their skill.[50]

The Commission seemed equally unimpressed by the medical profession's attitude on the feasibility of a doctor sedating the condemned person the night before an execution to ensure that he or she would be unconscious the next morning when the execution would take place. Said the report:

If the time were the night before, . . . this too would require unprofessional conduct from any doctor asked to give it. No doctor (*so we were told*) could ever properly give to anyone a larger dose than the maximum ordinarily used for therapeutic purposes. Such a dose would not be enough to make sure that the condemned man would be unconscious in the morning.[51]

The Commission, however, did not think there would be "any great difficulty in meeting the objections based on the doctor's professional code, if arrangements could be made – as they presumably could – for the dose to be a pharmaceutically standardised one which could be prepared by a layman."[52]

What emerges from the medical profession's attitude both in Britain and America is that, although there seems to be no fundamental objection to executions, the profession has no desire to be involved in the process. In America, "[m]ost physicians do not want to go beyond their present role . . . . They believe that the states should seriously consider returning to traditional methods of execution . . . . There is no doubt that the vast majority of physicians in America . . . believe that it is clearly wrong for a physician to kill."[53]

The British Royal Commission's somewhat irritated response to the medical profession's attitude is easily understood, as is the reluctance of the medical profession to participate in ritual killing. What is perhaps less easy to understand is why "a profession dedicated to preserving life when there is hope of doing so" has complacently accepted the institution of capital punishment, albeit by "traditional methods," as long as members of the profession did not become involved in it.

E. A matter of mislabeling

A bizarre – indeed almost surrealistic – case, *Chaney* v. *Heckler,* began in December 1980 when eight prison inmates under sentence of death in Texas and Oklahoma petitioned the Food and Drug Administration

(FDA) to take action against "the unapproved use of approved drugs in state capital punishment systems."[54] The FDA refused to intervene, claiming it had no jurisdiction over this particular use of drugs, and in September 1981 the petitioners filed suit in the U.S. District Court for the District of Columbia seeking to compel the FDA to act. On August 30, 1982, the District Court granted summary judgment in favor of the FDA.

The case went next to the U.S. Court of Appeals. That court reversed the lower court's decision, holding that the FDA had jurisdiction to regulate the state's use of prescription drugs for the purpose of causing death by injection and that the FDA had arbitrarily and capriciously refused to exercise its regulatory discretion to prevent use of drugs not proven "safe and effective" as a means of execution.[55]

The FDA's involuntary involvement arose because, in the Food, Drug and Cosmetic Act, Congress requires the Secretary of Health and Human Services or the Secretary's delegate, the Commissioner of Food and Drug Administration, to ensure that all "new drugs" are "safe and effective" for use under the conditions prescribed, recommended, or suggested on the official labeling.[56] The Commissioner had previously interpreted this requirement as imposing on FDA the obligation to investigate and take appropriate action against unapproved uses of approved drugs, when such unapproved use becomes widespread or endangers the public health.

Moreover, the FDA had used its power to investigate unapproved uses of drugs in situations analogous to use of drugs as a means of execution. For example, it had regulated the use of drugs administered to prison inmates in experimental clinical investigations.[57] The FDA had also investigated the use of drugs by veterinarians to put crippled and diseased animals to death; the FDA eventually required that applications be filed demonstrating the safety and effectiveness of chemicals used for this purpose.[58]

These analogies were not exact – there could be no exact analogy – but they were close enough to prove embarrassing. At any rate, the FDA's defense was sufficiently eccentric to suggest a degree of discomfort. It is not relevant here to consider that defense in detail, but two of the FDA's principal arguments deserve attention if only as examples of forensic fantasy.

The FDA argued that the state-sanctioned use of lethal injections came within a commonly recognized exception to the Food, Drug and Cosmetic Act's coverage, known as the "practice-of-medicine" exemption.[59] This exemption was clearly intended to prevent interference with physicians' treatment of their patients.[60] The suggestion that an exemption designed so as not to limit a doctor's use of drugs to treat patients should also prevent interference with the use of drugs to execute human beings is, to say the least, perverse.

Another FDA argument was that the use of drugs in lethal injections did not pose a "serious danger to public health," in contrast to the use of drugs for prisoner research or animal euthanasia. In support of this contention the FDA claimed that duly authorized statutory enactments which furthered proper state functions could not, as a matter of law, pose such a danger to the public and also that lethal injection statutes could not threaten the public health because by definition they applied only to a small number of persons convicted of capital offenses.[61]

A two-judge majority in the Court of Appeals, unimpressed by these arguments, ruled that the nonmedical use of lethal injections to execute prisoners did not fall within the practice-of-medicine exemption under the Federal Food, Drug and Cosmetics Act. With respect to the claim that the use of drugs in lethal injections posed no threat to public health, the court responded:

[T]his claim of rationality cannot stand next to FDA's earlier assertions that prisoners in clinical investigations and dogs in veterinary clinics were in "serious danger" from the unapproved use of approved drugs. If drugs used in these contexts pose a "serious threat" to the public health, then certainly drugs used to kill human beings pose such a threat. In short, the Commissioner presents no rational basis for concluding that lethal injections do not pose a serious health threat.[62]

The majority opinion did not confront the irony of condemning a practice designed to kill people because it might, in the process, also hurt them. There was, to be sure, precedent for this distinction in the FDA's jurisdiction over research with laboratory animals, and it would have been even more ironic if animals had achieved a level of protection under the food and drug laws unavailable to human prisoners. Yet it cannot be denied that the execution of prisoners was far from the minds of those who wrote this early consumer protection legislation, and nobody would argue that the FDA had jurisdiction over gas chambers, high-powered rifles, and other means of execution. Under such circumstances, singling out one of many lethal mechanisms for special scrutiny seems anomalous.

Then–Circuit Judge Scalia dissented from the majority's conclusion, although his opinion did not present the critique outlined in the previous paragraph. Judge Scalia acknowledged the inapplicability of the practice-of-medicine exemption, but argued that "FDA jurisdiction depends upon the existence of misbranding . . . which cannot be established under the facts of this case."[63] He also maintained that "the public health interest at issue is not widespread death or permanent disability, but (at most) a risk of temporary pain to a relatively small number of individuals."[64] The conclusion that lethal injections pose a serious danger to public health he described as "fanciful."[65]

One might disagree with Judge Scalia's quantitative assessment of the danger to health – it is not possible to tell how many persons might eventually be at risk – but in emphasizing the issue of misbranding or mislabeling, he did direct attention to the heart of the matter. The claims made for the practice of lethal injection represent an outstanding example of mislabeling. Furthermore, the jurisdiction of the FDA was invited by the attempt to put a therapeutic face on execution.

"I think and I hope," said Texas Governor Dolph Briscoe in May 1977, when he signed the state's lethal injection bill into law, "this will provide some dignity with death."[66] In so wishfully expressing himself, Governor Briscoe was doing no more than all the other official promoters of lethal injection, before and since, who have advertised it as "humane," "decent," and "seemly." In fact, killing human beings by lethal injection is plainly a squalid business; to talk about dignity in this connection, as we shall see, is patently an abuse of language. More than that, it displays an astonishing degree of moral insensitivity or dishonesty – or both.

According to law a drug is "misbranded" and impermissibly available to consumers unless its labeling bears adequate directions for use and such warnings against unapproved uses or methods of administration as are necessary for the protection of its users.[67] In this case the manufacturer's liability, if any, could at most be accessorial. But there can be no doubt of the liability of those responsible for state governments' use of prescription drugs for the purpose of causing death by injection.

In March of 1985 the U.S. Supreme Court overturned the Court of Appeals' judgment.[68] Justice Rehnquist, writing the opinion joined by six other members of the Court, rested the reversal of the Circuit Court on the discretionary authority of the FDA to refuse to institute enforcement action even if within the agency's jurisdiction. While labeling FDA intrusion in lethal injections an "implausible result," the Rehnquist opinion and the two concurrences in the judgment did not address the applicability of the food and drug laws to these executions:

In reaching our conclusion that the Court of Appeals was wrong, however, we need not and do not address the thorny question of the FDA's jurisdiction. For us, this case turns on the important question of the extent to which determinations by the FDA not to exercise its enforcement authority over the use of drugs in interstate commerce may be judicially reviewed.[69]

For these reasons, the Court's decision does not suggest that the FDA would have been wrong if it had used its authority to condition the use of lethal injections on the demonstration that they were safe and effective.

There is a certain poetic justice about the Appeals Court's decision in *Chaney* v. *Heckler* that is untouched by the action of the Supreme Court. Regardless of how the statutory language of the food and drug laws is interpreted, there was in fact mislabeling or misbranding in the states' legislation and in the claims made for lethal injections by its proponents. It is also ironically appropriate that the aid of the federal agency responsible for the protection of consumers should be sought by those who, in ordinary language if not in law, were destined to be the ultimate consumers of the injections.

The author whose work comes to mind here is, of course, Lewis Carroll. The trial scene at the end of *Alice's Adventures in Wonderland* [70] bears a number of similarities to the litigation and the controversy we have described. Some critics have seen the nonsensical nature of the trial of the Knave of Hearts as a metaphor for real and tragic features of human existence, and it has for this reason been compared with Kafka's *The Trial*.[71] In the *Chaney* case, too, the surface absurdities arise from, and direct attention to, a monstrous underlying reality.

The juxtaposition of inapposites reigns supreme in the search for "humane execution" and the claims to painless methods for the intentional infliction of human death. The attempt to make the administration of capital punishment a branch of veterinary medicine rendered the use of food and drug laws to halt such procedures far more fitting than first impressions would suggest. The fantasies of lethal injection proponents created the essential link between two wholly dissimilar areas of public law. *Chaney* involved a close legal question, after all.

The King of Hearts' confusion over whether Alice's evidence was important or unimportant, so that some of the jury wrote down "important" and some "unimportant," probably has a direct parallel in the confusion of observers on the use of food and drug laws to govern a method of execution. In this case we think those who wrote down "important" were right, because the phenomenon of lethal injection is an attempt to deny the antihistorical character of execution in late-twentieth-century America, an attempt that is simultaneously doomed to failure and likely to spawn other adventures in innovative denial. We shall return to this question after a survey of the subsequent history of lethal injection.

F. From theory to practice

It took just over five years to make the transition from the legislative authority to use lethal injection to the actual use of this method in Texas

Table 6.1. *Lethal injection legislation and executions by date, United States*

| | Before 1980 | 1980–2 | 1983 | |
			1st 6 months	2nd 6 months
Law	3	2	4	3
Executions	0	1	0	0

in December 1982. More than a year then passed between the first and second injection executions, but the practice resumed in earnest in March 1984, accounting for sixteen more deaths – thirteen in Texas, two in North Carolina, and one in Nevada – to this writing. The primary impact of these executions appears to have been that the practice has lost its novelty for supporters and opponents alike; executions by lethal injection seem no more – and no less – gruesome than contemporary executions by other means. Calls for lethal injection are less often heard in the media. Legislative enthusiasm for the practice has waned, and any mystique surrounding it did not survive the initial experience.

The first executions by this method were notable chiefly for what did not happen. They were neither occasions in the history of science nor landmarks in any principled debate about lethal injection as a means of execution. There were no reports of states that had passed or considered lethal injection legislation sending medical or scientific observers to Texas. Local medical authorities made no attempt to monitor the reactions of the condemned prisoners for pain or anxiety, or to calibrate the speed of the ultra-fast-acting barbiturates. Public officials made no claims about the efficiency or the humaneness of the executions as they did when they introduced the legislative proposals. It was almost as if the practice of lethal injection was a nonevent in the ongoing debate, producing no data or important news for either side: the equivalent of a space flight not being considered relevant by either supporters or opponents of the space program.

Nevertheless, the practice of lethal injection had a profound effect on the controversy. Thirteen of the seventeen states that ultimately passed injection laws had begun this process before the Brooks execution in Texas. The experience of execution did not deter state legislatures from reenacting legislation vetoed by the governor, as was the case in Illinois, or from passing optional lethal injection bills that were pending prior to execution, but public enthusiasm for lethal injection as a solution to the

1984		1985	
1st 6 months	2nd 6 months	1st 6 months	2nd 6 months
3	0	1	0
3	2	4	2

controversy surrounding the penalty of death effectively died with Charlie Brooks, its first victim. The change was almost immediate and substantial, as shown in Table 6.1.

The box score on legislation and executions is instructive in two respects. There is, first, very little overlap between the high season for lethal injection laws and the use of this method to kill. Eleven states passed such statutes between 1977 and 1983, a period that witnessed only one execution by lethal injection. Three more states, however, legalized the method in the first six months of 1984. As execution by injection became more common, enthusiasm for the practice waned. Since the middle of 1984, while the annual rate of lethal injections built to between five and six, the rate of which more states authorized the method diminished markedly.

It is perhaps significant that only two of the jurisdictions authorizing lethal injections did so after experience with executions in their states. The appeal of lethal injection seems stronger when executions are in prospect than when they are occurring in a jurisdiction.

G.   A preview of coming attractions

The principal value of this history is the way in which it excludes or eliminates. After *Gregg* the debate about capital punishment moved to a different level, a new universe of discourse. It was no longer only a debate about the death penalty as an abstraction, but about the concrete reality of executions.

It might seem at first that the debate about lethal injections is simply a rather specialized technical matter, irrelevant to the larger issue of whether the state should have the power to kill. Yet the participants did not seem to view it in that way. Indeed, on both sides of the dispute the issue was taken up with considerable fervor.

On one hand, the proponents of lethal injection saw it as a means of transforming and sanitizing the death penalty. Executions could be carried out "quickly, painlessly and decently" with no "unseemly" mutilation or distortion of the body and also without the more recent barbarous associations of the gas chamber.[72] Death penalty proponents hoped the change in tactics would legitimize the strategy.

Opponents of capital punishment had mixed reactions to the prospect of lethal injections. Some saw it as an attempt "to euphemize the deed."[73] "Killing people in cold blood," wrote John Conrad, "should be seen as intolerably revolting, whether done on a side street during a robbery or in the antiseptic conditions that can be arranged for anesthesiological extinction of life. There is no method of execution which is not an unnatural human invention."[74]

We think the real motivations in the debate about lethal injections are these: The proponents were striving to find a method of capital punishment that is acceptable to modern sensibilities, while its opponents hoped to show that the notion of modern methods of execution is a contradiction in terms. In this view, the real vice of electric chairs and gas chambers is not so much that they inflict pain as that they are visible anachronisms. Both sides of the controversy hoped, for different reasons, that lethal injections would bring executions into the twentieth century.

By midcentury, the means of execution employed in the United States were already regarded as atavistic. Two decades of disuse since then had rendered chambers and chairs the stuff of wax museum exhibits rather than the instruments of public policy. Thus to maintain an active execution policy required a means of killing less obviously discordant with today's institutions and values. It is fair to call the search for modern means of executions a public relations gesture only if it is acknowledged that this sort of "public relations" is of central importance. Capital punishment could seem appropriate only if a technique for taking life could be devised that appeared to be an authentic part of modern America.

This explanation helps to solve a number of the mysteries generated by the lethal injection controversy. No particular shortcoming that characterized conventional methods of execution was identified by the supporters of lethal injection, nor was the advantage of lethal injection over any specific existing means of execution ever an important element of the debate. The discussion of a "more humane" alternative proceeded with no reference to what was less humane about electric chairs, gas chambers, and hanging. The use of therapeutic drugs rather than nontherapeutic poisons, as a means of killing and the attempt to link death with science and medicine, make sense only if proponents of lethal injections are seen as pursuing a modern way to inflict death. The opposition to "high-tech homicide" is best understood as a passionate denial that the intentional infliction of death can be updated. The real dispute is about whether execution of any kind can be an acceptable part of modern institutions.

The interaction between the use of lethal injections and modern instrumentalities such as the FDA is thus more than a jurisdictional accident. Such conflict is preordained when therapeutic agents are commandeered to the nontherapeutic goal of inflicting death. Yet the selection of drugs was not fortuitous; the need was to define the enterprise of executing people in a way that was consistent with scientific progress and medical values. If prescription drugs had not been chosen, the instrumentality of "modern" executions might well have been the laser beam. In the end, the contradictory nature of a governmental system that simultaneously polices the pain levels involved in the destruction of laboratory animals while it permits the execution of humans runs much deeper than the statutory construction of our food and drug laws.

The main problems generated by real-world execution practices were a divisive impact on public opinion and the appearance of brutality. For more than five years the fantasy of lethal injection was pursued by its proponents as a solution to these problems. This fantasy was not defeated by counterargument or analysis of the execution process; it simply vanished when the injection process was instituted. Lethal injection, however, will remain a principal method of capital punishment in the United States for many years, even though the idea that spawned it – that executions can be made humane – has completely dissolved.

In retrospect, what is remarkable about the sudden disappearance of the lethal injection fantasy was not its vulnerability to experience, but its persistence in the minds of its advocates in the late 1970s and early 1980s. Did anyone really think that new technology and Madison Avenue terms could solve the problems and heal the divisions generated by executions? We believe the answer is yes, and that the level of unreality necessary to sustain such illusions is a chronic condition in debate about capital punishment.

Since 1977 we have not merely talked about putting people to death; we have also been doing it. In the 1980s, the more immediate and divisive context of the debate about lethal injections will affect every aspect of the death penalty issue in the United States as executions continue. The fox and hounds game in which fantasies are displaced by the reality of executions, and thus generate the need for further fantasies, creates a new instability in the list of issues involved in capital punishment. In this sense, lethal injection provides a preview of the way in which the social fact of executions will transform the dialogue about capital punishment. This transformation is the subject of Chapter 7.

Notes

1. Moran, "Execution Methods Based on Pragmatism," *Boston Globe,* June 7, 1985, at 14 (Letter to the Editor).
2. *Royal Commission on Capital Punishment 1949–1953, Report* 261 (1953) (hereafter *Royal Commission Report*).
3. *Id.* at iii.
4. *Id.* at 248.
5. *Id.*
6. *Id.* at 256.
7. *Id.* at 257.
8. *Id.*
9. *Id.* at 256.
10. *Id.* at 259–60.
11. *Id.* at 260.
12. *Id.*
13. *Id.*
14. *Id.* at 261.
15. *Id.* at 309; personal communication from C. P. Honey, Home Office, London, July 26, 1984.
16. *Okla. Stat. Ann.* tit. 22, § 1014.
17. *Idaho Code* § 19–2716; *N.M. Stat.* § 31–14–11; *Tex. Crim. Proc. Code* § 43.14.
18. Bureau of Justice Statistics, U.S. Department of Justice, *Bulletin: Capital Punishment 1983,* at 5, Figure 7 (1984).
19. Schwarzschild, "Homicide by Injection," *N.Y. Times,* Dec. 23, 1982, at A15, col. 1 (hereafter Schwarzschild, "Homicide by Injection").
20. *See* note 18.
21. *Quoted in* Schwartzschild, "Homicide by Injection."
22. Gardner, "Executions and Indignities – An Eighth Amendment Assessment of Methods of Inflicting Capital Punishment," 39 *Ohio St. L. J.* 96, 126 n.228 (1978) (hereafter Gardner, "Methods").
23. *Report of the Commission to Investigate and Report the Most Humane and Practical Method of Carrying Into Effect the Sentence of Death in Capital Cases* 3 (1888).
24. Beichman, "The First Electrocution," 35 *Commentary* 410, 413 (1963) (hereafter Beichman, "The First Electrocution").
25. *Id.* at 411.
26. *In re Kemmler,* 136 U.S. 436, 447 (1890).
27. *Id.* at 443.
28. Beichman, "The First Electrocution," at 417–18.
29. Gardner, "Methods," at 125–7.
30. *Id.* at 128–9; *Chaney* v. *Heckler,* 718 F.2d 1174, 1177–8 (D.C. Cir. 1983), *rev'd,* 105 S. Ct. 1649 (1985).
31. W. Bowers, *Executions in America* 33–5, Table 2–1 (1974); Bureau of Justice Statistics, U.S. Department of Justice, *Bulletin: Capital Punishment 1982,* at 2 (1984).
32. *Royal Commission Report,* at 259.
33. *Mont. Code Ann.* § 46–19–103(3).
34. *Wash. Rev. Code* § 10.95.180.
35. *N.C. Gen. Stat.* § 15–187.
36. *Royal Commission Report,* at 259.
37. *Id.*
38. *Id.*
39. *N.J. Stat. Ann.* § 2C: 49–2 (emphasis added).
40. *Id.* (emphasis added).
41. *Mont. Code Ann.* § 46–19–103(3) (emphasis added).
42. *Idaho Code* § 19–2716.
43. *See, e.g., id.*
44. *Ill. Rev. Stat.* ch. 38, § 119–5.

45. Hirsh, "Physicians as Executioners," *Legal Aspects Med. Prac.*, Mar. 1984, at 1, 3–4 (hereafter Hirsh, "Physicians").
46. *Id.*
47. *Royal Commission Report,* at 258.
48. *Id.*
49. *Id.*
50. *Id.* at 260.
51. *Id.*
52. *Id.*
53. Hirsh, "Physicians," at 2–3. Medical witnesses before the British Royal Commission also strongly favored traditional methods of execution (e.g., hanging); *Royal Commission Report,* at 247.
54. 718 F.2d 1174, 1177 (D.C. Cir. 1983), *rev'd,* 105 S. Ct. 1649 (1985). Originally, there were only two inmates on the petition; the remaining six joined by letter on January 12, 1981.
55. *Id.* at 1192.
56. 21 U.S.C. § 301 (1982).
57. 718 F.2d at 1180.
58. *Id.*
59. *Id.* at 1180–1.
60. *Id.* at 1181.
61. *Id.* at 1178.
62. *Id.* at 1190.
63. *Id.* at 1191–2.
64. *Id.*
65. *Id.*
66. *Id.* at 1198.
67. *Id.* at 1197 n.5.
68. 105 S. Ct. 1649 (1985).
69. *Id.* at 1654 (emphasis omitted).
70. L. Carroll, *Alice's Adventures in Wonderland* 128–47 (1946).
71. *The Annotated Alice* 15 (M. Gardner ed. 1965).
72. *Royal Commission Report,* at 255–6, 261.
73. E. van den Haag & J. Conrad, *The Death Penalty: A Debate* 192 (1983).
74. *Id.*

7

Life in a country that kills

This chapter addresses some social and political consequences of an active capital punishment program in the United States in the late 1980s. Chapter 8 deals with the longer-term future of the practice.

We do not have a national policy on capital punishment. Most of the fifty states are in a transitional period of unknown duration and indeterminate end. Under these circumstances, analysis of the impact of executions necessarily mixes both observation and prediction.

We begin by trying to locate current capital punishment policy in the United States along a continuum from the de facto abolition of recent decades to what could become a steady and active execution program. Next, we consider two competing scenarios for the short-term future of executions, one stressing the gathering momentum of executions and the other arguing that opposition to executions will grow as the practice increases and spreads beyond the South. We find elements of truth in both the arguments for momentum and for growing opposition. We argue further that the political climate surrounding executions differs so markedly from state to state that a specific analysis of different types of states is the only useful approach to discussing the short-term future of execution.

The period we consider – the next five years or so – will produce about 100 executions if current rates continue, roughly twenty a year. This leveling of the execution rate will not mean that important policy changes are absent from this short-term future. At the state government level, however, where most of the key decisions will be made, the foundations for longer-term policies are already being set in place.

A. Transition to the unknown

Margie Velma Barfield, a fifty-two-year-old grandmother and convicted murderer, earned at least footnote status in American political history by playing an important part in a close U.S. Senate race in North Carolina

126

between the Democratic governor and the Republican incumbent. The issue in that 1984 contest was not the candidates' position on capital punishment. Opponents of the death penalty would scarcely be engaged in close races for elective office in North Carolina, where support for capital punishment commands seventy percent majorities in public opinion polls.[1] Mrs. Barfield's claim to historical significance rests on the fact that, for the first time in many decades, a particular execution rather than the general question of capital punishment was the subject of a political controversy. The political significance of Mrs. Barfield provides an instructive point of reference for discussing the current status of capital punishment policy in the United States and its possible future.

Velma Barfield had been convicted of the 1977 murder of her fiancé by arsenic poisoning, one of four killings she admitted committing.[2] Before the summer of 1984, the only remarkable feature of the Barfield case, apart from the multiplicity of victims, was the gender of the defendant. Although several women are currently under active death sentences, no female had been executed in the United States for more than two decades preceding the Barfield conviction.[3] The matter became a political event when a State Superior Court judge set an execution date of November 2, 1984, four days before the general election. This was widely regarded as an attempt to embarrass North Carolina's governor and senatorial candidate James Hunt by forcing him to make a clemency decision prior to the election, and ensuring that unless clemency was granted the senatorial election would take place in an atmosphere colored by a recent execution.

Why an execution should prove embarrassing in a pro–capital-punishment state is neither mysterious nor solely the result of the special circumstances of the Barfield case. To be sure, Mrs. Barfield was a woman, and a grandmother at that; the killings were allegedly the result of an addiction to prescription drugs; and she had been rehabilitated in prison to the satisfaction of a number of citizens who were petitioning the governor for mercy.[4] But there was more than that to the governor's predicament. His opponent, the famously conservative Jesse Helms, could comfortably rest on his general support of capital punishment and withhold comment on the specifics of the Barfield case. Governor Hunt, on the other hand, found himself in the uncomfortable position of wielding the power to choose between life and death.

As we indicated in Chapter 5, the governor's decision not to prevent the execution is a classic example of passing the buck: But why was evasive euphemism and denial of authority necessary in the context of North Carolina politics? And what was no-win about the governor's no-win situation? Hunt's political predicament was succinctly described in the *New York Times* the day before he refused to grant clemency:

[M]any political experts say that a decision by the Governor to commute the sentence would be especially harmful to Mr. Hunt, who, like more than 75 percent of those in the state surveyed on the issue, has endorsed capital punishment. On the other hand, aides to Mr. Hunt privately say, the spectre of an execution and funeral on the eve of the election could turn off some of the Governor's supporters.[5]

The crux of Governor Hunt's problem was that he was caught in the transition from the general to the specific, from the idea of capital punishment to the reality of execution. Enacting a statute does not necessitate a funeral. Pronouncing a sentence of death does not generate media circuses, midnight vigils, detailed description of the defendant's last meal, final appeals, last words, and death agonies. Executions have consequences in the society at large and on attitudes toward the death penalty that are different in kind from general policy statements. We are only beginning to experience these consequences, yet understanding the nature of the shift from the abstract to the concrete is necessary for a balanced assessment of the future of capital punishment.

There have been sixty-two executions in the United States in the past nine years, but the distribution of executions over time and among the several states is far from uniform. Before 1983, no more than two offenders were executed, nationwide, in any single year since 1965.[6] The Supreme Court's determined effort to quicken the pace of final appellate review increased the number of executions in the United States to five in 1983, twenty-one in 1984, eighteen in 1985, and twelve thus far in 1986. What remains unclear is whether the 1984 total represents a midpoint in an accelerating momentum, or a high number produced by the backlog of prisoners whom the states really wanted to execute losing their federal court protection.

Executions thus far have been unevenly distributed among the states with capital punishment statutes. About three-quarters of the states have both capital punishment statutes and prisoners on death row, but only twelve have executed anyone since 1977. The distribution of executions among those states that have experienced executions since *Gregg* v. *Georgia* is also skewed. Four states – Florida, Texas, Georgia, and Louisiana – account for over seventy percent of all executions in the late 1970s and early 1980s. Outside the South, only Indiana, Utah, and Nevada have executed, a total of five times.[7] Further, the quickening pace of execution has not been accompanied by a parallel increase in the number of executing states.

While the annual rate of executions in the United States grew from two

Table 7.1. *Executions, new states executions, and states with death penalty statutes without executions, by year, 1981–5*

Year	Executions	States beginning executions	Death penalty states without executions (at start of each year)
1981	1	1[a]	31
1982	2	2[b]	30[f]
1983	5	4[c]	28[g]
1984	21	1[d]	27
1985	18	1[e]	25[h]

[a]Indiana.
[b]Virginia and Texas.
[c]Alabama, Georgia, Louisiana, and Mississippi.
[d]North Carolina.
[e]South Carolina.
[f]Includes Ohio, which enacted statute in November 1981.
[g]Includes Massachusetts, which enacted statute in December 1982, and New Jersey, which enacted statute in August 1982.
[h]Includes Oregon, which enacted statute in 1985; excludes New York and Massachusetts, whose statutes were invalidated by state supreme courts in 1984.

to five to twenty-one beween 1982 and 1984, the number of states beginning to execute each year actually declined. The two states that executed in 1982 both did so for the first time, and four of the five executions in 1983 were first executions in the responsible jurisdictions. While executions quadrupled in 1984, only one new state began to execute prisoners, and only one state without prior executions began the practice in 1985.

The right-hand column of Table 7.1 shows that the decline in initiating states is not simply a function of a reduction in the number of states with active death penalties but no prior executions. The four states starting to execute in 1983 constituted fourteen percent of the jurisdictions with death penalties in force and prisoners on death row. The single state to begin executions in 1984 represented four percent of the states eligible for that status at the beginning of 1984. And many of the nonexecuting states have large death row populations; California, Illinois, Pennsylvania, and Arizona ranked third, fifth, sixth, and eighth in that category as of August 1, 1986.[8] Thus, depending on the measure used, the United States has experienced both an increase and a decline in the adoption of capital punishment policy in the past two years.

At the midpoint of the 1980s, a fifth of all American jurisdictions have introduced capital punishment in earnest; about a quarter of all states remain officially abolitionist; and more than half of the states are in limbo, with capital punishment laws and death row populations, but no executions. There have been no executions in the Northeastern states, only two in the Midwest, and none in the Pacific states. The reality of executions, for most of the country, has yet to be experienced close to home. Indeed, as of the mid-1980s, the tone of the *New York Times* coverage of American executions resembles that of their foreign correspondents' reports.

Ten years after *Gregg* v. *Georgia* and nine years after Gary Gilmore's execution, there has also been little systematic consideration of where the United States is going in the immediate future or how far along we have come. That is the task of this chapter. What little discussion has occurred has been in terms of a single national perspective despite the substantial variations in policy and practice by region and by state. Our assessment of the next stage of capital punishment is organized around three contrasting versions of near-term trends: breaking the death row logjam, increasing opposition to execution, and a probable future in which both executions and social discord about execution increase.

B. Short-term scenarios

1. Momentum

The short-term future of execution policy in the United States can take various forms. At one extreme is a full-fledged return to an active execution policy, the momentum growing with each execution performed. The other extreme scenario is that public acceptance of capital punishment will be transformed into fervent opposition when implementation of the punishment becomes widespread. This section examines these two scenarios, and concludes that the most likely future of capital punishment will involve elements of both.

If America is regarded as one nation, a single community with a common ethos, it is possible to conceive that the community may soon become accustomed or acclimatized to the increasing use of the death penalty. Viewed in this light the growing numbers on death row represent a temporary obstruction, like logs jammed together in a stream. As momentum builds throughout the country, the breakthrough achieved in Florida over the past few years will finally expand and obliterate the logjam altogether.

This prefiguration is not entirely implausible. Public acclimatization to new governmental policies and practices is a perennial feature of political history. Moreover, execution can hardly be regarded as an innovation. Almost all nations have in the past inflicted the death penalty for some crimes. The resumption of executions may be seen less as a novelty than as the revival of an old American custom.

According to this scenario the resumption of widespread executions will be a manifestation of popular will. Those people, and they probably constitute a majority of the population, who believe that the best hope for crime control lies in "getting tough" with criminals by increasing penalties will embrace the new policy. The death penalty fits neatly at the end of the scale in a linear conception of punishment that regards each increased penalty as automatically producing an extra measure of deterrence. Those who think in such terms consider it axiomatic that, as James Fitzjames Stephens put it, "no other punishment deters men so effectively from committing crimes as the punishment of death."[9]

Proponents of this scenario acknowledge that the squeamish and tenderhearted will find a substantial increase in executions less easy to accept. But public concern is in part a function of media coverage, and there has been a notable decline in the attention paid by the media to individual executions in recent years as the number has mounted. In 1977 when Gary Gilmore faced a Utah firing squad, it inspired Norman Mailer to write *The Executioner's Song*.[10] Of the eighteen persons executed in 1985 none is likely to be the subject of a major publication. Even a genuine innovation like the adoption of lethal injection, despite extensive initial publicity, seems now to have lost its novelty for both supporters and opponents of the practicce, let alone those who were never particularly interested.[11]

The plausibility of the logjam scenario is difficult to assess, since it involves a number of empirical questions to which answers are unavailable. We do not know whether, if the locus of executions shifts from the Southern to the Northern states, general acceptance of executions will diminish and opposition increase. It may well be that an execution in California, for example, would not only have greater visibility, but would also have a very different impact on the California public than an execution in Georgia would have in California. We also do not know at what point in any state the diminishing marginal impact of each additional execution may be counterbalanced by the increasing salience of the greater number of executions that have taken place. Furthermore, there are other currently unanswerable questions about the possible reverberative or ripple effects of executions on the nature and intensity of citizen attitudes and reactions.

The logjam scenario has two further flaws. One is that is is unwarranted to assume that a homogeneous national pattern of similar execution frequencies throughout the nation will emerge. As we have seen, America is not simply a nation-state but a nation composed of many states, and nowhere is this more evident than in its execution policies.

For the other flaw in the scenario we must look at Florida, which has had sixteen executions since 1977, out of a death row population of 244 as of August 1, 1986.[12] If all death penalty jurisdictions were to follow the Florida example (eight executions in 1984) there would be about fifty-eight executions per year. The national death row population would be reduced from 1,765 to 1,707 – or by 3.3 percent – in a year. To destroy the logjam altogether within even five years would require about 300 executions per year, assuming *no* additional death sentences are imposed.

2. Reaction

Even a more modest execution rate than that evidenced by the current Florida figures would be regarded by many citizens, with some justification, as a "bloodbath." It has been decades since the death sentence was carried out in the United States with any semblance of regularity, and rapid escalation would inevitably renew the deep public division on capital punishment. Public opinion about the death penalty would be polarized, with very significant numbers opposed to the practice.

The ranks of opponents would extend far beyond the circle of religious idealists, liberal humanists, and civil libertarians who historically have formed the energetic core of the abolition movement. Capital punishment has long provided one of the most popular subjects for debate in those forums where students and tyro politicians test and sharpen their forensic skills. But frequent executions carry a potential for social conflict far transcending campus environs.

The possibility of broadening opposition to execution assumes importance because of its political context. After a period of conflict about the proper role of crime control in America, the decade since 1975 has witnessed an apparent law-and-order consensus in public opinion. The difference between the climate of opinion in the 1960s and that of the 1980s is not that a majority of the population only now supports strict law enforcement and the imprisonment of repeat felons. These policies always had majority support. The new consensus came about because the significant minority who opposed traditional law enforcement policy in the late 1960s and early 1970s either adopted the majority position or attached less importance to its opposition. This lessening opposition, usually by segments of the population at the liberal end of the political spectrum, has facilitated increased support of police, withdrawal of some procedural protections afforded defendants, and a doubling of the prison population without significant social friction. The present law-and-order consensus stands at risk if opposition to executions becomes an important part of the attitude of a significant minority toward government policy regarding crime and criminals.

That some such deepening and broadening of opposition to the death penalty may have begun already is suggested by the appearance of a new element in the abolitionist agenda and the emergence on the contemporary American scene of a public image – the death row hero. The psychological basis of this phenomenon was, incidentally, identified by Cesare Beccaria over two centuries ago.

Beccaria, the first notable writer to challenge the legitimacy of the death penalty, argued that executions provided a subject for compassion and abhorrence rather than "the salutary terror which the laws endeavor to inspire."[13] The example of barbarity presented by the legalized shedding of human blood, he maintained, provoked a tendency in the public to identify with the criminal.

This tendency is currently reflected in the activities of anti–capital-punishment groups whose members in recent years seem to have developed strong personal identification with the condemned. This identification goes beyond seeking legal counsel, typewriters, or transfers to facilities closer to hometowns and families. The songs and poems of convicted murderers acquire a mystique and are endowed with a presumption of aesthetic merit and unique insight. The condemned prisoner's complaints and protestations of innocence are accorded great weight. A process of idealization, of secular beatification, develops, in which the most unlikely candidates are invested with a kind of sanctity.

All this may seem extravagant, even ludicrous, but it should not be lightly dismissed. To do so would be to ignore its significance. The abolitionist sees the condemned as the most palpable victim of the government's willingness to take life in the name of justice. The murderer's crimes are past, his victims are beyond our capacity to protect or make whole. The taking of additional life is seen as gratuitous cruelty, and the condemned is transformed into a potential murder victim – the only such victim, moreover, whom persons of good will can support and attempt to save. In these circumstances the tendency to identify with the condemned is both understandable and understandably strong.

The idealization of the denizens of death row, however, obscures the most powerful argument against execution in a liberal democracy and the most fundamental of all arguments against the death penalty. "Men in their most secret hearts have every believed," wrote Beccaria, "that their lives lie at no one's disposal, save at that of necessity alone, which, with its iron sceptre, rules the universe."[14] The central case against state-imposed execution is the offender's humanity rather than that individual's prior good conduct, artistic ability, or whatever inventory of talents he or she may have revealed in this extreme situation.

It is irrelevant to the argument that prisoners on death row write poems, paint, are good to their mothers, or are able to persuade visitors that they were in another town when the execution-style slaying of the grocer and his wife occurred. What is relevant is that the condemned person thinks, feels, breathes, eats, and sleeps. It is the deliberate extinction of human life, including that of the ugly, the depraved, and those devoid of any ability to please, that is the essential wrong. Executions arrogate to political authority a power that no government should be given or take for itself.

Of course, the use of the death penalty provokes this kind of civil aberration by focusing attention on the offender's fate rather than that of the victim. And in so doing it is, as Beccaria saw, subtly injurious to the interests of the nation at large. "Only those are true and useful laws," he observed, "that do not alienate the minds of numbers of subjects, that unite and identify their own particular interests with those of the commonwealth."[15]

Frequent executions, by changing the subject – in this case from crime to punishment – have a deleterious effect on that larger consensus with respect to the legitimate authority of government in general and the administration of criminal justice in particular, a consensus that is the basis of social stability and solidarity. The process of identification with the condemned and a broadening distrust of government could affect many more Americans – a significant minority on whom true consensus depends – if the pace of executions quickens.

3. The emergent tug of war

Elements of both these scenarios will be intermingled in the years immediately ahead. But it would be a misconception to view this as a process of the increased momentum of executions producing a counterreaction of increased energy and commitment by abolitionists. What seems to happen is that both the momentum of executions and opposition to the death penalty increase simultaneously but independently, creating a discontinuous pattern of fits and starts in both public and political response. This momentum appears to be a mechanical process, operative at the individual state level, and more closely related to variations in political culture than to public opinion polls. By contrast, growing opposition to executions may be seen as developing in the larger national community, as less responsive to particular events, and as incremental in impact.

Table 7.1 shows a 1984 decline in the number of new states executing, but a dramatic increase in the number of executions. This suggests that, in some individual states that have been executing, the fact of three or four previous executions increases the likelihood and frequency of future executions. However, in bordering states during the early 1980s, there has been no bandwagon effect associated with the increase in the number of executing states. Executions in Texas lead more readily to more executions in Texas than to executions in Arkansas. If high execution rates in some Southern states have had any influence at all, it has manifested itself only in the death penalty policy of other Southern states. In relation to the number of additional states executing, the leveling off in 1984, 1985, and 1986 suggests the existence of boundary conditions or noncontinuous thresholds yet to be crossed.

General support for capital punishment remains high in public opinion, although the majority of the public polled do not live in states that execute.[16] On the crucial question of the salience of executions, particularly for those who oppose the death penalty, no data are available. The Barfield controversy and its role in a senate election, as well as the demonstrations that have been organized around particular executions, may be seen as modest indications of increasing salience among opposing groups; but they are very early indications. There may have to be more executions, and more states carrying out executions, before the processes that undermine the consensus on law and order become a significant force.

What is striking with regard to public opinion is the absence of any clear relationship between public sentiment, as reflected in the opinion polls, and execution practice in individual jurisdictions. There are not, and never have been, significant differences in public opinion poll results corresponding to those differences in execution practice that have been traditional in the United States.[17] Even more clearly evident in the post-*Gregg* years has been the lack of correlation between opinion poll majorities and state government execution practice. The South has a near monopoly on executions without any strong difference in public support for executions, and the concentration of executions in the South has *increased* rather than diminished as we have moved into the 1980s. Of the states initiating executions since 1982 all are in the South. Fifty-six of the past fifty-eight executions have taken place in Southern states.[18]

Table 7.2. *Recent executions by execution histories, most frequently executing states, 1950–9*

State	Rank by No. of executions, 1950–9	Rank by per capita executions, 1950–9	Combined rank, 1950–9	Rank by No. of executions, 1977–85
Georgia	1	2	1	3
Florida	5	4	2	1
Mississippi	6	3	2	10
Texas	2	8	4	2
California	2	13	5	–
South Carolina	10	5	5	10
Louisiana	9	7	7	3
Nevada	17	1	8	6
Arkansas	14	6	9	–
Alabama	12	11	10	10
Virginia	11	12	10	5
New York	4	22	12	–
Ohio	7	21	13	–
Arizona	20	9	14	–
Kentucky	16	14	15	–
North Carolina	13	19	16	6
Pennsylvania	8	25	17	–
Utah	24	10	18	10
West Virginia	17	18	19	–
New Jersey	15	23	20	–
Indiana	34	36	36	6

Source: Bureau of Justice Statistics, U.S. Department of Justice, *Capital Punishment 1982,* at 15, Table 2 (1984); Bureau of the Census, U.S. Department of Commerce, *Statistical Abstract of the United States, 1981,* at 10, Table 9.

We cannot offer a conclusive explanation for this striking fact but a preliminary suggestion might be that political culture rather than shifts in public opinion determine a state's propensity to execute. More specifically, the boundaries that separate most of the twelve states that have executed from those that have not appear to be the product of differences in governmental tradition, exemplified by a prior history of extensive executions.

As Table 7.2 indicates, the strong link between a propensity to execute and a history of execution policy is demonstrated by the fact that the four states accounting for over seventy percent of the executions in the 1970s and 1980s – Florida, Texas, Louisiana, and Georgia – were each ranked in the top seven states in executions in the United States between 1950 and 1959, sharing honors in that earlier decade only with the major population centers of California and two other Southern states.[19] Furthermore, this historical linkage extends beyond being another way of signifying that these are Southern states. The four execution leaders of the 1980s were also among the top six executing states of the seventeen Southern states between 1950 and 1959; and each of these states had more than twice as many executions in that earlier period as any other Southern state except Mississippi.[20] Controlling for state population only reinforces this dramatic pattern.[21]

Without detailed knowledge about why such patterns persist – after a gap in executions of fifteen years and the lapse of a quarter century – it is still striking to note that the high execution rate of the 1980s is a class reunion of those Southern states that had similarly high execution rates thirty years earlier. Even the exception seems to prove the rule: Mississippi, the only Southern state with anywhere near the 1950s number of executions in the four high volume states, has executed only once in the mid-1980s. But this decline has been accompanied by perhaps the most dramatic social and political change in all of the old South during the 1960s and 1970s.

The regional disparity and marked concentration in executions, however, was much *less* evident in the 1950s and 1960s, the years of waning use of the death penalty, than it has been in the mid-1980s. Further, this pattern of disparity has persisted for about a decade, unrelated to crime rates. What distinguishes states that have large death row populations but do not execute (for example, California and Illinois) from those states that do (Georgia, Florida, Louisiana, and Texas) is not public support for capital punishment as evidenced in the polls. Rather, it is government tradition, and this suggests that the most profitable approach to studying the transition period that lies ahead will be found in a separate analysis of different groups of states.

C. Patterns of state execution policy

The list of categories into which the states could be grouped in unmanageably long. We shall discuss five groups of states, ranked in ascending order of likelihood of execution in the late 1980s: (1) abolitionist states with no death penalty provisions before or after *Furman;* (2) de facto moratorium states with trends away from execution before the early 1960s and no executions since then; (3) "bellwether" states in the North with large death row populations but no executions since *Gregg;* (4) marginal states, all of which have capital punishment statutes and most of which have executed once or twice since 1976; and (5) frequently executing states, specifically, the four that have accounted for three-quarters of all executions in the past decade.

The list of categories may not be exhaustive; smaller states with death penalty legislation, such as Nebraska, Idaho, and Vermont, are not classified. On the whole, however, the classification scheme appears to explain the current status of execution policy in the United States and offer some insight into the future.

1.   The abolitionist states

There are a number of states of which none in the pre- or post-*Furman* years had authorized the death penalty. Although there have been occasional proposals for such legislation in some of them, none has joined any bandwagon. Alaska, Hawaii, Iowa, Maine, Michigan, Minnesota, Rhode Island, West Virginia, and Wisconsin fall into this category.

These states provide a striking demonstration of the hypothesis, outlined in Chapter 2, that holds that psychological reactance, rather than the power of public opinion, has been the principal motivating force behind the passage of death penalty legislation since *Furman*. The same public opinion trends observed in Ohio and Illinois can be expected in Michigan. There is no evident difference in culture between Iowa and Kansas. These abolitionist states seem as firmly bound to nonexecution as executing states are to their traditions. Only Oregon, where the penalty has come and gone before, has a post-*Furman* death penalty. Passage of a death penalty statute in any of the abolitionist states would represent not just a transition but rather a startling break with tradition. An execution in any of those states in the near future would be a major policy surprise.

2.   De facto moratorium states

These are populous states where, in most cases, the cessation of execution long predated the Supreme Court's intervention. The most notable examples are Massachusetts, New Jersey, and New York. Many are heavily urban with high rates of felony killings that led to executions in the post–World War II period. However, internal political factors significantly inhibited or prevented executions before the federal court moratorium in the 1960s. In these states government leaders have frequently clashed, with judges and some elected officials effectively obstructing any resumption of executions.

There has been considerable political controversy and "public support" for the death penalty in all these states. Indeed, public opinion poll results mirror those found in Southern execution states; but there has also been opposition *within* state governments, overt or covert, with some indication of positive political value in avoiding executions.

New York, then the nation's most populous state, had averaged about six executions a year in the 1950s, but executions diminished substantially in the early 1960s.[22] Both New York and Massachusetts introduced post-*Furman* statutes with provisions much more restrictive than the "aggravating circumstances" enacted by most states.[23] In both jurisdictions the state supreme court has invalidated the statutes authorizing the death penalty.[24] New Jersey adopted lethal injection as the method of execution in 1983, but no prisoner has been executed in that state for over twenty years.[25]

The de facto moratorium states in all likelihood will continue their nonexecuting policy. Barring major events in these states, political leadership with strong convictions against instituting an active execution policy will continue to maintain the current moratorium.

3. Bellwether states

These are populous states with big urban areas and major crime problems: California, Illinois, Pennsylvania, and Ohio. They are also states that, to date, have had no executions, but they do have substantial death row populations. If they follow the Southern pattern and start executing, this could have major consequences for future execution practices. Executing five percent of the death row population in these four states each year would result in twenty-two additional executions annually, approximately doubling the nationwide execution total.

Supreme courts in these states have played an important although not determining role in preventing executions. The initiation of executions in even one of these states might precipitate the kind of momentum to which we have referred. Conversely, it might generate the kind of opposition, based on the increased salience of execution, also discussed earlier.

4. Marginal states

The marginal states include those in the South and West that, considered in terms of their history and political culture, would appear to be the most likely candidates for leadership in pursuing active execution policies. They include Alabama, Arkansas, Mississippi, North Carolina, Oklahoma, South Carolina, and Virginia. Although Oklahoma has not executed since 1966, the other six have initiated executions, although not in large numbers. If such states as Alabama, Arkansas, Mississippi, or Virginia were to accelerate executions, they would probably contribute to a great increase the total number of executions. Through mid-1986, such an escalation has occurred only in Virginia, where five persons have been executed since 1977. If this execution policy continues, Virginia will quickly become a frequently executing state.

So-called marginal states may provide a laboratory for developing new institutional arrangements as part of the political process for coping with large numbers of scheduled executions. These states, most of which have crossed the line into active executions, will provide the quickest test of logjam theories and will reveal, if executions continue, under what circumstances opposition can be expected to occur. It was no accident, therefore, that the Barfield execution took place in North Carolina, a marginal state with one prior execution, and a reputation for modernizing quickly and thoroughly during the 1960s and 1970s – but also with the long-term legacy of a high execution rate. Many of the marginal states have rural areas, like Bladen County in the Barfield case, with courts that generate death sentences for cases in which prison terms would usually be imposed in metropolitan counties.[26] The absence of aggressive executive clemency or state supreme court intervention could produce a high number of executions, independent of the attitudes of most of the state's population. Only if allowing executions incurs adverse political reaction in urban areas will executive clemency seem prudent.

5. Frequently executing states

While these four states – Florida, Texas, Louisiana, and Georgia – have executed three times as many prisoners as all the rest combined, in none of these states has the number of executions, since 1977, exceeded one-tenth of the state's current death row population. In Florida the nation-leading total of sixteen executions is less than one-sixteenth of its death row population; and in Texas the ratio since 1980 is one execution for every fifteen current death row occupants. The backlog is large and growing fast. The state courts in these jurisdictions have maintained a hands-off policy and executive clemency is infrequent. In a very short time, either executions will continue to grow swiftly or significant administrative or judicial checks will develop. No intentional policy to control executions is currently in force in any of these high-frequency states, and as the number of executions increases, the impact on public opinion of large numbers of executions will receive an early test.

D. The federal system

Short-term predictions regarding capital punishment in the federal criminal justice system present no difficulty. Barring a catastrophic skyjacking incident or presidential assassination, there is no likelihood of an execution under federal jurisdiction in the next decade. Perhaps more interesting is the fact that there is little pressure from the Department of Justice, dedicated to capital punishment provisions in federal law, to have the death penalty utilized.

This is only partly explained by the absence of incidents that could generate eligibility for capital punishment under current federal laws. Fatalities resulting from robbery of federally insured banks and from kidnappings are not infrequent. A total of thirty-three executions did occur in the federal jurisdiction from 1930 through 1963;[27] but there is no significant effort to add to that total. Current federal statutes authorize death penalties for several offenses. However, the U.S. Congress has not acted swiftly to remove procedural barriers to death sentences and executions, nor has the Department of Justice made a federal death penalty or executions under federal jurisdiction a policy priority.

The reasons go beyond the national government's respect for state sovereignty. The federal administration can support state capital punishment provisions, approve from a distance the execution activities of the states, and collect whatever political dividends attach to that position without itself incurring any execution backlash. In effect they send surrogates to battle in the war on crime. Federal government leaders are thus much closer to the position Senator Helms occupied than that of then-Governor Hunt in the 1984 Barfield case. It would take extraordinary events to dislodge federal decision makers from a position of such manifest political comfort.

E. Constitutional litigation

Constitutional litigation in the federal courts played the major role in initiating and sustaining the moratorium on executions in the United States during the 1960s and 1970s. For some years after *Gregg* v. *Georgia,* as we saw in Chapter 4, constitutional guarantees were invoked to reduce the scope of death penalty legislation and to change the procedures for capital sentencing. In addition to regulating these standards and procedures, the U.S. Supreme Court's decisions also served to reduce death row populations by invalidating large numbers of then-current death sentences. *Furman* itself led to the invalidation of more than 600 death sentences; and a number of subsequent Supreme Court decisions struck down death sentences by the score and occasionally by the hundred.[28]

However, constitutional litigation in the federal courts is unlikely to play a major role in controlling either the frequency of executions or the population of death rows in the near future. This is a political rather than a substantive judgment, and it is also a tentative one. The history of the U.S. Supreme Court in dealing with these matters has been full of surprises and may continue to be so.

A number of problems with the standards governing capital sentencing and the procedures involved in the generation of death sentences raise substantial constitutional questions. The selection process currently used in the United States (described in Chapter 3) is subject to an attack based on the principles of *Furman*. For example, the fact that individuals with strong scruples against the death penalty are excluded from juries in capital cases gives rise to the possibility that such "death qualified juries" may be unrepresentative, as well as more prone to find defendants guilty, than juries drawn from a broader cross section of the population would be.[29]

The fact that homicides with white victims are far more likely to result in death sentences than are those involving black victims raises the specter of an unusual but troubling form of racial discrimination in the administration of the death penalty.[30] The lack both of meaningful standards for initial determination between life and death sentences and of coherent principles governing appellate review provides fertile ground for constitutional litigation.[31] Prosecutorial decisions to exclude racial minorities from juries, along with other questionable practices rooted in the wide band of prosecutorial discretion, also provide grounds for court challenges.[32] This list of potential objections to the current administration of the death penalty could be easily expanded.

The impact of a successful Supreme Court challenge – on any broad grounds, on the pace of executions, and on death row populations – could be profound. But just as the justices often tended in earlier years to accept expansive constitutional challenges because that would inhibit the practice of execution, so the pattern of decisions in the Supreme Court since the early 1980s suggests that the Court is now reluctant to participate in regulating the administration of capital punishment because of the effective embargo such intervention might place on the implementation of death sentences. *Deregulating Death,* a commentary on recent Supreme Court decisions in this area, demonstrates that the Court's recent decisions almost without exception have followed that pattern.[33]

Yet the Court's history of unexpected decisions over the past twenty years warns against categorically discounting the possibility of federal court intervention as a major determinant of policy in the near term. *McGautha* v. *California*[34] was the procedural challenge on which opponents of capital punishment rested great hopes in the Supreme Court. When the *McGautha* challenge failed, the arguments in *Furman* v. *Georgia* were given little chance of success, and in the wake of *Furman* few would have confidently predicted the result in *Gregg* v. *Georgia* and its execution-permissive progeny. Thus, given the clear pattern of decisions in recent years and the usually ample majorities supporting them, the legacy of uncertainty surrounding death penalty cases in the Supreme Court is, for the near future, the principal if not the only source of constitutional law encouragement for those committed to abolition.

F. Some lessons

Here are our major conclusions about the near future, based on the foregoing examination of the patterns of the recent past. First, political culture rather than public opinion apparently determines the passage of death penalty legislation and the occurrence of executions. For the present, we do not and cannot know why this is so, although it should be of considerable interest to political scientists.

Second, momentum effects seem to take place *within* states. In a populous state, the best predictor of further executions seems to be the fact that three or four executions have already occurred. So far, all our experience is confined to Southern states that have executed. No momentum has been generated in Indiana, where one execution took place in 1981 and one in 1985, or in Utah, with its sole execution in 1977; and recent as well as remote experience teaches that we should not generalize across regional boundaries. Nevertheless, the pattern is sufficiently clear to suggest that the initiation of executions in large non-Southern states may be a critical step in a transition phase. If California and Illinois begin executing, significant momentum effects will either be felt in those and other Northern jurisdictions, or the Southern pattern will be disconfirmed for the North.

Third, although we know where and when states have begun to execute, we do not really know why. There are states with large death row populations that are not executing. For each nonexecuting state it is possible to construct some profile of the roles that various institutions play in forestalling executions, although that will not be attempted here. Frequent executions in recent years seem tied to a pre-*Furman* history of frequent executions. But we are not able to delineate the institutional dynamics of that process, and we cannot explain the overwhelming influence of historical pattern on current behavior.

Perhaps a history of frequent executions, even fifteen and thirty years removed, serves as a kind of precedent, reassuring political actors that their own participation in executions in neither inhumane nor immoral. Such precedent could also provide a further argument to those who seek to put pressure to execute on reluctant governors or state supreme court justices, on the grounds that, historically, executions do not violate local community morality.

Two aspects of this "precedent" hypothesis deserve mention. First, the plausibility of this effect hinges on the existence of widespread moral uneasiness or ambivalence on the part of actors in all jurisdictions. Politicians and judges who are genuinely untroubled by or even enthusiastic about frequent executions do not need precedent to shore up their resolve; thus the existence of such indifference or enthusiasm in even one or two states would break the iron law that prior frequent execution policy was a necessary condition for current widespread execution practice.

The second aspect of the precedent hypothesis, related to our first point, is that the theory's main strength lies in the absence of alternative explanations. It might seem fanciful to suggest that the dead hand of execution practice in the 1950s should, through indirect psychological mechanisms, wield such power in the 1980s. But what alternative explanation is there? Why else would past history prove so reliable an index in the prediction of current practice?

Finally, it seems likely that active execution policy is much easier to forestall than it is to halt, once begun. Evasion and diffusion of responsibility of the kind frequently involved in the avoidance of first executions are common features of political life. The kind of conspicuous courage often required to bring about reversal of an execution policy is rare.

G. The later careers of brave governors

Neither gubernatorial leadership nor executive clemency can explain the slow spread of executions during the 1980s in states that we have called marginal in relation to execution policy. Opposition to the death penalty among political leaders has been confined to relatively safe jurisdictions, such as Massachusetts and New York. In the bellwether states – California, Illinois, and Ohio – popular wisdom says that such active opposition by a governor would be tantamount to political retirement, although the validity of this belief has never been tested.

The Hamlet-like hesitation and private doubt ascribed to some Southern governors never plays a prominent role in their public performances. When – and not if – the testing time comes in the bellwether states, their governors will face major political problems. The consequences of bravery, if there should be bravery, on the subsequent political careers of those displaying it would provide a significant indicator of the political cost of leadership in this field and hence the role it is likely to play in the future.

In theory, it is possible to discuss the recruitment of political leadership with respect to executions as a phenomenon independent of the climate of opinion in which that leadership will have to operate. In fact, this is not possible. The kind of people to be recruited and the roles they will have to play are largely defined by both public attitudes toward capital punishment and politicians' perceptions of those attitudes. In any sequence of events leading to successful leadership, even from the front, about executions, there is likely to be some malleability in the views of the general public and of designated elites that will precede any manifestation of courage by politicians. In this sense even "leadership from the front" is not quite that.

Even though widespread public support for the death penalty is a relatively recent development, and though the issue has not been important in recent political campaigns, it is generally assumed that support for capital punishment is politically "safe," and that opposition to executions erodes political popularity. There is no evidence to support these beliefs, beyond responses to general questions about legislation in opinion polls. This version of public opinion has rarely been tested in a political campaign. Opposition to capital punishment by governors in New York and Massachusetts has not resulted in their defeat, and since no Southern governor to date has taken an abolitionist stance, there has been no opportunity to test such a position at the polls.

Monolithic support for the death penalty may be the Gallup poll version of the Emperor's new clothes. The "macho" position on executions, fashionable in some elite segments of the Northern urban population, does not appear to be either deeply felt or durable enough to survive even a few executions close to home. The attitude of the broader general public is untested and difficult to gauge.

The political repercussions to confront the first brave governors may have a decisive effect on the extent to which bravery is contagious. But some tests of the consequences of political bravery are a near certainty in the short term. Without more aggressive intervention by the federal courts, state governors will be pushed into inescapable public positions in which crucial choices will have to be made, probably in a score of states that have not executed for twenty or twenty-five years. No fewer than five, and possibly as many as ten, state governors face the prospect of double-digit execution totals in the absence of personal initiative. Thus, these issues will inexorably become part of political campaigns.

A hiatus of leadership in the mid-1980s appears not only at the gubernatorial level. No one at any level has a ten-year plan or a five-year plan or even a one-year plan for execution policy. No one appears to have thought seriously about the future at all. This is partly due, of course, to deliberate attempts to shift the responsibility to someone else. It is also partly due to the continuing unresolved debate on capital punishment, and to the abdication and withdrawal of the Supreme Court as well as the lower federal courts from their previously dominant role.

Above all, however, it seems to be due to the fact that all those involved react as though they were the victims of circumstances not of their own making and beyond their control. It is as if everyone was waiting for the weather to change, without any science of meteorology as a guide; atmospheric conditions are seen as not merely uncontrollable, but as totally unpredictable.

Having failed to make any specific predictions about developments in the immediate future, it might seem incongruous for us to move, as we do in Chapter 8, to consider an even more remote prospect, but no contradiction is involved. As R. L. Stevenson said: "The obscurest epoch is today."[35] Forecasting the future career of an individual is not impeded by lack of knowledge about what he or she will be doing next week; and in this respect social forecasting is no different. Moreover, as historians can sometimes demonstrate, one effect of relative distance is the revelation of order and sequence concealed from those who lived through the events recounted. Speculating about the longer-term future can sometimes prove useful in the same way.

Notes

1. "Carolina Slayer Fails in Her Bid for a Reprieve," *N.Y. Times,* Sept. 28, 1984, at A17, col. 2.
2. "Clemency Plea Weighed in Carolina," *N.Y. Times,* Sept. 19, 1984, at A18, col. 2.
3. The last woman to be executed was Elizabeth Duncan, by California authorities in 1962. Schmidt, "Woman Executed in North Carolina," *N.Y. Times,* Nov. 2, 1984, at A1, A20, col. 4 (hereafter Schmidt, "Woman Executed").
4. Schmidt, "Woman Executed," at A20, col. 2.
5. Schmidt, "Decision on Execution Order a Key Issue in Carolina Race," *N.Y. Times,* Sept. 27, 1984, at A16, col. 1.
6. NAACP Legal Defense and Educational Fund, Inc., *Death Row, U.S.A.* 3 (Aug. 1, 1986) (hereafter *Death Row, U.S.A.*); Bureau of Justice Statistics, U.S. Department of Justice, *Capital Punishment 1982,* at 14, Table 1 (1984) (hereafter *Capital Punishment 1982*).
7. *Death Row, U.S.A.,* at 4.
8. *See id.* at 4–17 (lists of prisoners on death row for each state).
9. Stephens, "Capital Punishments," 69 *Fraser's Magazine* 753, 753 (1864).

10. N. Mailer, *The Executioner's Song* (1979).
11. *See* Chapter Six.
12. *Death Row, U.S.A.*, at 8.
13. C. Beccaria, *An Essay on Crimes and Punishments* 86 (W. Farrand trans. 1809).
14. C. Beccaria, *An Essay on Crimes and Punishments* (W. Farrand trans. 1880), *quoted in* C. Phillipson, *Three Criminal Law Reformers* 71 (1923).
15. *Id.* at 72.
16. The twelve states that have executed since 1976 contain only twenty-seven percent of the population in the United States. Bureau of the Census, U.S. Department of Commerce, *Statistical Abstract of the United States, 1981*, at 10, Table 9.
17. *See* Chapter 2.
18. *See Death Penalty, U.S.A.*, at 4.
19. *Capital Punishment 1982*, at 15, Table 2.
20. *Id.*
21. Ranked by number of actual executions, these four states were among the top nine executing states in the nation during the 1950s (*see* Table 7.2). When the number of executions is normed to population, this pattern remains consistent. In making our comparisons, we derived the average yearly population for the several states from the Bureau of Census statistics, *see Statistical Abstract of the United States, 1981*, by averaging the populations from 1950 and 1960. The four most executing states in the 1977–85 era were also among the top eight states ranked by per capita executions in the 1950s.
22. *Capital Punishment 1982*, at 15, Table 2.
23. *See Mass. Ann. Laws* ch. 265, § 2 (Michie/Law. Co-op. 1979); *N.Y. Penal Law* § 125.27 (Consol. 1975).
24. *Commonwealth* v. *Colon-Cruz*, 393 Mass. 150, 470 N.E.2d 116 (1984); *People* v. *Smith*, 63 N.Y.2d 41, 468 N.E.2d 879, 479 N.Y.S.2d 706 (1984).
25. *Capital Punishment 1982*, at 15, Table 2.
26. *See, e.g.*, Paternoster, "Race of Victim and Location of Crime: The Decision to Seek the Death Penalty in South Carolina," 74 *J. Crim. L. & Criminology* 754 (1983).
27. *Capital Punishment 1982*, at 15, Table 2.
28. *See* Bureau of Justice Statistics, U.S. Department of Justice, *Capital Punishment 1971–72*, at 1 (1974); Bureau of Justice Statistics, U.S. Department of Justice, *Capital Punishment 1977*, at 1 (1978) (265 prisoners removed from death row as a result of *Roberts* v. *Louisiana* and *Woodson* v. *North Carolina*); Bureau of Justice Statistics, U.S. Department of Justice, *Capital Punishment 1978*, at 1, 4 (1979) (over 600 removed from death row result of *Furman;* ninety-nine removed because of *Lockett* v. *Ohio*).
29. *See, e.g.*, Symposium, "Death Qualification," 8 *Law & Human Behav.* 1–195 (1984); Schnapper, "Taking *Witherspoon* Seriously: The Search for Death-Qualified Jurors," 62 *Tex. L. Rev.* 977 (1984).
30. *See, e.g.*, Baldus, Pulaski & Woodworth, "Comparative Review of Death Sentences: An Empirical Study of the Georgia Experience," 74 *J. Crim. L. & Criminology* 661 (1983); Baldus, Pulaski & Woodworth, "Monitoring and Evaluating Contemporary Death Sentencing Systems: Lessons from Georgia," 18 *U.C. Davis L. Rev.* 1375 (1985); Barnett, "Some Distribution Patterns for the Georgia Death Sentence," 18 *U.C. Davis L. Rev.* 1327 (1985); Gross & Mauro, "Patterns of Death: An Analysis of Racial Disparities in Capital Sentencing and Homicide Victimization," 37 *Stan. L. Rev.* 27 (1984).
31. *See, e.g.*, Dix, "Appellate Review of the Decision to Impose Death," 68 *Geo. L.J.* 97 (1980).
32. *See, e.g.*, Paternoster, "Prosecutorial Discretion in Requesting the Death Penalty: A Case of Victim-Based Racial Discrimination," 18 *Law & Soc'y Rev.* 437 (1984).
33. Weisberg, "Deregulating Death," 1983 *Sup. Ct. Rev.* 305.
34. 402 U.S. 183 (1971).
35. R. L. Stevenson, *Familiar Studies of Men and Books: Literary Papers* 451 (1922).

8

The path to abolition

America has outgrown the death penalty, but is reluctant to acknowledge that fact in the 1980s. Yet, if there is any continuity in the civilization of this country, then the end of executions is inevitable. How this is to be accomplished, and when, are questions surrounded by profound uncertainty. They are also the topic of this chapter.

A. Was Durkheim wrong?

The retention of the death penalty in the United States represents a striking exception to Emile Durkheim's "laws of penal evolution:"[1] Durkheim identified "two causes of the evolution of punishment – the nature of the social type and of the governmental organ."[2] He claimed that "the intensity of punishment is the greater the more closely societies approximate to a less developed type – and the more the central power assumes an absolute character."[3] In addition, he said: "Deprivations of liberty, and of liberty alone, varying in time according to the seriousness of the crime, tend to become more and more the normal means of social control."[4]

He acknowledged, however, that the movement from less to more developed societies, and from absolutist to more liberal political regimes, did not always coincide. Thus, "it happens that, in passing from a primitive type of society to other more advanced types, we do not see punishment decreasing as we might have expected, because the organization of government acts at the same time to neutralize the effects of social organization."[5] In other words, when one of the causes of the evolution of punishment is absent, the progressive moderation of punishment might not occur. What makes America the remarkable exception is that, being neither an undeveloped society nor under an absolutist government, it still retains a method of punishment characteristic of an earlier stage of development.

148

A hypothetical Martian visitor, less biased than we are but familiar with trends in the rest of the developed world and cognizant of American history, would probably conclude that fifty years from now the abolition of capital punishment in the United States will long have been achieved. If the same detached observer were asked about executions over the next five years, however, he or she would predict no significant progress toward abolition of the death penalty. Public opinion, political pressures, the abdication of the federal courts, and the undisciplined performance of other decision making institutions all combine to create a climate in which there will probably be more, not fewer, executions in the near future.

If abolition is inevitable in the long run but highly unlikely in the short term, how will the gap be bridged? One thing is certain: Whatever social mechanisms and contingencies may be involved, the transformation of a society committed to reintroducing the death penalty into one engaged in reestablishing abolition will prove far more difficult and divisive than the continuation of the 1960s moratorium on executions would have been.

Our discussion of abolition in the United States of the midfuture has four parts. First we examine four circumstances that will not bring about the abolition of capital punishment. Second, drawing on our earlier analysis of abolition in other countries, we outline some of the steps necessary for nationwide abolition in the United States. Third, we consider some of the residual social fears about abandoning the death penalty, the so-called hard cases. Finally, we discuss the benefits of abolition to American society and government.

B. False promises

By whatever means abolition does occur in the United States, we can say with reasonable certainty that there are four ways in which it will not happen. It will not happen as a consequence of a major decline in the rate of violent crime that might inspire a more tolerant and magnanimous attitude toward those convicted of homicide. It will not happen because of a dramatic abatement in the ideological conflict between the proponents of hard- and soft-line approaches to crime control policy. Nor will it occur because of research findings that would constitute proof that the death penalty is no more a deterrent to murder than is imprisonment. Finally, abolition is extremely unlikely to come about because of a single precipitating event – for example, the execution of an individual subsequently proved innocent, or the intervention of a charismatic political leader.

Even if violent crime rates were to decline significantly, they could never decline enough. No level of violent crime low enough to abate the public's fear of assault or criminals will ever be achieved in the real world. It is significant in this regard that South Dakota, with crime rates about one-tenth that of, say, New York or North Carolina, passed death penalty legislation after *Furman*.[6] This phenomenon should not be surprising. The public is much more cognizant of crimes when they occur – especially through sensationalized media coverage – than it is of crimes that do not occur.

Further, the ideological conflict permeating the death penalty dispute will not be resolved by the mass conversion of those favoring the death penalty. Support for capital punishment is not comparable to preference for a particular political party or football team. Its proponents want to give government the ultimate weapon in the war on criminal evil precisely because it is ultimate. Opposition to capital punishment emanates from fear of the ways in which modern governments may employ their power to the detriment of the individual citizen.

These different views of the proper role and limits of governmental power are both pervasive and antithetical. Just as executions will always provoke opposition and resistance, so too will a period without executions inspire fears that society has inadequate protection from violent criminals, fears that may not dissipate for decades or even for generations. The idea that there might be some kind of reluctant accommodation between hard-liners and liberals, with the former relinquishing the death penalty in exchange for liberal support for other harsh crime control measures, might seem plausible in the abstract. But its plausibility rests on the false assumption that the real issue is crime control rather than the feelings of potency and security that accompany the use of governmental power in its ultimate form. On this deeper issue, there is no room for compromise.

Nor will this matter be resolved by the discovery of conclusive evidence that the death penalty is not a more effective deterrent to homicide than is imprisonment. This is so for two reasons: First, nonexperimental research, which is all that is possible in the study of the deterrent effects of capital punishment, cannot furnish invulnerable conclusions. Research will always have shortcomings; methodologies will always be subject to criticism. Second, as Thorsten Sellin explained to the Royal Commission on Capital Punishment in 1951, the question of whether the death penalty was to be abolished or retained has never been determined by the evidence but on beliefs and sentiments little influenced by evidence about ulilitarian effects.[7] The death penalty controversy, like most other political controversies, cannot and will not be resolved by equations.

Finally, it is improbable that abandonment of the death penalty will result from some singular event or political act such as a dramatic miscarriage of justice, for example, the execution of an innocent person; or a decisive action by some brave governor that will prove to be a crucial turning point. Such events or acts have in the past played an incremental role in the movement toward abolition in particular countries, but the abolitionist movement has existed for centuries, and with steadily increasing force, since Beccaria published *On Crimes and Punishments*[8] in 1764. Specific events may slightly accelerate or retard the movement, but only general and profound social change can alter long-term results. Moreover, the most instructive demonstration of the need for abolition and the control of governments in modern history – the Nazi regime – has already happened. A more powerful object lesson is unlikely to occur in the midrange future.

C. Elements of abolition

The history of capital punishment, both in the wider context of the Western world and in the United States, suggests a number of factors that will characterize the abolition of the death penalty in this country whenever it happens. Among them are the following: the nationalization of the issue in the federal system; the phenomenon of political leadership from the front; and the felt necessity for retaining the penalty for some crimes, in some specific circumstances, during a considerable portion of the initial phase of what would be, in fact, the aftermath of abolition. All of these factors were discussed in our earlier analysis of abolition in other nations. They are conditions that apply with special force to the United States in the 1980s and beyond.

1. Nationalization

Debate about whether the death penalty in America should be regarded as a national or a local issue could proceed endlessly and on a variety of different levels. Most criminal justice responsibilities in the United States are vested in state and local governments, including the definition of most crimes, the great majority of police forces, and ninety percent of prisons and jails. Execution policy conforms to this pattern. Ninety-nine percent of all executions since 1930 have been conducted under state and local jurisdiction.[9]

Federal authority overrides state and local law when local policies conflict with federal interests, or with shared values of sufficient national significance to produce federal legislation. When the federal government chooses to intervene, its authority to do so under existing precedent is unlimited. If the practice of execution conflicts with constitutional values or with strong federal interests, abolition can be achieved by either Congress or the federal courts. Thus, the exercise of federal power to nationalize the issue of capital punishment is a matter of will rather than ability.

The only nation-states with genuinely federal governments to have had experience in these matters are Switzerland and Australia. Their case histories point up the existence of a gap of many decades between abolition of the death penalty in the first jurisdiction to take this step, and the last to do so. This pattern seems independent of prevailing public attitudes; federalism itself appears to serve as a prescription for a protracted process of abolition and for long-term, if restricted, retention of the death penalty.

The long period between the beginning and the end of the abolition process in federal systems does not constitute proof that the allocation of power to the states necessarily defers the end of executions. A sixty-year gap between the first and the last state to abandon execution could as easily occur because decentralized power enables the process of abolition to begin earlier as because it delays culmination to a later date. Indeed, both Switzerland and Australia experienced a complete cessation of executions earlier than did other European and Commonwealth countries. One function of federalism with respect to power over criminal justice in the United States undoubtedly was to facilitate the initiation of abolition in the nineteenth century.[10]

The only safe generalization that can be made about the effect of decentralized power is that it fosters diversity among the units that make up the federation. It can thus delay and diminish the impact of dominant historical trends in those units, although it will not necessarily affect the ultimate results.

However, viewed in the context of the worldwide movement toward abolition of capital punishment, the persistence of state and local power over execution policy has proved a major inhibitor of that trend in America in recent years. Indeed, there is a distinct possibility that the practice of execution has become almost as much a celebration of states' rights as a matter of criminal justice policy.

The doubling of the number of death sentences in the South in reaction to *Furman* (discussed in Chapter 5) can be seen as the use of death penalty policy to express hostility toward the national government's power. Moreover, the persistence of a higher level of death sentences since *Gregg,* and the continued clustering of actual executions in states of the old Confederacy, provide additional evidence that executions represent a manifestation of state autonomy that continues to influence state and local decision makers even when federal restraints on the freedom to execute have been removed. Thus, unless the states' rights struggle spontaneously ends, nationalization of the death penalty issue appears to be a necessary component in the timely achievement of abolition.

Of the two most obvious methods of wielding national power to curtail the states' use of the death penalty – constitutional adjudication in the federal courts and legislation in Congress – the former has been historically both more frequent and easier to achieve. But this type of judicial legislation based on the Eighth Amendment has two drawbacks: the reluctance of Supreme Court justices to lead conspicuously from the front, and an awkward inability of the Court to experiment or take deliberate intermediate steps toward abolition. By contrast, Congress has the institutional ability to enact gradual measures such as a moratorium, and also the explicit authority to do so under the fifth section of the Fourteenth Amendment. On the matter of leadership from the front, however, the Congress is characterized by consistent timidity, lacking a tradition of moral leadership such as that evinced in the British Parliament, and sheltered by the historical pattern of Supreme Court leadership. Congress is thus an unlikely place to look for the initiation of federal abolition.

Still, a legislative solution at the federal level can occur in some circumstances. Strong presidential leadership is one such possibility. If Congress itself cannot lead from the front, American history is replete with examples of presidential initiatives being followed by that body into new territory. A strong Supreme Court initiative might also move Congress to react with compromise measures, such as a moratorium, that could be perceived as less drastic than total abolition. But our experience with civil rights suggests the likelihood of at least a ten-year gap between the Supreme Court and Congress with respect to moral leadership in politically unpopular directions. Although this gap may have narrowed, there is no reason to think it has been eliminated.

The capital punishment issue is already nationalized in a number of important respects: The mass media and the public react more strongly to an execution in Texas than to one in South Africa. A national scorecard on executions seems to have significance for both opponents and proponents of the practice. Furthermore, the long history of federal court restraint on executions leads the public to believe, with some justification, that executions now taking place under state authority also carry some federal mandate.

When considering which levels of government determine execution policy, it is a mistake to bifurcate the possibilities into state power and initiative on the one hand and sudden and total federal preemption on the other. The decline of executions since the 1930s in the United States is attributable to a mix of federal and state policy. Constitutional standards and federal courts still play an important role in every death penalty case. There are also analogous areas of federal–state regulation in which a question was nationalized only after a particular stage had been reached by the states.

The U.S. Supreme Court's decision in *Roe* v. *Wade*[11] is a stark example of the abrupt nationalization of the abortion question – but the Court's ruling came *after* a majority of all American states had liberalized their grounds for legal abortion in less than a decade, and *after* four states had introduced provisions of the sort nationalized by the Court for abortion on demand. Justice Blackmun's opinion for the majority emphasizes that the relationship between the changes at state level and the Court's action was neither coincidental nor unimportant.[12]

The Blackmun opinion in *Roe* characterizes the Court's action in creating a national right as conforming to a contemporary trend. Moreover, that action was taken after a moral consensus favoring the prohibition of abortion had been effectively rejected in the majority of states. This pattern of centralized decision making confirming an already evident trend in the states is not an unlikely scenario for federal court action on capital punishment. In fact one can read both Justices Stewart and White, as well as Justice Brennan, as conceiving that to be the Court's role in overturning discretionary death penalties in *Furman*.

Capital punishment by whatever method has become a national issue. The long-term future of abolition in this country will probably witness even greater federal dominance over the controversy, with the courts or Congress, or both, playing a substantial role. Even the current period of state-level domination of the issue is itself a policy of the federal government, in this sense only one of many succeeding phases of federal policy determining the allocation of power on capital punishment issues.

2.   The search for leadership

However, and whenever, the death penalty is abolished in the United States, that step will be taken with limited public support and will be contrary to the manifest weight of public opinion. The evidence for this assertion can be found both in the twentieth-century history of abolition in every nation where public opinion on abolition has been studied, and in public opinion surveys in every region of the United States. Although majority opinion opposes the ending of executions, democratic govern-ments, nevertheless, abolish the death penalty.[13] Thus, an almost inherent element of abolition is that responsible agents manifest a willingness to act against public opinion.

If such leadership is a necessary condition to achieve abolition, what sort of people are willing to demonstrate it and where are they located in the authority structure of American government? As we have suggested, potentially unpopular steps are more often taken at the national level than by state or local governments; more often by the judiciary than the executive; and still less frequently by the legislature. The legislative branch is also less prone to follow executive initiatives in the United States than in parliamentary governments in all but the most ascendant periods of presidental leadership, because of weakened ties between American presidents and political parties and the political fortunes of legislators associated with presidents.

Finally, the long history of judicial intervention in the capital punish-ment controversy and a number of other minority rights issues may have inhibited the development, in other branches of both state and federal government, of the will to confront perceived popular opposition. While formal responsibility for execution policy is vested in individual state governments, there is in 1986 no office at any level of either state or federal government in which the occupant is expected to define his or her task to include responsibility for death penalty policy.

Under these circumstances, the most likely path to change is through the Supreme Court, whose exercise of moral leadership is supported by a long historical tradition. Failing that, state governors are the political officials most likely to regard the death penalty policy as being a crucial part of their responsibility and, therefore, to take action.

Inevitably, some governors will attempt to exercise the powers of their office in the direction of abolition, a strategy that might be contagious if it proves politically successful. This process, of course, is far more likely to occur in abolitionist and de facto moratorium states than in states where executions are more frequent, and it should be remembered that state governors have very few models for this sort of bravery in recent Ameri-can experience.

One factor, however, that might induce state governors to assume leader-ship is the existence of opposition to executions by opinion-leading elites. Minority opposition to the death penalty can be a political problem if it emanates from people who count. Furthermore, there is a tradition of defer-ence to the organized legal and medical professions in matters of moral judgment that might be influential and exploitable in this connection.

Ultimately, the leadership from the front that results in elimination of the death penalty will almost certainly emanate from the Supreme Court, but when that happens, the societal response will be largely determined by political leadership in other branches of the federal government and at the state and local levels. Furthermore, brave governors and even brave senators will have to take important roles in demythologizing the politics of capital punishment long before the Court acts to end executions.

The demythologizing process has already begun in some Northern states. The crucial tests with regard to halting the spread of executions will take place in some of the bellwether jurisdictions discussed in Chapter 7. However, any real hope of using political processes to reduce the number of executions must involve the chief executives in those frequently executing states where the logjams have already been broken. Thus, the major moves toward abolition in the midterm will be contingent on antiexecution politics at the state level, but decisive leadership and full nationalization eventually will come from the Supreme Court.

3. Saving graces

A useful, if not always necessary, factor in the abolition process has been a lengthy transition period between the end of executions and the formal repudiation of all capital punishment. There are still Western countries where the formal finishing touches to abolition have not been applied, but which are as safe from the hangman as any of their neighbors. A number of methods to achieve de facto abolition are available.

An inventory of such devices would include: an executive declaration suspending executions; a legislative moratorium of indefinite or fixed period; formal abolition coupled with a commitment to reevaluate and, if necessary, reintroduce the punishment at a later date; and abolition for civil crimes, with retention for crimes against the security of the state – for example, treason, espionage, or killing the Chief Executive. Devices of this kind may prove not merely useful but essential in the American context.

Moreover, such measures are best suited to executive leadership, particularly at the state level, but they are less available to the Supreme Court. Thus the most likely locus for their use is in state governments, where tactical stratagems and experiments are politically possible and have in the past been used in pursuit of abolition.

On the other hand, some federal strategies may be effective in promoting abolition. One such tactic is to impose procedural requirements on the practice of execution until the point is reached at which capital punishment falls into desuetude. This is something of a charade, but it is a useful charade that served its purpose until the reversal in *Gregg* v. *Georgia*.

The procedural pendulum may swing back again until a combination of high principle and formal requirements once again brings about effective abolition. Insofar as *Furman* is still good law, a successful attack on the death penalty as "cruel and unusual punishment" in violation of the Eighth Amendment is also still available as a mechanism to create de facto abolition. This tactic, of course, will not achieve a formal break with *Gregg* v. *Georgia* on the constitutionality of the death penalty under any circumstances. That will come much later than the actual end of executions.

4. In sum

This account of the abolition of capital punishment in America is incomplete in a number of respects. Notably, we lack a timetable, but if conjecture is in order, we would surmise that the last execution in the United States is more likely to take place in fifteen years than in fifty years; and it is not beyond possibility that executions will cease in the near future. Significant early indicators will occur at every level of government, although it is probable that the Supreme Court will ultimately preside over the formal disestablishment of the death penalty.

The mechanism that will bring an end to executions is also a matter of speculation; there is insufficient evidence for even an informed guess. However, the government act that ends executions will probably precede the unequivocal renunciation of capital punishment by a substantial period of time.

One explanation for the imprecise character of our predictions about future developments is simply the inability to envision history in advance. But the timing and pattern of the abolition process depends largely on other political choices that will be made in the coming years. Thus, a significantly disparate and more precise forecast of the time at which the Supreme Court would put an end to executions might have been possible if the 1984 presidential election had been differently decided. Developments in abeyance for the duration of the Reagan Court might quickly have come to pass during a Mondale administration.

Although the 1984 election was focused and decided on other questions, its impact on the short-term outlook for constitutional adjudication is evident. A number of critical events will take place in the coming years, not the least of them being national elections. To estimate in advance what form they will take or what their consequences will be for the political pattern of the abolition process or the timing of the end of executions is impossible.

But there is no doubt that the end will come. Although both the public mood and the ideology of governments fluctuate dramatically in relatively short periods of time, in the history of the Western world those fluctuations occur within a larger continuous movement of developing social and political trends. Thorsten Sellin sees the movement for abolition of capital punishment as arising from "beliefs in the personal value and dignity of the common man that were born of the democratic movement of the eighteenth century."[14] In this longer-term perspective the transience and marginal significance of current fashion is clear.

When the 1980s come to be viewed in retrospect, events that have already occurred are likely to assume a very different significance from that attributed by current commentary. Indeed, some developments now appearing as dramatic reversals in direction, seen in their true relations to other events of our time, will probably be recognized as having contributed to the end of capital punishment.

Predicting that the Supreme Court of the United States will preside over the end of executions in the relatively near future is hardly the way to acquire a reputation for political common sense. There are literally no indications in the Court's recent performance or the political content of the mid-1980s to support this prognostication. Instead, we are the willing prisoners of our method. Historical trends will produce the pressure for abolition and the national Supreme Court seems the path of lowest resistance to achieving that objective. We see the Court changed not by personnel or a single event but by a sense of the necessity of living up to history's demands.

D. Hard cases

So far in this chapter our predictions have been cast in descriptive rather than didactic terms, identifying elements in a probable path to a preordained destination. Yet many observers – including even those who do not quarrel with our assessment of the general direction and prevailing tendency of long-term trends – still question whether American society at its present stage can accept or afford the social consequences of the renunciation of the death penalty.

Their objections commonly take the form of posing "hard cases": crimes or criminals or social conditions for which only the availability of the ultimate sanction seems to provide an appropriate response. Those concerned about the societal consequences of irrevocable relinquishment of capital punishment nominate five varieties of hard cases. For purposes of exposition we call them: the unique deterrent; the heinous crime; the institutional killer; the victim's mother; and the unforeseen case.

We do not view these hard cases as merely debating points to be rhetorically rebutted and put to rest. They represent genuine concerns often arising from deep convictions. To ignore them or dismiss them as inconsequential is to overlook the fact that they help both to elucidate the nature of resistance to abolition and to explain why it has not been achieved.

1. The unique deterrent

Proponents of the unique deterrent thesis will often acknowledge the absence of any reliable evidence that the threat of capital punishment has even a marginal deterrent effect on homicide rates.[15] They raise the possibility, however, that the total unavailability of the capital sanction may embolden potential offenders currently restrained from committing murders even in nonexecuting states, and also will leave us unilaterally disarmed in the face of possible new types of crime or new kinds of criminals who may be unresponsive to any lesser penalty.

The belief that the death penalty is a unique deterrent is based on deeply rooted intuition and is seen as self-evident. It has probably never been more clearly expressed than in James Fitzjames Stephen's often quoted article, "Capital Punishment," published in 1864:

No other punishment deters men so effectually from committing crimes as the punishment of death . . . this is one of those propositions which it is difficult to prove, simply because they are in themselves more obvious than any proof can make them. It is possible to display ingenuity in arguing against it, but that is all. The whole experience of mankind is in the other direction. The threat of instant death is one to which resort has always been made when there was an absolute necessity for producing some result. . . . "All that a man has he will give for his life." In any secondary punishment however terrible, there is hope; but death is death; its terrors cannot be described more forcibly.[16]

The whole human experience may tell us that the threat of instant death would for most normal human beings be transcendentally terrible. But the inference that the relatively remote possibility of death in the distant future, which is what the existence of the death penalty means in practice, must therefore be a singular and irreplaceable deterrent to murder, represents a spectacular non sequitur. The British Royal Commission on Capital Punishment wisely decided that it was "important . . . not to base a penal policy in relation to murder on exaggerated estimates of the uniquely deterrent force of the death penalty."[17]

2. The heinous crime

The specter of the heinous crime is invoked by those who espouse capital punishment as retribution, on the grounds that an important function of punishment is to provide a fitting or appropriate reprisal for an offense. These individuals claim that some crimes are so outrageously evil or wicked that they demand condign punishments.

Political scientist Walter Berns supports the death penalty not because it is a deterrent, for "the evidence on this is unclear and besides, as it is usually understood, deterrence is irrelevant."[18] Rather, he supports it because he believes the function of punishment is to pay the offender back. He cites a number of cases, such as those of Richard Speck, Charles Manson, and Elmer Wayne Henley (the last of whom, with Dean Allen Corle, killed some twenty-seven young men in Houston, Texas). Henley, he notes "was sentenced to 594 years in prison, but it is questionable whether even that sentence is *appropriate repayment* for what he did."[19] His conclusion is that justice requires the death penalty. "I am aware," he says, "that it is a terrible punishment, but there are terrible crimes and terrible criminals."[20] There is, of course, no rebuttal to the assertion that some crimes are terrible; they are. But put in that way Berns's argument, far from suggesting a rational basis for penal policy, irresistibly calls to mind Samuel Johnson's rejoinder to a similar analogy in a different context: "It might as well be said 'Who drives fat oxen should himself be fat.' "[21]

Berns's argument confuses the retributive notion of matching the gravity of the offense to the severity of punishment with the societal need for vengeance. We discuss the latter in the next section. As to the former, matching terrible crimes with terrible punishments is both impossible to achieve and morally perverse. The death penalty cannot be graduated in accordance with the viciousness of the crime, and retaining it in order to pay back offenders with equivalent atrocity is, as Beccaria observed, not to serve justice but to "extend the beastly example."[22]

3. The institutional killer

Another hard case pressed by those involved in the maintenance of control in penal institutions is that of the violent, aggressive prisoner convicted of homicide, who has killed a guard or another inmate while in prison and presents a threat that he will kill again. Such prisoners, it is said, represent an immediate danger to staff or other inmates and an impossibly difficult control problem. The death penalty is nominated as the only feasible solution.

In a statement before the U.S. Senate Committee on the Judiciary in November 1983, Norman Carlson, Director of the Federal Bureau of Prisons, argued that such cases demonstrate "the need for that ultimate sanction."[23] The death penalty is needed because "inmates who murder, then murder again, must be held accountable"; "another life sentence adds nothing to the scales of justice"; and "there is no justice because the assailants are not punished."[24] Such retributive considerations are discussed above.

Mr. Carlson also argued that without the death penalty "there is no meaningful deterrent," and "there is no safety because there is no deterrence."[25] The deterrent effect of the death penalty is considered in the Appendix, but in this context it should be added that many of "the small number of dangerous and violent criminals" to whom he referred would have already demonstrated that the threat of the death penalty did not deter them from murder.

Moreover, what Mr. Carlson referred to as "a critical problem we face in the management of the Federal Bureau of Prisons" is not confined to penal institutions. Psychiatric hospitals contain many highly dangerous patients who present similar problems in regard to custodial control and the protection of staff and inmates, which are resolved without killing the patients. The use of death as a means of institutional management can no more be justified in prisons than in mental hospitals.

4. *The victim's mother*

The victim's mother provides a more specific referent than is usual in the discussion of the functions of punishment – the unmet need for retribution or adequate requital on the part of those close to the victim. A standard feature of the media circuses surrounding recent executions is the television interview with a member of the victim's family who asserts that he or she will not be able to sleep or resume a normal life until justice has been done and the murderer put to death.

This demand for what is called retributive justice, although it is not easily distinguished from vengeance, occasionally finds a place in more sophisticated arguments for an active execution policy as something requiring legitimate satisfaction. As Justice Stewart said in *Furman:*

The instinct for retribution is part of the nature of man, and channeling that instinct in the administration of criminal justice serves an important purpose in promoting the stability of a society governed by law. When people begin to believe that organized society is unwilling or unable to impose upon criminal offenders the punishment they "deserve" then there are sown the seeds of anarchy – of self-help, vigilante justice and lynch law.[26]

162 II. Futures and consequences

For many, the prospect of unappeased moral outrage and thwarted instinctive appetite for reprisal on the part of both the families of victims and the community at large is a powerful argument against abolition of the death penalty. It is also demonstrably erroneous, deriving its plausibility from a paradox that relates to the peculiar circumstances of the retention of the death penalty in America at this moment in history.

The victim's mother cries out for the murderer to be executed and is dissatisfied with any lesser penalty, precisely because the death penalty is available as the most substantial response to willful killing in the United States at this time. Because it is available, any lesser penalty would depreciate the significance of the crime and would confer second-class status on the life, and the circumstances of the death, of the victim. The frustrated response and the outrage are a function of the existence of the death penalty.

Undoubtedly, if some kind of torturous method of execution involving severe physical pain were authorized as a legal penalty for murder, then the family and loved ones of many victims would feel cheated if the offender who caused their loss was accorded a painless death. Similarly, if the penalty of death were available for some rapes, then rape victims and those close to them would feel denigrated by the application of noncapital sanctions.

When capital punishment is abolished, the demand for it will persist as long as the experience of executions is a recent memory – but for little longer. When executions cease to be a proximate memory in society, the families and friends of homicide victims will continue to demand the most severe penal consequences that can be attached to that form of crime. And they will be similarly frustrated and outraged when, as will sometimes happen, the maximum penalty is not imposed.

Here lies the supreme irony involved in the practice of capital punishment in America today insofar as it is intended to fulfil a retributive function and satisfy vindicatory or vindictive needs. To reserve the capital sanction for one in a thousand killings, to confine its application only to those who kill during robberies, or only to those who kill police officers, or kill whites, is, in the majority of homicide cases, to increase personal and social frustration in those close to the victim by disparaging their anguish and depreciating the significance of their loss.

It has been said that "capital punishment for murder exerts a moral influence by indicating that life is the most highly protected value."[27] Viewed in this light the demand for the retention of the death penalty might be seen as representing fear that human life would be devalued by abolition. Yet abolition has precisely the reverse effect as far as the majority of homicides are concerned.

The experience of abolition in other Western nations demonstrates that insofar as it is true that there is "an instinctive feeling in most ordinary men that a person who has done an injury to others should be punished for it,"[28] then that feeling is not tied inflexibly to particular penalties. The gradual erosion of support for capital punishment in the wake of abolition indicates that adjustment to a penalty scheme with one less terrible punishment can be achieved without social trauma.

5. The unforeseen case

Finally, there is an objection to the total abolition of capital punishment that draws on our limited ability to foresee the future and, in particular, to anticipate what appalling criminals and monstrous crimes may be forthcoming in the years ahead. Some suggest that the time may come when a crime so demoniacal and atrocious occurs that the unavailability of the death penalty would provoke massive social disaffection and disequilibrium.

In the American context, such dire premonitions may not seem altogether implausible, but the available evidence in 1986 discounts these phantasmic visions. In our country, we have the experience of contiguous American states with and without capital punishment. Furthermore, over a score of developed industrial countries have an abolition policy that has not given rise to what proponents of this objection see as the opening of a Pandora's box, releasing into the world some unprecedented malignancy. This extensive experience demonstrates that the unforeseen case, which would stampede mature societies into retrieving the gallows, seems never to occur; the Mephistophelean master criminal never appears.

Still, the worry about surrendering the ultimate deterrent cannot be easily dismissed, nor should it be. It is a lesson that can never be taught; it can only be learned. That is why the saving grace of retaining the death penalty on the statute books for some special category or categories of crime, or for unforeseen circumstances, is a useful device and should probably feature in any realistic abolitionist program. In this way, acknowledgment of the hypothetical hard case makes experiment possible and enables the lesson to be learned.

E. The benefit of virtue

The end of executions in America will not be achieved without time, effort, and social discord. There is an obvious question to ask regarding the effects of abolition. Will it be worth it? What social benefits will be associated with it in this last outpost of executions in the West? Also, the cost–benefit question raises the wider issue of how one can evaluate the relationship between executions or their absence and larger social progress.

We regard the end of the death penalty in the United States as a high priority reform in the criminal justice system and in the broader social framework within which it operates. Yet the criminal justice system abounds with problems urgently demanding attention, many of them involving unnecessary suffering for large numbers of people. What is there about this question that demands the significance we have accorded it?

We suggest that the benefits that will accrue should be viewed as negative, symbolic, and representative. They will be negative in that removing this excrescence from the body politic is analogous to the removal of a wart from the human body. What is achieved is the diminution of suffering when the wart has been excised rather than any sudden access of well-being. The negative benefits of ending executions extend beyond the simple fact that they no longer have to be performed. There can be no tasteless media coverage of executions that do not occur; no hypocritical attempts to represent the deliberate taking of human life as medical treatment; no ambivalent defensiveness; and, within a relatively short time, no social divisiveness relating to death as a punishment.

The principal advantage of abolishing the death penalty is that it will no longer be there to disfigure our society, but the social dividends that will be earned by abolition are not wholly negative. They are also symbolic and qualitative, rather than quantifiable, units of social utility. This is true both of the practice of execution and its abolition. Mass destruction may work well as an instrument of social control but the deliberate taking of individual human lives coupled with elaborate judicial procedures is not an efficient tool for social management. As a means of incapacitation the prison, the Gulag, and the labor gang are far more cost-effective. So the benefits of capital punishment are symbolic: They lie in the statement executions make about the relationship between the government and the offender; in the vindication of absolute and ultimate power appropriated to governmental ends, even if this only happens in a small number of cases.

The symbolic value of abolition in Western society is the message of forbearance in modern governments, armed with an abundance of lethal technology, deliberately choosing not to kill in the face of criminal provocation. It is a statement about the proper limit on governmental power, a conception of the nature of democratic government with implications far beyond the field of criminal justice. Here lies the crucial connection between the cataclysmic lessons of the Nazi regime and the rejection of the death penalty throughout Europe when that regime ended.

The fact that there are terrible crimes and terrible criminals reinforces the moral value of governmental restraint. Failure to execute in the face of ordinary homicide does not carry the moral force of refusal to respond in kind to some of the monstrous crimes that are a too frequent feature of late-twentieth-century civilization. The more terrible the crime, the more forceful the statement of governmental restraint. In this sense, Rudolph Hess and Sirhan Sirhan are preserved as exhibits in a museum of limited governmental force that maintains the liberty of all of us.

The abolition of capital punishment should not be seen as an instrument for the achievement of social progress in the form of wider recognition of a broader human rights agenda. Rather than facilitating further reform, usually the abolition of the death penalty *represents* progress that has been achieved. It constitutes the kind of statement that only a progressive society can make. It provides countries throughout the world with an index of the degree of recognition accorded to human rights.

The hanging of prisoners does not make South Africa a backward country; rather it provides a good indicator of the level of respect for human rights in that country. By the same token, the health and welfare of the common person in Scandinavia, France, and Great Britain are not significantly advanced because of the absence of executions. Yet the same social forces that facilitated abolition have helped to define citizenship in these countries in ways that have enhanced social welfare, and the same perception of the proper limits of governmental power provides protection against political abuses that threaten citizens who commit no crimes.

Is America, then, at the same stage of moral and political development as South Africa? Does this country need to develop much further to reach the level of civilization at which the abolition of the death penalty will be acceptable? An argument could be made in support of that proposition, but it would be based on a profound misunderstanding of the real situation in the United States.

Executions in America are an anomaly, not only in relation to the progress achieved in other Western countries but also in relation to America's own development. We have in fact already outgrown the social and political conditions in which capital punishment can continue to be practiced. The revival of an active execution policy would involve an appalling regression. There is a defensive quality about contemporary demands for executions even from the most articulate advocates, an uneasy awareness that what is being sought is not the revival of an obsolete penal method but a reversion to moral primitivism. In the end, by discarding capital punishment, American society will be catching up with itself.

Notes

1. *See* Durkheim, "The Evolution of Punishments," in *Durkheim and the Law* (S. Lukes & A. Scull eds. 1983).
2. *Id.* at 107.
3. *Id.* at 102–3 (emphasis omitted).
4. *Id.* at 114 (emphasis omitted).
5. *Id.* at 107.
6. U.S. Department of Justice, FBI, *Crime in the United States: Uniform Crime Reports* 58, 60, Table 5 (1985).
7. Royal Commission on Capital Punishment, *Minutes of Evidence* 656 (1951), *quoted in* T. Sellin, *The Penalty of Death* 87 (1980).
8. C. Beccaria, *On Crimes and Punishments* (H. Paolucci trans. 1963) (hereafter C. Beccaria, *On Crimes and Punishments*).
9. Bureau of Justice Statistics, U.S. Department of Justice *Capital Punishment 1982,* at 15, Table 2 (1984).
10. *See* Chapter 2.
11. 410 U.S. 113 (1973).
12. *Id.* at 139–40.
13. *See* Chapter 1.
14. T. Sellin, *The Death Penalty* 15 (1959).
15. *See, e.g.,* van den Haag, "The Death Penalty Once More," 18 *U.C. Davis L. Rev.* 957, 965 (1985).
16. Stephen, "Capital Punishment," *Fraser's Magazine* 753 (1864).
17. Royal Commission on Capital Punishment, *Report* 24 (1953).
18. W. Berns, *For Capital Punishment* 8 (1979).
19. *Id.* at 9.
20. *Id.* at 8–9.
21. 4 *Boswell's Life of Johnson* 331 (G. Hill ed. 1934).
22. C. Beccaria, *On Crimes and Punishments* at 50.
23. Carlson, Statement Before the Subcommittee on Criminal Law, Senate Committee on the Judiciary, *Restoration of Capital Punishment Under Federal Law* 1 (Nov. 9, 1983).
24. *Id* at 4.
25. *Id* at 5.
26. *Furman* v. *Georgia,* 408 U.S. 238, 306 (1972).
27. Andenaes, "The General Preventive Effects of Punishment," *U. Pa. L. Rev.* 967 (1966).
28. A. Goodhart, *English Law and the Moral Law* 92 (1958).

Appendix: deterrence and the death penalty

One of the most widely used arguments in favor of the death penalty is that it is "a social necessity because it effectively deters people from committing murder."[1] Indeed, the deterrence issue has been described as "traditionally the most important single consideration for both sides in the death penalty controversy."[2] It might seem anomalous, therefore, that we have relegated the question of deterrent efficacy to an appendix. We have done this for three reasons.

First, it will be clear to those who have read this far that the crucial question in relation to the death penalty concerns its legitimacy and propriety rather than its efficacy. It is preeminently a political and a moral question, not an empirical one.

Some social policy issues may be settled simply by reference to empirical data and the inferences drawn from their analysis, but the issue of whether or not the death penalty should be prescribed by law for any crime is certainly not one of them. In facing that issue we confront not one but two fundamental moral questions: not merely whether we regard the idea of putting a person to death for a crime as morally acceptable, but also whether the state should be granted the power to terminate human life. We do not deny that, in general, "the deterrent efficacy of punishments should play *some* role in deciding on rational grounds whether they are morally appropriate,"[3] but in the case of capital punishment, we believe it has no role.

Second, the motivating force behind the abolitionist movement, both in this country and those other countries of Western culture that have finally abandoned the death penalty, has not, as a matter of fact, come from advances in the scientific assessment of the comparative deterrent effectiveness of different penalties. Rather, it has come from development in prevailing attitudes and beliefs regarding what is moral and just. As Hans Zeisel pointed out: "Nowhere was the worldwide decline of the death penalty significantly connected with arguments about its effectiveness or lack thereof."[4] Similarly, when executions cease in America it will not be because of the findings of deterrence research.

It is true that the prospect of unpleasant consequences is the fuel that powers the machinery of deterrence. It is also true that, in framing punishment policy, the differential effectiveness of various threatened consequences or penalties is an important consideration. But although the decision about what form those penalties should take may be conditioned by that consideration, it is never determined by it.

Forms of punishment like breaking on the wheel, burning at the stake, branding, and mutilation were not abandoned because they had proved ineffective. They would not be readopted if an anthropologist were to discover some remote tribal territory where these penalties were still employed and which appeared to be relatively crime-free as a consequence.

Some years ago Chief Justice Cornelius of the Supreme Court of Pakistan claimed that in Saudi Arabia the cutting off of hands as a punishment for theft had "proved to be an extremely effective deterrent against that form of crime."[5] The Chief Justice may have been confusing deterrence with incapacitation, and the evidence he offered to support his assertion was tenuous, but these were not the reasons why his recommendation fell on deaf ears in the West. It would not have been adopted even if empirical investigation had demonstrated the correctness of his claim.

What is true of maiming is true also of taking human life. The question of the death penalty is not one that requires further empirical investigation for its resolution. Both those who oppose and those who support capital punishment by appealing to research findings, as well as those who lament the inconclusiveness of these findings, sometimes seem to imply that if only further information or more precise data were available the matter could be quickly settled.

They may do so because, as Sellin suggests:

[I]t is characteristic of modern man, reared in an age of scientific orientation, that he wishes to use scientific thoughtways in the approach to his problems. He does not like to be considered irrational. When he formulates public policies he wants to think that such policies are based on scientific facts . . . .[6]

It may thus be understandable that some of those concerned with the death penalty issue should see it as turning on the question of deterrence, because in that aspect it might be susceptible to scientific investigation.

Our third reason for avoiding detailed discussion of deterrence is simply that this issue, unlike most we encountered, has received sustained attention in prior academic writing, including our own.

That being said, we acknowledge that "no issues raised by the controversy over the death penalty have been more hotly contested than those that focus on its efficacy as a deterrent."[7] Further, reasonable people have regarded the evidence regarding deterrent effectiveness as an important factor in deciding whether the death penalty should be regarded as morally permissible. Nor is it unlikely that some support for the death penalty has been generated, or more probably reinforced, by claims about research that purport to demonstrate the effectiveness of executions as a deterrent to murder. Finally, in death penalty cases in the Supreme Court, estimates of the deterrent effect of capital punishment have been prominently mentioned in briefs and referred to in justices' opinions.

It is for these reasons that we conclude with this brief appendix, which is intended only as an introduction to the issue of deterrence as it relates to the death penalty in the United States. More detailed and comprehensive treatments are available in the literature.[8]

For these limited purposes, we first discuss issues of definition that bear on the discussion of capital punishment and criminal homicide. In section B we summarize the major published research on capital punishment and homicide in the United States prior to 1970. Section C discusses the work of Isaac Ehrlich in the mid-1970s. Section D contrasts Ehrlich's work with earlier findings as well as studies generated by some of his critics. Section E reports the findings of a National Academy of Sciences review panel as well as our own conclusions about the statistical evidence on homicide and capital punishment. Finally, section F puts the statistical materials in the broader context of social policy toward homicide.

A. Definition

According to sociologist Jack P. Gibbs: "[T]here are nine properties of punishment that could be relevant in stating the deterrence doctrine as a theory."[9] However, we are not here concerned either to formulate a general theory of deterrence or to provide a definition of deterrence that would be invulnerable to criticism. It is sufficient for our purposes to provide a definition that indicates how we are using the term and also to draw certain important distinctions.

1. General deterrence

For the present purpose we shall adopt the definition used by the National Academy of Sciences Panel on Research on Deterrent and Incapacitative Effects: "*Deterrence* is the inhibiting effect of sanctions on the criminal activity of people *other than* the sanctioned offender," and includes all "the internal psychological mechanisms by which sanctions discourage crime" such as "the normative validation and moral definition effects of punishment."[10]

This effect is often referred to as "general deterrence" to distinguish it from "special deterrence," which refers to the effect of punishment on the person punished. In considering the deterrent effect of capital punishment on homicide we are concerned with general deterrence, with the effects of the threat of execution on potential offenders. In the case of the death penalty there is no special deterrent effect, in terms of crimes averted, on the person executed; although there is of course an absolute *incapacitative* or *preventive* effect.

2. Absolute and marginal deterrence

It is important to distinguish between absolute and marginal deterrence. This distinction has in the past been frequently overlooked in the discussion of deterrence and the death penalty. Absolute deterrence refers to the inhibiting effect of a particular criminal sanction. Marginal deterrence refers to the inhibiting effect of one criminal sanction as compared with another.

In the capital punishment debate the issue is not that of absolute deterrence – whether or not the death penalty is a deterrent. It is that of marginal deterrence – whether it is a more effective deterrent than the alternative sanction of imprisonment.

To obtain evidence on the absolute efficacy of the death penalty as a deterrent to homicide it would be necessary to compare the homicide rate in a jurisdiction where homicide is a capital offense with the rate in a jurisdiction where it is not even a criminal offense. So it is not suprising that all the available evidence relates to the marginal deterrent efficacy of the death penalty.

Once the issue has been narrowed to a question of capital punishment as a *marginal general deterrent,* it can be further specified in two significant respects. One concerns the alternative penalty and the other concerns the target behavior to be deterred. The alternative penalty against which the threat of executions should be judged is protracted imprisonment, for this is the alternative in every state in the United States for cases in which execution might be considered. The target behavior is criminal homicide, the only crime for which capital punishment is authorized in the states and the focus of the vast majority of existing studies of threat of execution as a general deterrent.

The cumbersome but more precise restatement of the empirical issue addressed here is whether the threat of execution is a superior marginal general deterrent to criminal homicide, compared to the threat of a protracted prison term. So stated, the issue lacks theoretical scope. We cannot investigate the entire range of deterrent effects of criminal punishment. We cannot determine whether the death penalty might be a marginal general deterrent when compared to short terms of imprisonment or fines. We cannot discuss the impact of threatening death rather than alternative punishments for economic crimes or other forms of law violations.

B. Early evidence

One of the earliest and best attempts to explore the comparative effectiveness of the death penalty and imprisonment as a deterrent to homicide was carried out by Thorsten Sellin for the Model Penal Code Project of the American Law Institute. Faced with the task of trying to extract some meaning from the data on punishment policy and homicide rates in the United States, Professor Sellin adopted the method of matched group comparison.

Matching in this context means selecting areas that, although different in punishment policy, are as similar to each other in all other respects as is possible. This is important because homicide rates in the United States vary in a distinct regional pattern, so differences in location and variations in social conditions, operating independently of any differences in punishment policy, may have a significant influence on homicide rates and thus invalidate any conclusions about the effect of the death penalty.

Sellin sought to control for these differences as follows. Groups of contiguous states, "closely similar" in "social organization, composition of population, economic and social conditions, etc.," were matched wherever at least one of the states in a group differed from the others in the group in maximum penalties for homicide.[11] The rates of homicide in states with capital punishment were compared with those in states without capital punishment only within these clusters of similar jurisdictions.

The results of this exercise are shown in Table A.1, which represents an adaptation of the data provided in Sellin's study.

The conclusion drawn from these matched group comparisons was that capital punishment did not appear to have any influence on the reported rate of homicide. As Sellin put it: "The inevitable conclusion is that executions have no discernible effect on homicide death rates."[12] Since that conclusion was based on a deliberate attempt to eliminate differences other than those in punishment policy that might influence the homicide

Table A.1. *Comparative crude homicide death rates in states with and states without the death penalty^a – average annual rate, 1940–55*

Midwest

Matched group 1			Matched group 2			Matched group 3		
	D	D			D		D	
Michigan	Indiana	Ohio	Minnesota	Wisconsin	Iowa	North Dakota	South Dakota	D Nebraska
3.5	3.5	3.5	1.4	1.2	1.4	1.0	1.5	1.8

New England

Matched group 1			Matched group 2		
	D	D		D	D
Maine	New Hampshire	Vermont	Rhode Island	Massachusetts	Connecticut
1.5	.9	1.0	1.3	1.2	1.7

^{a}*Death penalty states are marked with a D.*
Source: adapted from the tables provided in T. Sellin, *The Death Penalty* 25, 28 (1959).

rate, it is much more reliable than a nonmatched interstate comparison would have been.

Still, there are two problems associated with this type of study. First, it is possible that there are unknown or unidentified variables that may invalidate the presumed similarity of the areas compared. Second, it is possible that differences in punishment policy are *systematically* related to other variables that influence crime rates, and it may be that there are no areas that differ with respect to punishment policy and do not also differ in what may be related respects.

In practice, the closer a comparison comes to an ideal matching exercise, the more distant becomes the probability that overlooked or uncontrolled-for differences between comparison units will have an invalidating influence. Moreover, the application of Sellin's cluster comparisons over a large number of clusters of states lends greater credibility to his conclusions. Because his comparisons were repeated a number of times and yielded a consistent lack of significant difference in each repetition, the imperfections inherently associated with matching techniques would be important only to the extent that we might suspect a consistent and systematic relation between the presence or absence of the punishment policy variable he was studying and other factors that might influence the crime rate.

The danger that false inferences may be drawn from comparisons will always exist, though in varying degrees. However, it is sometimes possible to find independent evidence that may either corroborate or run counter to a comparative inference. It may thus be possible to test the validity of such an inference by examining the evidence of studies that run parallel to the basic comparative exercise.

An example can be found in the study of police safety that Sellin made in the course of his research into the deterrent effectiveness of the death penalty. In this study he set out "to test the claims of the police that the death penalty makes the lives of policemen safer."[13]

He compared the data on killings of police in death penalty states and abolition states "of quite similar traditions, populations, and culture . . . bordering on one another."[14] He found it "impossible to conclude that the states which had no death penalty had thereby made the policeman's lot more hazardous."[15] He found also that "the same differences observable in the general homicide rates of the various states were reflected in the rate of police killings."[16] This parallel finding confirmed the conclusions of the earlier general comparative study.

In addition to these comparative researches Sellin and his associates conducted other studies designed to determine whether the death penalty exercised any influence on the rates of capital crimes. In particular they examined "the rates of capital crimes in specific states or countries that have experimented with abolition in order to observe the effect of the abolition or the introduction of capital punishment on such rates."[17] Once again his conclusion was that the death penalty "exercises no influence on the extent or fluctuating rates of capital crimes."[18]

Retrospective studies, such as comparing crime rates in particular jurisdictions before and after changes in punishment policy, may be hindered by confounding possibilities: Rates of crime may fluctuate independently of any change in penalties; conditions leading to changes in penalties may themselves independently influence the crime rate or produce other social responses which do so.

As a further check on the findings of his first two approaches, Sellin employed a third method of testing the deterrent effect of capital punishment on homicide. He called this "a case study of deterrence," which involved examining the specific effect of highly publicized executions on homicides in a particular locality, Philadelphia.

His hypothesis was that the death penalty's deterrent effect should be demonstrable after well publicized executions, and that the effect should be most noticeable in the community where the offense occurred, where the trial aroused wide publicity, and where the offender lived and had relatives, friends, and acquaintances.

The assumption was that deterrence should manifest itself by a decline or at least a temporary drop in homicides after such widely publicized executions. Five cases were selected that met the specifications and also occurred as somewhat isolated events, providing sixty-day periods free from other executions of local interest, both before and after the execution.

Sellin found a total of 91 homicides in the "before execution" periods and 113 in the "after" periods. He also found that if the five 120-day periods were combined, there were 105 days free from homicides during the sixty day periods before the execution and 74 in the periods after the executions. He concluded that the data provided no evidence of a measurable deterrent effect.[19]

This case study does not, of course, constitute powerful evidence that capital punishment lacks a marginal deterrent effect. It is subject to the confounding possibility that exists in all before-and-after analyses – that homicide rates may fluctuate independently of executions. Moreover, Sellin's figures indicate that in the ten-day periods immediately after execution there was a total of sixteen days free from homicides compared with only nine such days in the ten-day periods immediately before executions. This might be consistent with publicized executions having a short-term delaying effect, but no net deterrent effect in the long term.

Both comparative and retrospective studies, as well as studies of the short-term response to executions in a single jurisdiction, are admittedly imperfect. Nevertheless, Sellin's combination of the three techniques, all of which are vulnerable, but vulnerable in different ways, is vastly superior to a research strategy based on a single method. The imperfections of individual methods may to a large extent be canceled out when different, if equally imperfect, methods are used in independent assessments. Although Sellin's study has been criticized for its simplicity, his adjunctive use of different assessment methods represents a recognition of the complexity of the problem lacking in some more statistically sophisticated later work.

C. Later evidence

Thorsten Sellin's most forceful critic has been Isaac Ehrlich, who argued that the statistical methods used by Sellin to infer the nonexistence of the deterrent effect of capital punishment did "not provide an acceptable test of such an effect and consequently do not warrant such inferences."[20] Two of his principal criticisms were that Sellin compared different jurisdictions on the basis of their statutes regarding capital punishment rather than their practice of executions; and that he failed to hold constant factors other than the death penalty that might influence the rate of murders. "Pairs of neighboring abolitionist and retentionist states," he has written, "such as Illinois and Wisconsin, Michigan and Indiana, or Massachusetts and Rhode Island, differ in their economic and demographic characteristics, in their crime rates and law enforcement activity, and presumably also in their medical services available to victims of aggravated assaults."[21]

Ehrlich himself employed regression analysis, taking into account such variables as the arrest rate in murder cases, the conviction rate of murder suspects, the rate of labor force participation, the unemployment rate, the fraction of the population in the fourteen-to-twenty-four age group, and per capita income, in an attempt to isolate the death penalty effect on the capital crime rate. He applied his analysis to aggregate data for executions and homicide rates for the United States as a whole in the individual years from 1932 to 1970, during which time executions decreased and homicides increased, particularly during the 1960s.

He concluded: "[T]he empirical analysis suggests that on the average the tradeoff between the execution of an offender and the lives of potential victims it might have saved was of the order of magnitude of 1 for 8 for the period 1933–67 in the United States."[22] The divergence between 1960 and 1969 is shown in Figure A.1.

Ehrlich's study attracted a great deal of attention for a number of reasons: He was the first to employ regression analysis as a means of estimating the death penalty effect. His findings ran counter to almost all the available evidence on the matter. Finally, prior to its publication, the study was introduced to the Supreme Court by the Solicitor General of the United States in *Fowler* v. *North Carolina*[23] as evidence in support of capital punishment.

The study also attracted a great deal of criticism on methodological grounds, particularly in relation to the fact that the deterrent effect appeared to be a function of the mathematical specification of Ehrlich's model. Critics also raised questions about variables omitted from his analysis and the possible effect of these omissions on his findings.

In particular, it was pointed out that crime increased generally during the 1960s. Lawrence Klein and his associates noted that:

While the FBI reported murders and non-negligent manslaughters to have increased by 74 percent from 1960 to 1970, burglaries increased by 142 percent, auto-thefts by 183 percent, and larcenies ($50 and over) by 245 percent . . . the only . . . [crime] potentially deterrable by capital punishment is the one that showed the most modest gain, even though executions came to a halt by 1967.[24]

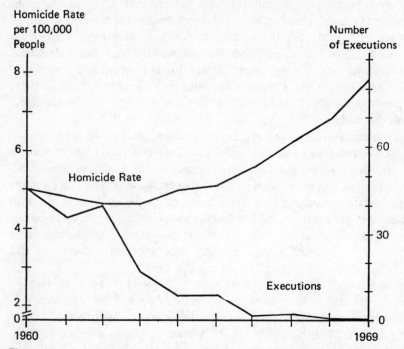

Figure A.1.   U.S. homicide rate and number of executions, 1960–9. *Source:* Zeisel, "The Deterrent Effect of the Death Penalty: Facts v. Faiths," 1976 *Sup. Ct. Rev.* 317, 337.

This, the authors said, "suggests to us that the strength of Ehrlich's statistical relationships between executions and homicides depends significantly on changes during this recent decade in variables omitted from the analysis, variables that would explain the increase in crime generally."[25]

The most damaging criticism, however, came from Brian Forst, who demonstrated that Ehrlich's time-series analysis of aggregate United States data (unlike Thorsten Sellin's study) ignored important regional differences. Forst analyzed changes both over time and across jurisdictions in the crucial decade of the 1960s and concluded: "The finding that capital punishment . . . does not deter homicide is remarkably robust with respect to a wide range of alternative constructions."[26]

The implications of Forst's study in relation to Ehrlich's thesis that the reduction in executions in the 1960s caused the growth in the capital crime rate have been succinctly stated by Hans Zeisel. If Ehrlich's thesis was correct "then no such growth should obtain in the states in which there could be no reduction in executions because there had been none to begin

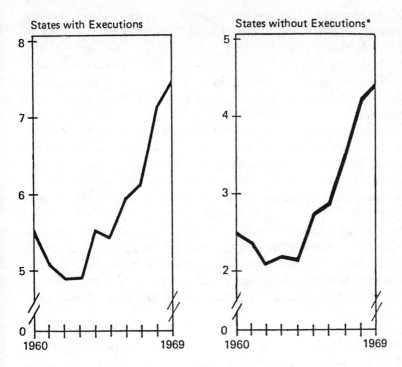

States with Executions   States without Executions*

Figure A.2.   U.S. homicide and execution rates, 1960–9. *Source:* same as for Figure A.1.

with."[27] Yet, as Zeisel showed graphically (reproduced in Figure A.2), the growth in the capital crime rate during the 1960s was as great in the states previously without executions as in those previously with executions.

D.   *Sellin* v. *Ehrlich*

According to Klein, Forst, and Filatov: "Sellin's study of selected pairs of states and Ehrlich's time-series analysis of aggregate United States data represent two fundamentally different empirical approaches to the testing of the hypothesis that capital punishment deters homicide."[28] It might be more precise to say that Sellin's matching technique and Ehrlich's multiple-regression analysis represent two different approaches to taking account of the influence of factors other than the death penalty that might influence the rate of murders.

Both matching and regression techniques are imperfect methods for eliminating differences, other than those in punishment policy, that may influence a crime rate. Sellin's comparison of clusters of neighboring states closely similar in social organization, composition of population, and economic and social conditions is vulnerable to the criticism that there could be many variables that might invalidate the presumption of close similarity of the states being compared. Ehrlich's analysis is equally vulnerable to the criticism that it may neglect a number of variables that might significantly affect the homicide rate.

As we observed some years ago: "[V]ery few, if any, studies done on the impact of criminal law variations on crime give us reason to believe that most of the many factors which should be included in such a statistical analysis are present and accounted for."[29] We also warned that the statistical complexity of the more sophisticated analytical techniques may lull the researcher "into a false sense that all relevant variables have been accounted for, or that natural variations are in fact present," so that the use of such techniques becomes more dangerous than helpful.[30] Although that warning referred to multiple-correlation analysis rather than the multiple-regression technique employed by Ehrlich, the greater sophistication and complexity of his analysis does not diminish but instead reinforces its appropriateness.

Moreoever, there are good reasons for thinking that factors not used by Ehrlich in his regression model are significantly related to the homicide rate. Such obvious variables as the decline in the time served in prison for homicide and offenses that often result in homicide, increased gun availability, and the availability and quality of emergency medical services were omitted from the regression model. Thus, despite the fact that Ehrlich's findings were termed "stunning and memorable,"[31] these omissions alone make his conclusion – that the increase was attributable to the decline in executions – somewhat less impressive.

Since Ehrlich's original paper on the deterrent effect of capital punishment appeared, a number of other studies have been published, including attempts to apply econometric techniques to cross-state data. One of these, by Ehrlich himself, examined the evidence on the cross-sectional patterns of murder in 1940 and 1950 and found that "the cross-sectional studies on balance reinforce the findings of the substantial restraining effect on murders of punishment in general and capital punishment in particular."[32] He also said: "[P]erhaps the main policy implication of the present study lies in the support it lends to the general deterrence hypothesis."[33] Peter Passell reported on 1950 data for forty-one states and 1960 data for forty-four states. He found five variables related systematically to the homicide rate: the conviction rate; the average term of imprisonment for murderers; poverty; age; and racial migration. As for the execution variable, he reported that "students of capital punishment must look elsewhere for evidence confirming deterrence. We know of no reasonable way of interpreting the cross-section data that would lend support to the deterrence hypothesis."[34]

E. The National Academy of Sciences panel

A review of the evidence on the deterrent effect of capital punishment on homicide was conducted by a panel established by the National Academy of Sciences in 1975. The panel was convened in order to provide "an objective technical assessment of the available studies of the deterrent and incapacitative effects of sanctions on crime rates."[35] It was also asked to identify gaps in knowledge and provide some guidance for future research.

Panel members were drawn from the disciplines of political science, sociology, psychology, economics, criminology, and law, and from the methodological areas of statistics, econometrics, and operations research.[36] Its assessment of the available evidence was aided by a number of papers commissioned by the panel, including literature reviews and further analyses of data that had already been reported and published.

With regard to capital sanctions the panel's report includes a commissioned paper by Lawrence R. Klein, Brian Forst, and Victor Filatov entitled "The Deterrent Effect of Capital Punishment: An Assessment of the Estimates." This paper comprises a review of the available studies done in this area of inquiry, discussion of methodological issues raised by those studies, and an assessment of the suitability of presenting available estimates as a basis for judicial and legislative decisions about capital punishment.

The principal emphasis in the paper is on Ehrlich's time-series analysis. His cross-state analysis is referred to only in a footnote, remarking on the differences between Ehrlich's and Peter Passell's cross-state results. "One cannot help but be puzzled," the authors observe, "that two apparently similar approaches would yield such strikingly different findings."[37] Concerning Ehrlich's time-series analysis, the review is critical of his theoretical model, the omission of factors that may have affected the homicide rate during the period studied, and the soundness of his conclusions.

The authors characterize Ehrlich's findings as suggestive and provocative; but also as fragile, too uncertain, and at best, tentative. They conclude that "we see too many plausible explanations for his finding a deterrent effect other than the theory that capital punishment deters murder."[38] Their own final verdict is that "the deterrent effect of capital punishment is definitely not a settled matter, and this is the strongest social scientific conclusion that can be reached at the present time."[39]

The panel's report on the question of whether capital punishment has any deterrent effect beyond that associated with imprisonment is noncommittal. Ehrlich's analyses provide "no useful evidence on the deterrent effect of capital punishment"; and the panel concludes that "the current evidence on the deterrent effect of capital punishment is inadequate for drawing any substantive conclusions."[40]

There is one striking difference between the conclusions of the authors of the commissioned paper and those of the panel itself. Although Klein, Forst, and Filatov maintain that Ehrlich's results are not sufficiently powerful, robust, or tested to be used to pass judgment on the effectiveness of the death penalty, their verdict on his research is not wholly negative. They congratulate Ehrlich and others for "opening up a fascinating area of research with much scholarly potential," and express the opinion that "it remains to pursue this line of research to the point at which it can be used in the future for making important contributions to legal policy."[41]

By contrast, the panel did not recommend undertaking further studies on the deterrent effect of capital punishment. The nonexperimental methods to which this research is necessarily limited, they reported, could not meet the rigorous standards of proof required for any policy use of the results. The panel concluded that "research on this topic is not likely to produce findings that will or should have much influence on policy makers."[42]

Our own conclusions differ from those of the Academy's panel in two respects but concur with them in a third. Our first difference relates to the inferences that can be drawn from the many studies, both over time and cross-sectional, which have dealt with the effect of the death penalty on homicide rates. Those studies do not disprove the existence of any marginal deterrent influence; the data and the various methodologies are respectively too ambiguous and too problematic for that difficult task. Nevertheless, and this is of considerable significance, the accumulated evidence places a low upper limit on the amount of marginal deterrence that could have been achieved by capital punishment practices then in effect (and that has remained undetected).

The presence or absence of the capital threat and the low levels of execution accompanying that threat have not produced any significant variation in homicide rates. Given these circumstances, the effect that can plausibly be attributed to the threat of the death penalty is much less than the potential deterrent effect that might be expected or argued for in the absence of any data. There is room for debate only about whether the marginal deterrent effect is nil or very small in relation to total homicide volume. In making the transition from deterrence theory to policy implications it is important to recognize that the effect cannot be major.

Our second area of disagreement may be no more than a matter of emphasis. If the panel intended to discourage any further research on the effect of executions on homicide rates we would demur. The concentration of executions in a few states and the differential timing of changes in execution policy offer opportunities for time-series studies that might shed further light on the existence or magnitude of general deterrent effects. We think such research should be pursued.

We do, however, agree with the panel's conclusion that research on the deterrent effects of capital punishment "is not likely to produce findings that will or should have much influence on policy makers."[43] But the reason we do not think that evidence from deterrent research will be relevant to policy has little to do with methodological issues or the failure of nonexperimental research to meet required standards of proof.

Whether the deterrent effect of capital punishment on homicide is slight (the most that it could be) or nonexistent is inconsequential. Modest deterrence can be achieved by other means and the prevention of homicide can be pursued by methods other than deterrence, as we argue in the next section. Once we discount the possibility that capital sanctions have a significant influence on homicide rates, further research on the subject may prove useful for other purposes but will be irrelevant to the determination of proper public policy regarding the death penalty.

F. Policy implications

While interpretations of statistics about the behavioral effects of the death penalty differ, there is wide consensus that neither the research findings relating to capital punishment and homicide rates, nor any of the inferences drawn from them by scholars engaged in or commenting on that research, have policy implications regarding the desirability of executions in the United States. No student of general deterrence has nominated the death penalty as a uniquely effective marginal deterrent to murder.

Ehrlich and others involved in the econometric analysis of data relating to crime and punishment have not confined their investigation to the deterrent efficacy of the death penalty. Ehrlich's own earlier work dealt with the effect of variations in prison sentences that he found to be an effective crime deterrent.[44] In relation to homicide the most that he has claimed is that "capital punishment has a differential deterrent effect over and above *the actually enforced imprisonment terms.*"[45]

Thus, even if one accepts his general deterrence hypothesis, with its basic proposition about the influence of "prospective gains or losses" on the propensity to commit murder,[46] no inference regarding the necessity for the death penalty is warranted. Those seeking deterrence solutions to the problem of homicide will find plenty of room for a substantial increment in "prospective losses" when, as one Philadelphia study found, the average minimum sentence for second degree murder was two years' imprisonment.[47]

These considerations make clear the problematic character of one of the most superficially attractive arguments against abolition, which has been most forcefully, and frequently, advanced by Ernest van den Haag. It is based on Isaac Ehrlich's assertion that "an additional execution per year over the period in question (1933–1967) may have resulted in 7 or 8 fewer murders,"[48] described by van den Haag as "well proven."[49] The reasoning is that when we abolish capital punishment we risk the lives of potential victims who might have been spared if murderers were executed.[50]

Although van den Haag described Ehrlich's conclusions as well proven, Ehrlich himself did not. He explicitly stated that his observations "do not imply that empirical investigation has proved the preventive effect of capital punishment."[51] Moreover, neither Ehrlich nor anyone else has provided any evidence that capital punishment is a more effective deterrent to homicide that long prison terms. It is not that the evidence is inconclusive; it does not exist. We have no empirical data to tell us what the differential deterrent effects of disparate periods of incarceration are vis-à-vis the death penalty.

Van den Haag said: "[I]t seems immoral to let convicted murderers survive at the probable – or even at the merely possible – expense of the lives of innocent victims had the murderer been executed."[52] "I do not want to risk their lives for the sake of the lives of murderers."[53] Yet in employing the death penalty, it can just as easily be argued that we are not risking the lives of potential victims for the sake of the lives of murderers; we are taking the lives of murderers without any evidence at all to suggest that this will preserve the lives of potential victims better than any available alternative.

In short, we are killing people on the basis of a hypothesis that, far from being "well proven," has never been investigated. It has been rightly said that "anyone who purports to set out a justification for the institution of punishment has got to come to terms with the problem of action in a state of ignorance,"[54] an observation that applies with transcendent force to capital punishment. If anything "seems immoral" in this context, it is enthusiastic advocacy of the death penalty coupled with unconcern about that problem.

Moreover, consideration of levels of alternative punishment does not exhaust the range of possibilities in relation to the reduction of criminal homicide. Evidence regarding the relationship between handgun availability and the death rate from violent assault is much more persuasive than the evidence adduced regarding variations in penalties. This is not merely because the underlying psychological theory is more plausible than the postulate on which the econometric analysis is based: "The decision to commit murder . . . is considered to be the result of an independent either/or choice among alternative actions by a potential offender . . . murder would be expected to occur if the expected utility from committing murder to that person exceeds the expected utility from alternative pursuits."[55] It is also because the evidence of the effects of weapon availability came from the study of individual acts of violence rather than studies of aggregate statistics of violent crime in different jurisdictions at different points in time.

Evidence regarding the marginal deterrent efficacy of capital punishment in relation to murder is not imperfect merely because it is not definitive; it is worse than that. It is at the lower end of the spectrum of circumstantial evidence on those issues where only comparisons between areas and over time are available.

At the same time evidence regarding weapon dangerousness and weapon availability as contributors to the volume of homicide is ignored. The supporters of capital punishment are not usually enthusiastic about gun control measures. Ernest van den Haag, one of the most outspoken advocates of the death penalty, acknowledged: "[W]e have no proof of the positive effectiveness of the penalty,"[56] but said flippantly that "outlawing handguns is not likely to be more effective than outlawing alcohol: zip guns are even easier to produce at home than bathtub gin."[57]

Supporters of the death penalty often speak as though saving lives was one of their principal objectives. It is hard, however, to reconcile this enthusiasm for taking lives as a means of saving lives – based as it is on the disputed hypothesis of the above-zero marginal deterrent effect of executions – not only with opposition to gun control, but also with the absence of interest in such a direct method of saving lives as the improvement of interstate emergency medical services, or the availability of guns.

Nor is gun control an isolated instance of a life-saving criminal law initiative that has not proved notably attractive to supporters of executions. It is estimated that each year more persons die in alcohol-related traffic accidents than do victims of total reported murders and nonnegligent homicide. Students of deterrence have long noted the potential of variations in law enforcement to save lives in high volume crime.[58] Yet the enthusiasm for using the criminal law as an instrument of public health has rarely led proponents of execution to attach high priority to social control of drunk drivers.

It is quite clear from the literature that neither proponents nor opponents of the death penalty, when they consult the products of deterrence research, are engaged in a disinterested pursuit of the truth. Moreover, if that were their objective they would be looking in the wrong place. Neither are they, when they review the statistical evidence, anxious to discover what the policy implications of that evidence might be. This is just as well because no policy implications spring unmediated from even the best kept crime statistics.

Those who are already firmly committed to well-defined policies are not interested in hearing about possible alternatives. What they are looking for is evidence to support their convictions. Frequently they seem to treat the annals of deterrence research as arsenals from which they can obtain weapons and ammunition with which to launch attacks on their opponents.

Very few come to oppose or support capital punishment as a result of analysis of the statistical evidence, although the great nineteenth-century criminological pioneer Gabriel Tarde, in this as in other respects a singular figure, did so. He originally favored the death penalty, describing it as "the most logical, most concise, and even . . . the most humane solution of the penal problem in so far as social monsters are concerned," and said of the idea of abolition: "There can be no better example of human silliness than the frankly fictitious passion lavished upon this subject."[59] But he changed his mind when, as Director of the Bureau of Statistics in the Department of Justice in Paris, he found virtually no relationship between rates of criminal activity and the severity of punishment.

Such conversions are rare, however; and the fact that they are rare is a reflection of the real nature of the dispute between those who support and those who oppose the death penalty. It is not now, and never has been, about the relationship between the death penalty and homicide rates.

Notes

1. T. Sellin, *The Death Penalty* 19 (1959) (hereafter T. Sellin, *The Death Penalty*).
2. H. Bedau, *The Courts, the Constitution and Capital Punishment* 108 (1977) (hereafter H. Bedau, *Courts*).
3. Bedau, "Deterrence: Problems, Doctrines and Evidence," in *The Death Penalty in America* 102 (H. Bedau 3d ed. 1982); *see also* Lempert, "Desert and Deterrence: An Assessment of the Moral Bases of the Case for Capital Punishment," 79 *Mich. L. Rev.* 1177 (1981).

4. Zeisel, "The Deterrent Effect of the Death Penalty: Facts v. Faiths," 1976 *Sup. Ct. Rev.* 317, 340 (hereafter Zeisel, "Facts v. Faiths").
5. Cornelius, "Crime and the Punishment of Crime," 6 *Exerpta Criminologica* 11 (1966).
6. T. Sellin, *The Death Penalty,* at 15–16.
7. H. Bedau, *Courts,* at 93.
8. *See* J. Gibbs, *Crime, Punishment and Deterrence* (1975) (hereafter J. Gibbs, *Crime*); F. Zimring & G. Hawkins, *Deterrence: The Legal Threat in Crime Control* (1973) (hereafter F. Zimring & G. Hawkins, *Deterrence*).
9. Gibbs, "Preventive Effects of Capital Punishment Other than Deterrence," 14 *Crim. L. Bulletin* 34, 35 (1978); *see also* J. Gibbs, *Crime,* at 95–144.
10. National Research Council Panel on Research and Deterrent and Incapacitative Effects, *Deterrence and Incapacitation: Estimating the Effects of Criminal Sanctions on Crime Rates* 3, 16 n.4 (1978) (hereafter National Research Council, *Deterrence*).
11. T. Sellin, *The Death Penalty,* at 23.
12. *Id.* at 34.
13. *Id.* at 53.
14. *Id.*
15. *Id.* at 57.
16. *Id.*
17. *Id.* at 63.
18. *Id.*
19. *Id.* at 50–2.
20. Ehrlich, "The Deterrent Effect of Capital Punishment: A Question of Life and Death," 65 *Am. Econ. Rev.* 397, 398 (1975) (hereafter Ehrlich, "Deterrent Effect").
21. Ehrlich, "Deterrence: Evidence and Inference," 85 *Yale L.J.* 209, 223–4 (1975).
22. Ehrlich, "Deterrent Effect," at 398.
23. 428 U.S. 904 (1976).
24. Klein, Forst & Filatov, "The Deterrent Effect of Capital Punishment: An Assessment of the Estimates," in National Research Council, *Deterrence,* at 346 (hereafter Klein, Forst & Filatov, "Assessment").
25. *Id.*
26. Forst, "The Deterrent Effect of Capital Punishment: A Cross-State Analysis of the 1960's," 61 *Minn. L. Rev.* 743, 763 (1977).
27. Zeisel, "Facts v. Faiths," at 330.
28. Klein, Forst & Filatov, "Assessment," at 341.
29. F. Zimring & G. Hawkins, *Deterrence,* at 267–8.
30. *Id.*
31. H. Bedau, *Courts,* at 99.
32. Ehrlich, "Capital Punishment and Deterrence: Some Further Thoughts and Additional Evidence," 85 *J. Pol. Econ.* 741, 742 (1977) (hereafter Ehrlich, "Further Thoughts").
33. *Id.* at 780.
34. Passell, "The Deterrent Effect of the Death Penalty: A Statistical Test," 28 *Stan. L. Rev.* 61, 80 (1975).
35. National Research Council, *Deterrence,* at 16.
36. One of us (Zimring) served on the panel and wrote a paper for it dealing with policy experiments in general deterrence during the 1980s. *See* National Research Council, *Deterrence,* at 140–86.
37. Klein, Forst & Filatov, "Assessments," at 342 n.6.
38. *Id.* at 358.
39. *Id.* at 359.
40. National Research Council, *Deterrence,* at 62.
41. Klein, Forst & Filatov, "Assessments," at 359.
42. National Research Council, *Deterrence,* at 63.
43. *Id.*
44. Ehrlich, "Participation in Illegitimate Activities: A Theoretical and Empirical Investigation," 81 *J. Pol. Econ.* 521 (1973).

45. Ehrlich, "Further Thoughts," at 778 (emphasis added).
46. Ehrlich, "Deterrent Effect," at 398–9.
47. Zimring, Eigen & O'Malley, "Punishing Homicide in Philadelphia: Perspectives on the Death Penalty," 43 *U. Chi. L. Rev.* 227, 234–5 (1976).
48. Ehrlich, "Deterrent Effect," at 414.
49. E. van den Haag & J. Conrad, *The Death Penalty: A Debate* 128 (1983) (hereafter *Debate*).
50. van den Haag, "In Defense of the Death Penalty: A Legal–Practical–Moral Analysis," 14 *Crim. L. Bulletin* 51, 58–9 (1978) (hereafter van den Haag, "Defense").
51. Ehrlich, "Deterrent Effect," at 416.
52. van den Haag, "Defense," at 59.
53. E. van den Haag, *Debate,* at 300.
54. Griffiths, "Book Review," 79 *Yale L.J.* 1428 (1970).
55. Ehrlich, "Further Thoughts," at 743.
56. E. van den Haag, "On Deterrence and the Death Penalty," 60 *J. Crim. L., Crime & Pol. Science* 147 (1969).
57. E. van den Haag, *Punishing Criminals* 154 (1975).
58. *See, e.g.,* J. Andeneas, *Punishment and Deterrence* (1974); F. Zimring & G. Hawkins, *Deterrence.*
59. G. Trade, *Penal Philosophy* 530, 566 (R. Howell trans. 1912).

Index